Steadicam: techniques and aesthetics

Dedication

To my parents

Giorgio and Milena

who instilled in me the joy of knowing and creative curiosity

Steadicam: techniques and aesthetics

Serena Ferrara

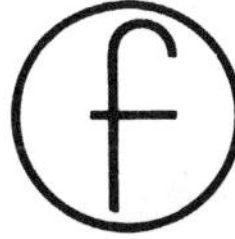

Focal Press

OXFORD AUCKLAND BOSTON JOHANNESBURG MELBOURNE NEW DELHI

Focal Press
An imprint of Butterworth-Heinemann
Linacre House, Jordan Hill, Oxford OX2 8DP
225 Wildwood Avenue, Woburn, MA 01801-2041
A division of Reed Educational and Professional Publishing Ltd

A member of the Reed Elsevier plc group

First published 2001

British Library Cataloguing in Publication Data
A catalogue record for this book is available from the British Library

Library of Congress Cataloguing in Publication Data
A catalogue record for this book is available from the Library of Congress

ISBN 0 240 51607 9

Printed and bound in Great Britain
Composition by Scribe Design, Gilingham, Kent

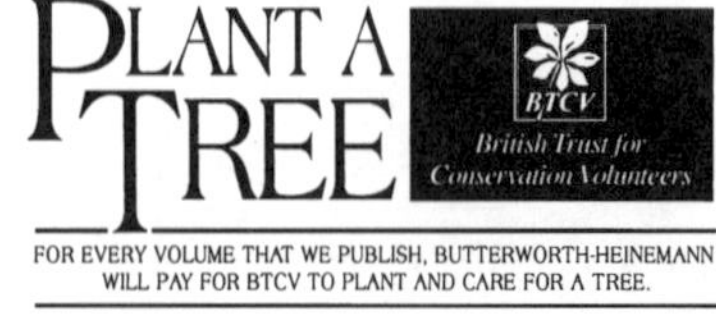

Contents

Foreword

I have just been on the most rewarding Steadicam job of my career. I'm 58 years old and I bicycled to work every day in Paris, as eager and excited as a kid. The last shot, at the end of the last day was, I believe, my lifetime-best work; and may have shown a glimpse into the future of my invention.

La Traviata, live from Paris, June 3rd and 4th, 2000. Four separate half-hour segments broadcast live to 120 countries from four historic Paris locations. Photographed by Vittorio Storaro, produced by Andrea Andermann, directed by Giuseppe Patroni Griffi and conducted by Zubin Mehta. The world press called it 'a mad risky high-wire act' on the part of the largely Italian crew.

Via microwave our shots flew across Paris to a monitor on Zubin's podium in the 'Salle Wagram'. A fixed camera beamed his conducting back to TV screens hidden on the set. The performers' voices were captured by tiny hair-mikes and sent to Zubin's earphone and we heard the RAI orchestra on hidden speakers. The whole works was mixed in real time, in six different video formats, and uplinked by satellite to every corner of the globe.

Act I, from the 17th century mansion which is now the Italian Embassy, was a ballet for three Steadicams and two dollies – each precisely choreographed to avoid being seen by the others. Act II required three Steadicams, two dollies and a crane in Marie Antoinette's 'Hameau' at Versailles and includes an amazing 10 minute continuous Steadicam take by French master Valentin Monge (who shot part of it while walking on his knees in high grass!). Dollies and cranes were used exclusively for Act III, so we had time to get the Steadicams to the last location, and at 11.30 p.m., in a tiny apartment on Isle St. Louis overlooking Notre Dame, I had the great joy of shooting the entire finale of Act IV as a single 25 minute uncut one-take Steadicam shot, in extreme emotional intimacy with the performers, as 'Violetta' approached her death at the window on the stroke of Notre Dame's bells. I had never done 'live' before and had never 'pulled' my own zooms while operating Steadicam. The adrenalin rush of the former and the amazing power of the latter were a revelation to me.

After five weeks of rehearsal the live broadcasts came off perfectly, with but one brief video glitch in Act I, and the euphoria afterwards was astonishing. By the time my long, long shot faded to black most of our 90 crew members had made their way to the apartment and crowded inside, popping champagne corks and shouting our names as cheering rose from the crowd outside on the quay. The *New York Times* called this *La Traviata* production 'a work for solo, orchestra and Steadicam' and that's just what it was.

Steadicam graduated from tool to instrument a long time ago but the *New York Times* statement implies that in the hands of an artist a brilliantly operated Steadicam can have an emotional impact of the same magnitude as music or lighting or art direction, and can seriously augment acting and direction. Storaro's brilliantly designed Steadicam sequences could be profitably studied by people from all of the above disciplines, as well as, of course, Steadicam operators, for whom once again we may have inched up the bar.

The late Ted Churchill 'invented' the modern profession of 'Steadicam Operator' in 1980 with the publication of his famously funny pamphlet *The Steadicam Operator's Manual of Style*. Ted was a genius of self-promotion. He anointed our fledgling occupation 'The Last Great Job in the Business' and became its first journeyman celebrity. Ted, in effect, invented Us (in the same sense, according to Harold Bloom, that Shakespeare invented Humanity).

Thereafter we were a profession. He imagined a future in which Steadicam Operators starred as the laconic, heroic cowboys of the movie biz (Ted called himself an 'Arty Pack Mule'), and shucks, it all came true.

That summer I taught the first ever Steadicam Workshop, in Rockport Maine, to pass on what I had learned during my year on *The Shining*. Half of the students were beginners; the rest, including Ted, had either taught themselves or learned by lurching around my Philadelphia townhouse. Ted handed out the first edition of his pamphlet (to great acclaim) and his demeanour, wardrobe, dialogue and instant freeze-dried mythology were soon memorialized in his full page ads and much imitated to this day.

Ted himself would have loved the work on *La Traviata* but I'm not certain that some of our early cowboy-fiddlers would have had the patience for it. Practicing a single shot for four weeks, with the ensemble-artist discipline of the 'violin-operator' was a new experience for me, but as I settled into it, frame by frame, an intense collaboration developed between myself and the artists, between the intersecting optical and emotional trajectories of our work, which was simply more affecting than the sum of its parts. And there, I think, is where Steadicam is headed – beyond the physical stabilizing effect of the hardware to the undreamed-of artistry of its future operators.

Victorian gentlemen used to require a week of full-time instruction to wobble along on a bicycle, whereas kids today learn to ride in about 15 minutes. The trick of balancing on two-wheels was an exotic concept back then, but of course is now quite commonplace. Likewise, most people today have seen Steadicams being operated somewhere or other, and students now arrive at week-long Steadicam workshops already primed to acquire the basic Steadicam balancing trick – controlling the angle of the upper body so that the arm truly lifts 'up', thus floating the camera serenely within reach.

Steadicam operating requires, if not strength, an unusual combination of physical and mental agility – the ability to coordinate variously high exertions by the legs, back and hand, with delicate, artistically directed manipulations by the opposite hand (picture trying to simultaneously move and play a piano!). Your overworked brain has to ration and distribute your attention circularly between a dozen incompatible tasks; between composition and navigation, between the story-telling dynamics of the moving camera and the mundane need to not fall down. One reason it's the 'Last Great Job in the Business' is simply because it uses everything you've got. A great Steadicam shot is, like other great human performances, primarily an act of the will. It requires feats of concentration and highly schooled instincts, yet (with the exception, of course, of Glenn Gould playing the piano) it usually ends up looking quite elegant, if seldom altogether effortless.

Serena Ferrara contacted me several years ago to request an interview for her Doctoral Thesis. I was impressed with her knowledge of film and its history, but certainly never expected her to show up as a student at the 1998 workshop in Umbria. I have observed that women, particularly those who have been dancers, are quicker than men to learn the balancing act that must be performed by the upper body, if the exertion required is to be manageable. However, Serena was the tiniest of all the 1000 or so people that I have taught, weighing herself not much more than the average Steadicam, and so we all expected her to be a dilettante, to give it a brief 'doctoral' try and retire to the sidelines to take notes. Serena, however, never backed off – her nerve and perseverance were inspiring, and she made it through the entire course, looking improbably graceful, if, at times, a bit like a miniature Margot Fonteyne trying to hold Nureyev aloft for minutes at a time.

Serena has gone on to write an important and equally graceful book about what we jokingly called, and now are beginning to believe might actually be, the 'Noble Instrument.' *Steadicam: techniques and aesthetics* is an uncanny literary companion to my long-term fascination with the physics, aesthetics and history of camera movement. I think 'obsession' is too strong a word, but I admit to having been inordinately preoccupied with these matters for most of my adult life. I am therefore gratified to see how comprehensively she has assembled all of it: the fossils and bones of my first experiments, the early instruments with their vestigial bumps and bits, the most complete deconstruction yet of the parade of models that followed, and all the stories and anecdotes and diagrams in between, including obscure interviews that light up missing pieces of the story and abundant references to the movies that tie it all together.

Serena advantageously arrived at the workshop with her thesis in hand, and was therefore able to test her academic conceptions of 'cinema' against torrents of real-world information from the front. Her book will therefore be invaluable to anyone who expects to learn how to operate Steadicam, since it straddles the intellectual chain-link fence that often separates theory from practice. I give a lecture periodically on the 'Moving Camera' at film schools and festivals, and I plan to crib shamelessly from her chapter on 'Semiotics and Narrative', and from her numerous, sometimes surprising, interviews.

Altogether, *Steadicam: techniques and aesthetics* is an excellent book in a field that is still distinctly under-populated. It is the first to combine insights from the world of film scholarship with hard-won Steadicam skills and lore obtained from real, and distinctly analog, life.

Garrett Brown
Philadelphia, September 2000

Preface

The idea for this book developed from my curiosity about the Steadicam, the cinematographic tool that, more than any other, has revolutionized how films and television are made. Steadicam is a balancing system for the hand-held camera that allows the operator to move anywhere and film continuously while keeping the image steady. This device has brought a new point of view to filmmaking with regard to stories, characters and events, and has had a great influence on narrative and shooting techniques.

I first encountered the Steadicam while watching televised events in which an operator could be seen on stage 'wearing' a device with a camera on top and walking in a strange, sort of diagonal manner as he circled the performer, while the screen projected a smooth and enveloping dolly shot. Intrigued, I chose the Steadicam as the subject of my thesis[1] and discovered that books or publications dedicated to it were practically non-existent. The small amount of technical information available dated from the time of its debut, when Garrett Brown, its inventor, led a series of workshops with Vittorio Storaro and other important directors of photography, in which the uses to which the device could be put were described and a short demonstration film made. It was at this point that the idea of eventually writing a book that would fill the gaps in the small amount of literature available on the Steadicam took hold.

The first source I turned to for direct knowledge of the Steadicam was also the most important. Garrett Brown, in fact, very kindly agreed to an interview, which is included in Part Three of this book, and I began to glimpse the many facets of this fascinating and revolutionary device. This book, consequently, aims to present the Steadicam as comprehensively as possible, describing it on different levels: historical (its birth, history and the first experiences with it), technical (its structure, how it works and how it has evolved over the years) and narrative (with an analysis of some 'exemplary' films). The final section includes a series of interviews undertaken by the author, published here for the first time, with movie industry professionals, including directors of photography and Steadicam operators. A number of different views of the Steadicam are presented and the discussion is left open.

It is important to remember that it is the operator, the director, the director of photography, the actors and so on, who construct the images seen on the screen and who generate the emotion that make a movie not merely a technical accomplishment but something which captures the viewer.

Notes

1 Ferrara, S. (1997). *La Steadicam come generatrice di effetti e come istanza narrativa.* (*The Steadicam as creator of effects and narrative voice.* Thesis in History of Cinema.) Università degli Studi di Pisa: Facoltà di Lettere e Filosofia.

Acknowledgements

I would like to take this opportunity to thank Garrett Brown, that extraordinary inventor, who made time in his busy schedule to read the manuscript of this book and make numerous invaluable suggestions.

I would like to thank all the people who believed in my work and offered their time and ideas to help me complete it. First among these are my parents, my sisters, my brother and my partner.

Elisabetta Cartoni was the force behind my 'practical and direct' experience with the Steadicam.

Karen Craig was more than just my translator; she also helped revise and assemble the book.

I would especially like to thank all the people I interviewed for this book, who gave me their opinions, ideas and, above all, their time: Garrett Brown; Larry McConkey, John Carpenter, Ed DiGiulio, Caroline Goodall, Mario Orfini, Nicola Pecorini, Giuseppe Rotunno, Vittorio Storaro and Haskell Wexler.

Finally, I am grateful to the following people for their help (in alphabetical order, as they were all equally important): Lou Adler, Silvana Agueci, *American Cinematographer*, Cinema Products, Frank Dellario, Focal Press (Beth Howard, Margaret Denley), Antonio Franco, John Jurgens, Gabriella Giaconi, Erwin Landau, Alessia Moretti, Emma Parker, Nicola Piegaia, Riccardo Piattelli, Rodolfo Tritapepe, Mirco Vettori, Nicola Zani and also to the Istituto Cinematografico dell'Aquila 'La Lanterna Magica'.

Part One

History and Techniques

1
The moving camera

Camera movement: an historical overview

Any discussion of the technical aspects of cinema and the possible ties between technique and narration needs to be prefaced by an account of the most significant passages in the evolution of filmmaking techniques.

Framing, that is to say selecting the portion of space and the viewpoint in order to follow a certain moment of the action from the best possible position, implies making a selection on the basis of ability to portray the events that are occurring and fulfil the narrative aims. Actually, this is only true for films that aspire to be 'straightforward' and 'descriptive'. In other cases, framing may not have illustrative potential as its sole concern, but will involve artistic taste and dramatic devices such as arbitrarily altered proportions, the desire to render the subject unrecognizable and so on.

Staying in the realm where the criterion of choice is the desire to relate events as they occur, an important early realization – in 1896, Eugene Promio, the operator for the Lumière Brothers, was impressed with the beauty of the images of Venice captured by his camera while he travelled along the canals on a gondola – was that perhaps the shot which is determined by and determines the point of view cannot be made from only one spot. The camera may need to move, rotate, elevate or otherwise alter its position or angle relative to the object of our interest in order to catch all desired aspects. Furthermore, this must not be done only by moving the camera from one spot to another and keeping it immobile during shooting; it is natural to catch the movement of the scene also with the movement of the camera.

Right from its beginnings, cinema aimed to entertain and amuse the public. At first, films told stories using only one shot, then a number of shots in sequence, while at the same time adding a diversified point of view with respect to the subject.

In the early years of filmmaking, shooting was done in the studio. The studios were housed in open or glass-ceiling buildings that provided natural illumination for the sets. Only later was artificial lighting used:

> The surface of the stage was slightly tilted, like in regular theatres, in order to exaggerate the size of the objects and the depth of the scene. No one had realized yet that placing the camera in a slightly higher position and varying the angle of the optical axis could achieve the same result. The tilted floor had the drawback that after a few hours of work, the actors and technicians complained of aching ankles and were noticeably tired. Nevertheless, it was still difficult to understand the mechanics of certain situations.
>
> For a long time, in fact, dolly shots continued to be made by moving the scene on rollers, with all the difficulties that this engendered, instead of simply putting the camera on three or four wheels to be able to move it freely relative to the scene.[1]

The earliest movies consisted of one shot with the camera fixed in a hypothetical central seat in the audience, which was considered the ideal position. Later, at the end of the nineteenth century and in the early years of the twentieth century, films with multiple shots were made, which lasted longer and had more complex stories. The subjective vision of the character was used as a motivation for the cuts between frames and to link various situations. Thus, a movie showed first a character and then what the character was seeing, with perhaps some visual tricks to underline the subjectivity of the vision, such as a view through binoculars using a cut-out.

In 1910, cameras on tripods that previously could only perform horizontal pans were provided with movable heads, which allowed them to execute both horizontal and vertical movements. Experiments began to be made with moving the camera; it was put on impromptu wheeled conveyances or on cars, ships and trains, in order to give the illusion of movement.

In 1912, the arrival of the very first real dollies, movable platforms on wheels that supported the camera, its operator and at times an assistant, further increased the possibilities of filming with a moving camera.[2] The dollies moved on tracks, at first made of wood and later metal, allowing motion over rough or uneven surfaces. They could also be pushed on four rubber-coated wheels by the grips, using a steering device.

The camera was no longer glued to one spot, a mere witness to the action taking place before it; now, with these means of support, it could move giving a range from long shots to very close-up shots. The need to attract the public and arouse their interest reveals itself in the early filmmakers' efforts to find new effects and narrative devices as they developed techniques that would allow them to fulfil the intentions of the author. In addition, filmmakers began to be more aware of lighting, using it not simply to expose the film but as an active contribution to the construction of the story.

To explain the action frequently required giving the audience a series of different viewpoints and often a viewpoint that moved. Cameras were pushed, pulled or mounted on any moving contraption imaginable, in order to follow, pass, overlook or stop beside the subject – techniques developed by trial, error or inspiration to tell the story in the best possible way, whether by mechanical or organic means.

Besides the problem of creating the image, there was also that of recording the sound. The music and explanatory captions that accompanied the first films were no longer sufficient to illustrate the stories, the public needed to hear the 'dialogue'; therefore, a system for synchronizing the film and the soundtrack was invented. The soundtrack was attached along one edge of the film between the perforations and the frames,[3] guaranteeing the synchronization of sound and image. The tools required to put such a system into practical use were considerably improved as a result of research done on radio technology and, in 1927, Warner Bros released the first 'talking' film: *The Jazz Singer*. From this point on, the camera had an electric motor to synchronize it with the sound-recording device and, as it now needed to be connected to a power supply, it ceased to be an object held freely in the operator's hands.

The advent of sound had a revolutionary effect on filmmaking techniques and camera design, which was still basically that of the pre-war models, changed accordingly in terms of both concept and use. During the 1930s, both the camera crank (which relied on the constant and uniform movement of the operator's hand for the advancement of the film) and the spring (mechanical advancement of the film by winding up a spring), were replaced by an electric motor. Because of the motor, the sound camera was quite noisy and consequently the operator had to stand with the camera and tripod in a soundproof box during shooting. This led to the development of the sound blimp, a sound-absorbing covering for the camera that allowed the operator and the camera greater freedom of movement.

Throughout the 1930s a number of technological advances were made in tripods and camera accessories in general. Whereas the early tripods could only accommodate horizontal and vertical movement of the camera (pans and tilts), the modern ones developed in those years were also capable of roll movement. The camera could be moved practically in any direction imaginable.[4]

To hear and see better, to know more ... films attempt to satisfy these narrative requirements in order to provide the most complete artistic realization possible. Camera movements became more complex as, in its turn, the narrative tone became more complex and symbolic.

The use of the dolly became widespread; a version called the 'railroad' dolly was built for use in train corridors and, in 1929, the crane made its debut – a more imposing structure than the dolly with an arm that could reach as high as 15 m. The crane was created in response to the need for spectacular camera movement and to give the spectator a better view of the action. It consisted of a large trolley with a long projecting arm, at the end of which was a platform that held the camera and the operator. This machine made it possible to combine a number of camera movements in more complex dynamic arrangements (i.e. to pan and boom together). The spectacular images that resulted made it an indispensable tool.

The camera now moved through space: it could be moved forward, backward, to the right or left, up and down and also diagonally and in a circle. It is important to remember that all this movement was achieved through the work done by grips, who had to deal with the bulky and heavy equipment and counterbalances necessary for the various manoeuvres and which only later was made lighter and easier to use.

The end of the 1940s saw the development of the crab dolly, which provided even greater flexibility for manoeuvring:

> a crab dolly can be steered by all four wheels interconnected to turn together, as well as by the usual two-wheel steering. Hence it can be instantaneously turned from a movement tracking straight forwards to a 'crabbing' movement sideways at 90 degrees to the original path.[5]

This process of optimization of all equipment used on set and on location continued, so that it slowly evolved in those years to respond to various needs. However, even after the Second World War the fundamental aspects of such equipment still mirrored the structures that had been defined with the advent of sound.

The official debut of television in 1936 conditioned the course of technical research in the years that followed. Having established itself during the 1950s as a means of providing both entertainment and information with news programmes and services following events around the world, television found that in order to be present at events and report them, it needed to film quickly and efficiently, using camera operators who could go anywhere.

The new kind of reportage made it necessary to shoot with more agility, which required more easily handled equipment and smaller crews for location shooting. Consequently, research aims now included the building of lighter cameras and better accessories.

In 1953 a lens was introduced to the market, destined only for the 16 mm camera, but which would later become an indispensable accessory of every movie camera: the zoom lens. As it is a lens with a variable focal length, it can give the illusion of movement by passing from one degree of magnification to another, i.e. by going from a short focal length (wide-angle) to a long focal length (telephoto lens) it appears that one is moving closer. Actually, as opposed to the dolly that really moves through space and maintains a consistent sense of depth and a natural variation of perspective, the zoom lens only appears to make a travelling shot as the observation point does not change and only the magnification varies, enlarging or diminishing the object viewed.

Looking back, we can see that cinematic equipment was evolving in the direction of ever-greater freedom of camera movement. In fact, the 1960s saw the development of many different devices and techniques in this sense, which also gave new inspiration to filmmakers who were quick to take advantage of the new technology.[6] For example, the camera car (a truck set on shock-absorbing springs and adapted to hold the camera) was increasingly used for shots of automobiles and of objects seen from the passengers' point of view.

Filmmaking profited from various technical developments such as the zoom lens, lighter-weight cameras and improved lighting equipment. Since these had the effect of speeding up filming, they were particularly useful in the production of low-budget movies. A perfect example is the use of the hand-held camera, which came to embody various movements in the history of cinema, such as 'free cinema' and 'nouvelle vague'.

> The movement of the hand-held camera moves with leaps and bounds, jerking in a discontinuous and irregular way. This type of movement, which is necessarily present in many films of 'reportage', becomes widespread during the second half of the 1950s with the diffusion of 'cinema verité', which used it to create a more direct and immediate relationship with reality.[7]

The advantage of this kind of shot is that it does not require the positioning of a tripod, the responsibility for the shot being entirely the operator's, who can act without delay, using existing light or a fairly approximate lighting set-up. In addition, as there is no significant presence at the location, the need to obtain permits is eliminated and the crew can leave the site as soon as the shoot is finished.

Various braces and harnesses were developed to fix the camera to the operator's body so that he could hold the camera without fatigue. However, these did not prevent the camera from jerking, and so devices for smoother movement, such as the gyro stabilizer, were designed. One of these, built originally for military binoculars, was positioned under the camera and guaranteed a certain horizontal stability for hand-held shots. The inconveniences of this set-up were that it was impossible simultaneously to shoot pans and tilt shots owing to the direction of rotation of the gyroscope, and it resulted in considerable extra weight for the operator to carry on top of the already substantial weight of the cameras of that time (also because the average production used the 35 mm camera and not the lighter 16 mm).

At the same time, research continued into the remote control of camera angle, which made it possible to obtain shots in positions and situations previously considered impossible. The Louma, a crane with varying lengths of 'arm' that can be put together on location, was the first to provide a remote-controlled pan and tilt head for the camera at its end. This increased the expressive possibilities for filmmakers, since it was sufficiently light and portable to be erected in places where it would be impossible to erect a normal crane.[8]

In the 1970s researchers focused on further separating the camera from the man and began using computers to automate various functions. This meant, however, giving over much of the responsibility for making the shot to machines and computers, as happened with John Dykstra's motion-control work in *Star Wars* (1977).

At this time, Garrett Brown's work on the Steadicam finally (and paradoxically) made it possible to obtain a true reunion of man and real-time image-capturing machine: hand-held and movable, as if a direct part of the operator's body; smooth as a dolly shot, but without the arbitrary mechanical constraints of rails and wheels. As Garrett Brown says

> Camera as Fonteyn, operator as Nureyev would be the ideal – a dance partnership capable of any vector of graceful motion within the range of the operator's hands, arms and legs. Camera as simply an instrument of the operator's expression in three dimensional space – capable, as operators get increasingly skilful, of going nearly anywhere and doing nearly anything that can be imagined ...[9]

Types of camera movement

The importance of camera movement varies according to the narrative requirements of the shot or sequence. It often plays a fundamental role in the construction and development of the story. The main types of camera motion are:

1 Angular
   - *Pan shot* – the camera is rotated around its vertical axis.

- The *whip pan* is a very quick pan, in which it is almost impossible to perceive the intermediate images between the beginning and the end.
- *Tilt* – the camera turns, from a fixed point, towards the top or the bottom (the horizontal is blocked).
- *Roll* – the camera is rotated around an axis along the line of sight of the lens.

2 Spatial
- *Boom* – the camera is moved up and down on its vertical axis.
- *Tracking* – linear motion of the camera by means of a dolly (the platform on which the camera is mounted on rubber wheels or rails according to the type of ground and desired effects); a translational movement. Tracking can be:
  - *forward* – to give the effect of forward movement or to approach a subject and focus the viewer's attention on it; to precede the character
  - *backward* – to pull away from the subject to reveal the larger scene, to diminish the subject's importance; to follow
  - *transversal* or circling – the camera moves transversally or laterally on its own axis to place the subject in three dimensions, to see various sides of the subject or to simply pass by
  - *to accompany* – both the camera and the actors are moving.
- *Camera car* – the tracking can be done from a camera car.
- *Aerial shot* – the camera is on an aeroplane, helicopter, etc.
- *Crane and dolly* – the camera is fixed above the arm to facilitate upward and downward movements or 360° rotation, thus combining various movements. The crane and dolly are very stable, mounted on a wheeled platform that holds a mobile arm. They differ in the size of the arm and the maximum height reached, the dolly having a maximum of 4 m and a crane more than 15 m. There are also mini-dollies of more reduced dimensions, which are easier to control.
- *Zoom* – although an optical movement, zoom gives the illusion of moving closer to and further away from the subject by magnifying the image.
  - *zoom in* – the camera seems to close in on the subject
  - *zoom out* – the camera seems to move away from the subject
  - *snap zoom* – a zoom movement into the subject done at maximum speed.

The function of camera movements

When discussing camera movements, it is necessary to explain their function in movies. In fact, besides following the actor's movements, illustrating and depicting the setting and travelling through space, they may also serve the purpose of generating the 'sense of creation' of the film. The film unfolds before our eyes in a certain way thanks to the camera, which chooses for us what is 'important': it enters a room, lingers on certain objects, exits through a window, descends three floors of a building and in the doorway picks up again a character who is just coming out ... Merely by how it moves, it creates suspense, tension and is able to convey the feeling of time and space.

There are many ways to use camera movement that aid in the construction of the story and, as with framing, in obtaining the best possible portrayal of what is happening.

> Camera movements, whose main purpose is that of maintaining the central element of the 'profilmic'[10] and directing the viewer's attention to it.[11]

As well as the 'justified' use of a camera's movement, such as in following a character, it can also be used as a cinematic device to indicate the presence of the narrator, the person who holds the threads of the story, organizes the spaces, knows what is happening. In this case, the movement chosen no longer appears to serve the purposes of the story, but is used by the narrator to evidence his otherwise subdued presence. The camera movements may respond to such a need by anticipating events, waiting, abandoning the action before its conclusion, following the 'internal movement' of the creator of the story.

Camera movement can thus be divided into two main categories: 'motivated movements', those that follow the path of a character or a moving object whilst maintaining a certain distance, viewpoint and speed relative to the subject; and 'free movements', in which 'detached from the action of the scene, the camera moves independently through space'.[12]

Within a film, this division is not clear-cut, precisely because often a movement begun in one way (i.e. following a character) is transformed into another, so changing its function. Furthermore, this might not be particularly noticeable, so that it is difficult to catch the meaning of the camera moves unless one is analysing them in detail. As with other manifestations of cinematic technique, there can be various levels of interpretation; consequently, the result is tied to a sequence of meanings and the value assumed by a move is determined by the role the move has been given. For example, the camera may seem to be following a character but it will then linger, even if for just an instant, on the empty space from which the character has just departed (for example, in *The Shining*, Danny in the corridor ... see Chapter 2). Although this seems to assign a descriptive role to the movement, it is actually evidence of the presence of a gaze from above, pointing to something which, precisely because the spectator can not clearly identify it, creates tension.

Often, in fact, the role of the camera movement is to take on 'the gaze of the character', to create that mechanism by which the movement of drawing nearer or further away is determined by what the character is seeing (as for example in *The Untouchables*). Thus, the gaze of the character is incarnated in the structure of the movement itself of the camera towards, or away from, something. Such movements take on particular characteristics according to the situation. Each encounter is a surprise, mitigated by slowness if the movement is one of measured discovery, or exaggerated by frenzy if the movement forward has the rapid, jerky style of the hand-held camera.

Numerous effects can be obtained. In the subjective shot, in which the character's gaze and the camera's vision coincide, the movement gains a particular tension and the development becomes imperative, exactly because greater or lesser knowledge is dependent on its going forward: the viewer tends to identify with what he or she sees and his/her gaze moves and learns synchronously with the camera.

Film, intended as a large-scale look at life and objects, is a transposition onto the screen of precisely that movement of the eyes and person which is natural in real life but exceptional when depicted on film. Normally we pay selective attention to what we see, unlike the global and total vision of a film. A shot catches many more elements than does the human eye; consequently, the time the spectator needs to perceive and comprehend it must be taken into account.

Camera movement, like other cinematic elements such as editing, should not exceed a certain speed (unless it is justified by narrative requirements) because the time needed to 'read' the image is determined by the physiology of the eye and the brain. The speed involved in the process of building the rhythm of the film, on the other hand, can exceed perceptible levels and exacerbate the viewer's appreciation of the image, in order to follow the rhythm of 'creative time'.

Notes

1 Bernardo, M. (1983). *La macchina del cinematografo*. Gruppo Edit, Forma, p. 82.
2 '*Cabiria*' Giovanni Pastrone, 1914. Pastrone was the first to use the dolly with new narrative intent that showed the three-dimensional effect of the huge scenographies. A new name was given to the dolly shot – 'alla Cabiria'.
3 System patented by A.C.G. Petersen and A. Poulsen in 1924.
4 This was due to various new kinds of heads: friction heads, in which the operator's movement is blocked by a series of gears that are regulated separately; and gear heads, in which the horizontal and vertical rotation movement is assured by two cranks that precisely reduce the movements, decreasing the amount of physical effort necessary.
5 Salt, B. (1992) *Film Style Technology: History and Analysis*. 2nd edition. London: Starwood, p. 231.
6 The Spider Elemac, a little dolly which can be moved in any direction.
7 Rondolino, G.-Tomasi, D. (1975) *Manuale del film*. Torino: Ed. UTET, Libreria, p. 122.
8 Salt, B. (1992) *Film Style Technology: History and Analysis*. 2nd edition. London: Starwood. 'Film style and technology in the 1980s: The idea of using the panning and tilting movements of cameras gained more and more ground during this decade. The Louma crane, ... was joined by various other devices incorporating electric motors driving a pan and tilt head that could be attached to any standard camera support system. These came to be called generically "hot heads"... '.
9 Personal communication, February 2000.
10 Rondolino, G.-Tomasi, *op. cit.* p. 50 'Each shot is always the result of choices made at two levels. The first is that of the *profilmic*, meaning everything which is in front of the camera, which is there for the purpose of being filmed and is a concrete part of the story being told (settings, characters, objects). The second level which determines the characteristics of a shot is the *filmic*, which has to do with discourse, properly called the language of cinema, or, more simply, the ways in which the profilmic elements are portrayed'. *op. cit.*
11 Rondolino, G.-Tomasi, *op. cit.*
12 Rondolino, G.-Tomasi, *op. cit.*

2 The Steadicam

Invention of the Steadicam

> The STEADICAM was conceived as a stunt camera, designed for running shots over rough ground, but by the time of its feature debut in 1975, we were beginning to realize that we had underestimated its potential.[1]

In the early 1970s camera operator Garrett Brown began thinking about a way to improve the stability of hand-held camera shots, with the idea of building a support for the camera that would isolate it from the jerking caused by the operator's movements. The need for such a support became apparent to him during work on a shot he was directing. A very unwieldy and heavy dolly was being used for the take, which needed slow and descriptive pans. Brown thought that there must be a simpler way to achieve the same results.

The first step was to conceive a support for the camera that would be easier to handle, and that would allow a hand-held camera to be as stable as one mounted on a dolly. To circumvent the problem of the hand-held camera inevitably capturing the movements transmitted to it by the operator, Garrett began to look for a way to disconnect the camera from the operator's body. So, he mounted the camera on a post, for support, and put weights on the other end of the post to balance the camera's weight.

> I wanted to improve the look of my hand-held shooting. I was intrigued and built a long 't-bar' rig of plumbing pipe, which was stable in all directions as one ran around the countryside. It was clumsy and rolled a lot, but the footage looked surprisingly good. I suppose if I had been satisfied with this gadget (which gets re-invented from time in this business, e.g. 'Shaki-cam' and 'Pogo cam'), the project would have ultimately fizzled, but I couldn't quite leave it alone.[2]

Later, he added a handle to position the camera exactly at the balancing point and improved the structure, replacing the rigid post with a long parallelogram, creating a 'minicrane' (Figure 2.1).[3]

In order to support this contraption, he added a system of cables and pulleys, which brought all the weight to bear on the operator's shoulder.

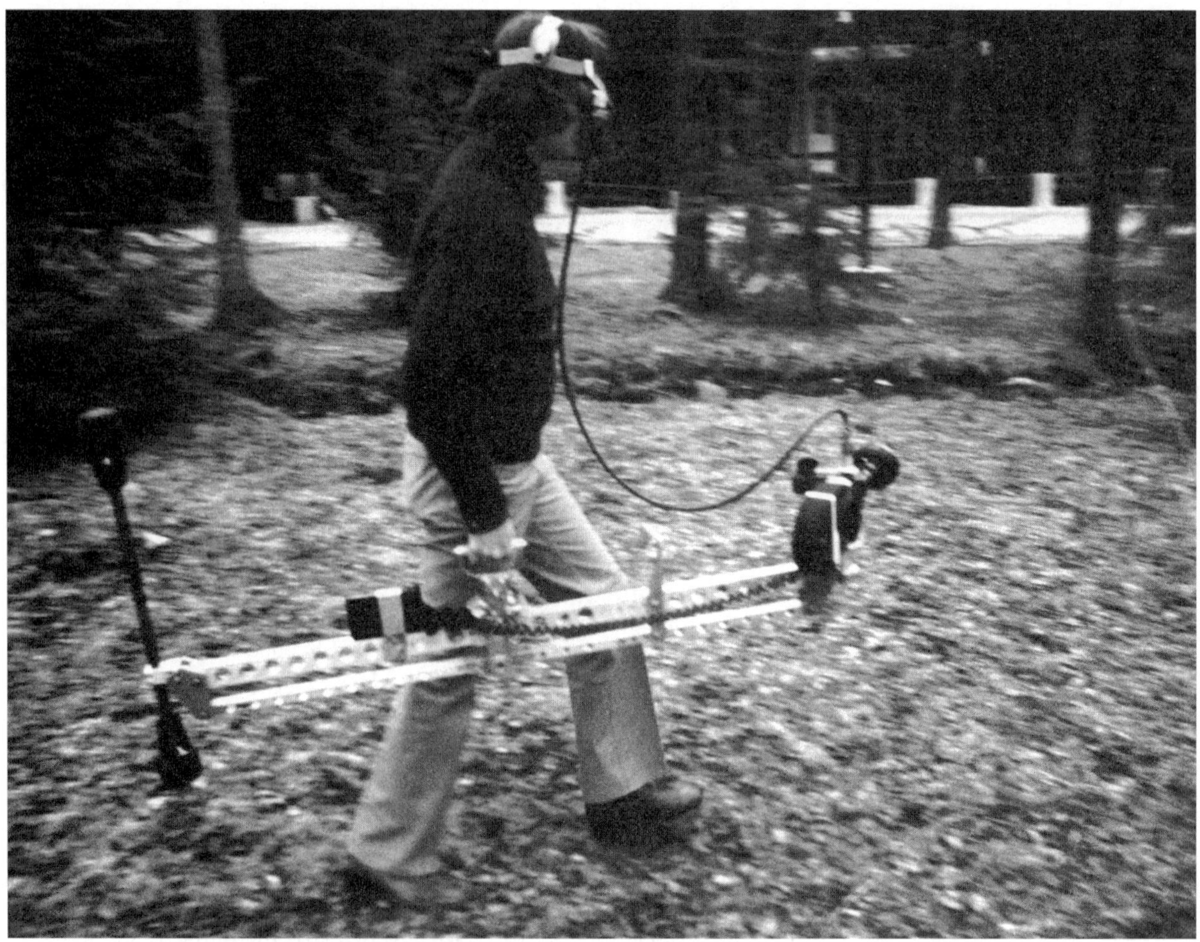

Figure 2.1 First trials with the parallelogram-crane version of the 'Pole Rig', using heavy weights to stabilize Garrett's ACL 16 mm camera. Note the first 8-mm-thick version of the fibre optic viewfinder and the lack of a 'vest'. Photo: Garrett Brown collection

What he wanted was a piece of equipment that would give him the same quality of movement as a dolly, that had the capacity to 'boom' the lens height continuously from above the head down to ground level with the camera mount kept parallel to the ground, and which would allow the camera to be moved in all directions while still remaining isolated from all movements of the operator. The idea was on track but the structure turned out to be excessively heavy and unwieldy, despite giving good results on film (Figure 2.2).

Garrett had to take another look at his creation, make some compromises with regard to his expectations (i.e. stop insisting that the camera could move from above the head down to the feet) and solve the main problem: the weight and size, which were too inhibiting for the operator. After a number of attempts, Garrett had the key – success would require a *combination* of several unlikely devices: an **expanded camera**, with its various parts separated from each other to increase their inertia; a '**gimbal**' (a series of bearings and rings that provide support but do not transmit angular influences) connected to an '**arm**' made of a double parallelogram of spring-loaded links to carry the weight (instead of the operator's own arm) and to isolate the camera from unwanted lateral and vertical movements as the operator walks, runs or climbs stairs. Finally,

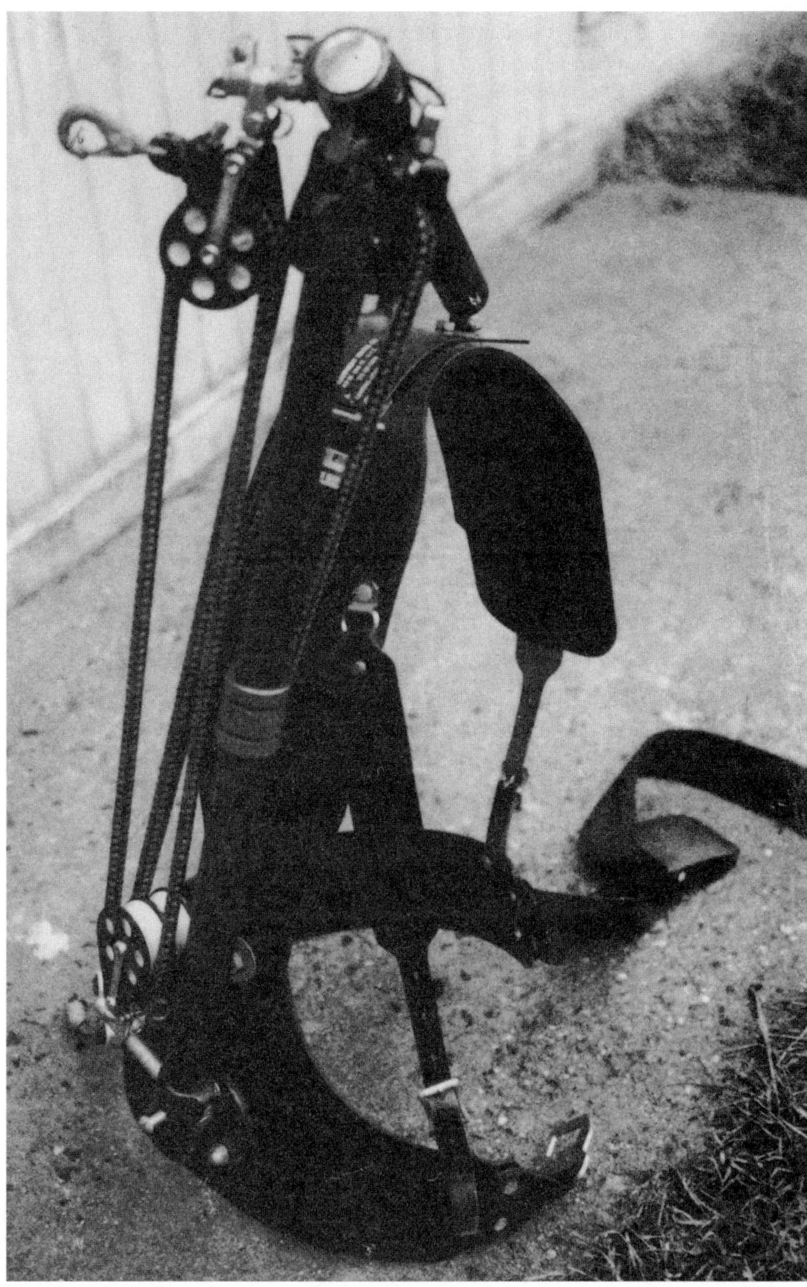

Figure 2.2 The first 'vest', showing Garrett's 'endless-bunji-cord' suspension built to relieve the awful load of the parallelogram-crane stabilizer of 1972. Photo: Garrett Brown collection

Garrett realized that he could no longer keep his eye on a viewfinder without causing the camera to bump and jerk, and so the last piece of the puzzle was the addition of a method to **monitor** the image (originally by means of a fibre-optic tube, but eventually by a video screen). These four items became the basis for Garrett's original patent, and he found that when (and only when) all four were combined, the result was astonishing – a device capable of eliminating the operator's unwanted motions and producing a shot as smooth as if on wheels (Figure 2.3).

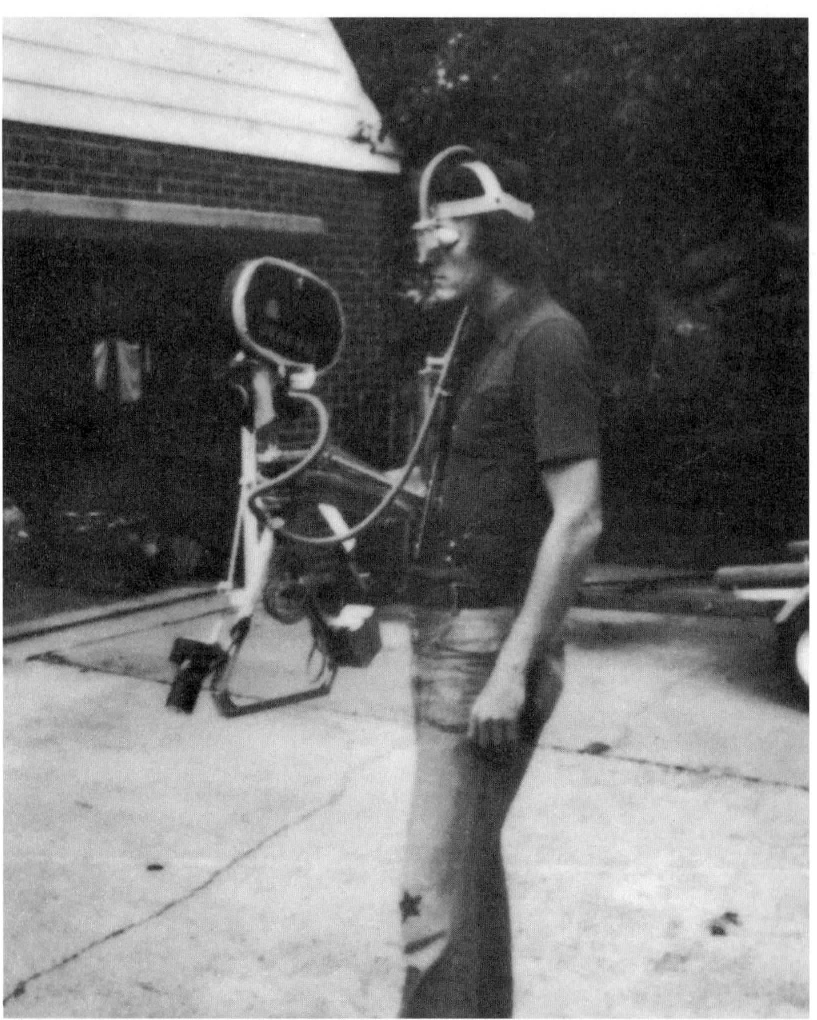

Figure 2.3 1973. The first prototype. Note the helmet to hold the fibre optic viewfinder in contact with Garrett's eye. Photo: Garrett Brown collection

As Garrett recalled later,

> I did finally emerge with 'The Invention'. I had a model of the arm, made with parts from a couple of parallelogram desk lamps, and a sketch of the absolute minimum configuration for mounting the camera, battery, magazine and monitor. I believed it would work well for fast-moving shots, but doubted it would ever give the dolly much competition for precision (remember, I was used to versions with the inertia of the Chrysler Building). At worst, I thought it could be simpler, smaller and lighter and therefore had a chance to be sold, so I decided to build one final version.[4]

After a series of prototypes, Brown created the 'Brown Stabilizer', which was later given the name Steadicam (see interview with Ed DiGiulio p. 140). The description for the US patent, granted on 12 April 1977, reads:

> A portable camera equipment system especially adapted for operation by a camera operator in motion and capable of being hand-guided, the system being of improved stability against angular deviation in pan, tilt and roll, and substantially free-floating in a manner to isolate

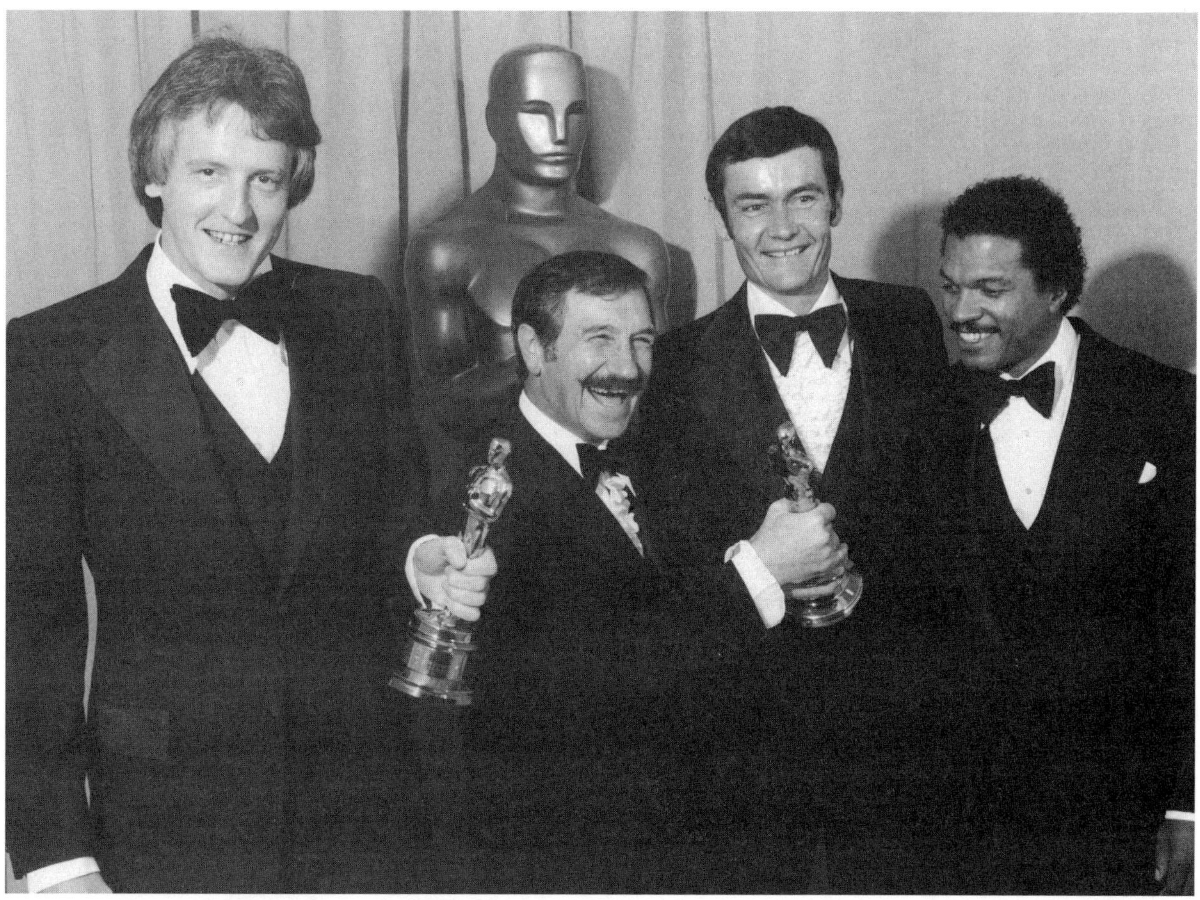

Figure 2.4 Garrett Brown, Ed DiGiulio and John Jurgens celebrate the 1977 Oscar for Steadicam, with presenter Billy Dee Williams. Photo: Garrett Brown collection

> the equipment also from unwanted lateral and vertical movement caused by the motion of the camera operator using the equipment.[5]

In 1978 this invention brought Garrett Brown and Cinema Products Corporation an Oscar (Figure 2.4), a success repeated eleven years later with the awarding of an Emmy.

The first-generation Steadicam

The first-generation Steadicam system[6] (Figure 2.5) was made up of a body brace worn by the operator (operator's vest), to which an articulated arm (stabilizer support arm) was attached. At its other end, the arm supported a post on top of which were mounted the camera and the viewfinder, while the lower portion held the battery pack for the power supply (Figure 2.6).

Since 1975 the Steadicam has evolved considerably as its designer has continued to experiment with it, making use of his own experiences and those of other operators. Today, the Steadicam is a highly perfected system for supporting the camera that makes it possible to shoot while moving or standing still, with the operator completely isolated from his equipment and yet 'wearing' it. It is available in different models to fit both movie cameras (16, 35 mm) and video cameras.

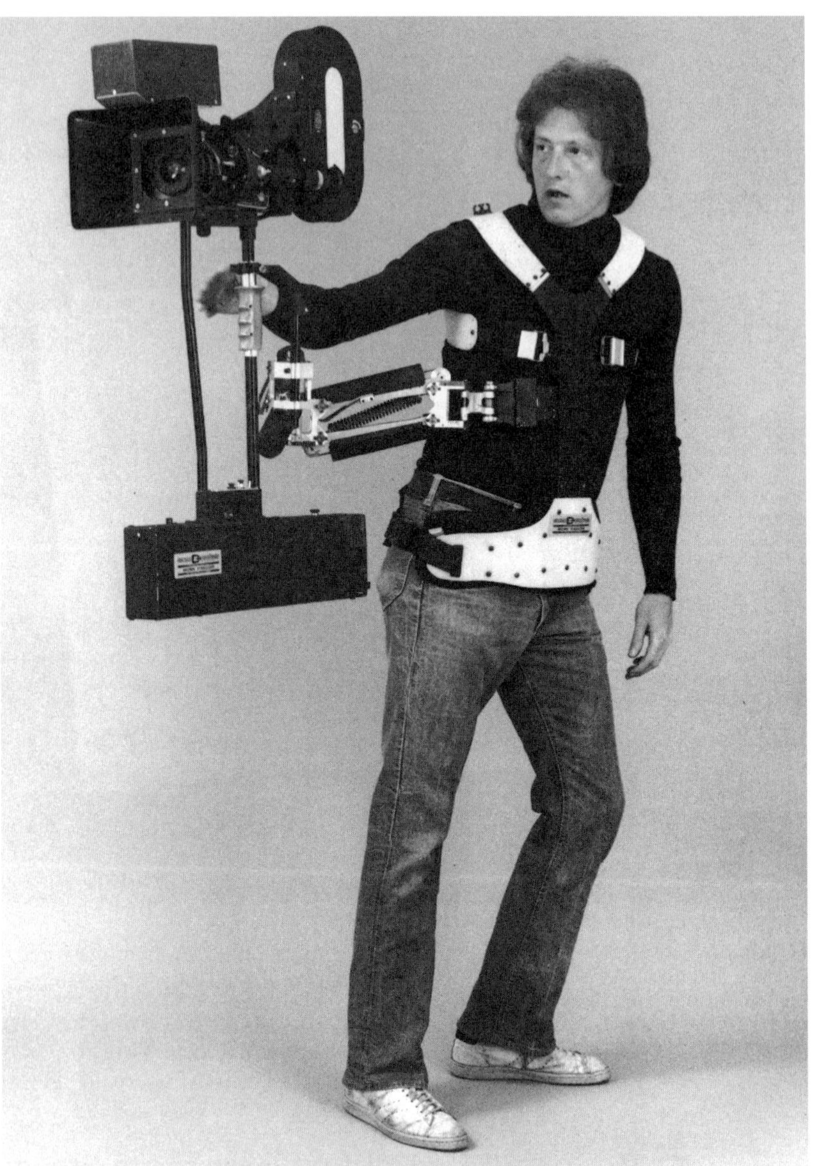

Figure 2.5 The first commercial model – the CP-35, with its built-in Arriflex camera. Photo: Garrett Brown collection

Steadicam structure

The Steadicam consists of the following (Figure 2.7).

1 The *Camera Operator's Vest*. This effectively distributes the weight of the Steadicam system (including the camera and lenses) over the operator's shoulders, back and hips. The vest has straps for adjusting the fit and has velcro closures for ease of use. The stabilizer support arm, attached to the frontplate on the lower right or left side as desired, links the vest to the rest of the system.
2 The *Stabilizer Support Arm*. This is a support system that parallels the complete range of the operator's arm movements and

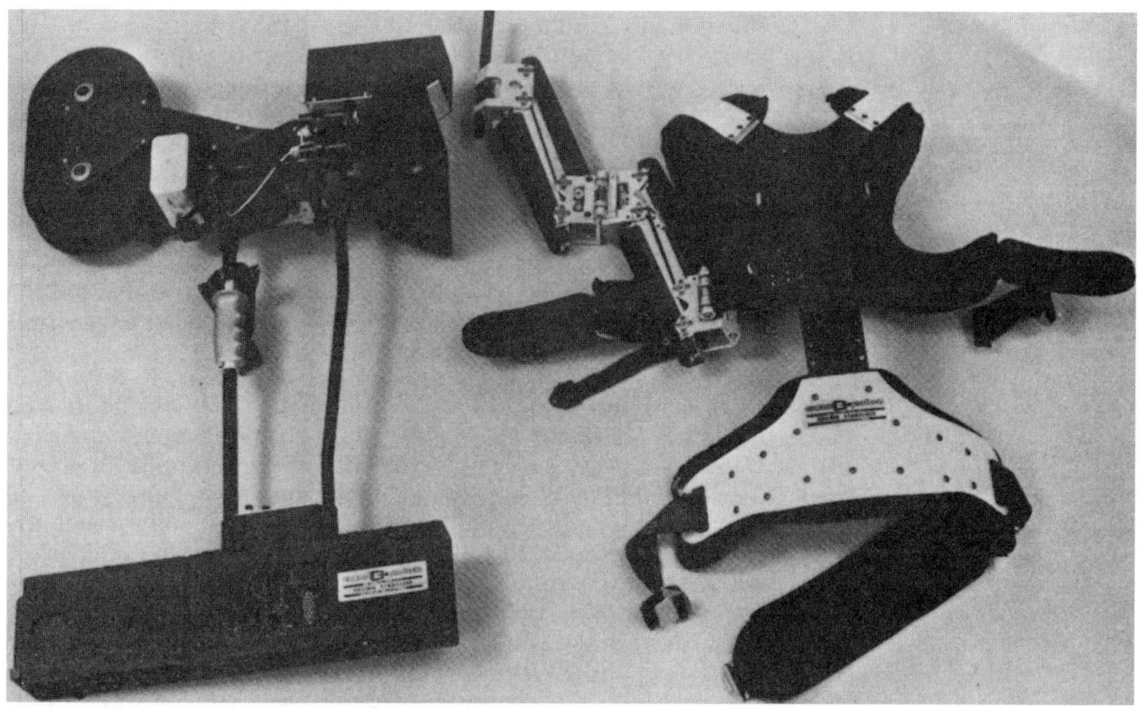

Figure 2.6 The complete Steadicam–35 system. Photo: Garrett Brown collection

Figure 2.7 The components of the Steadicam: vest, arm and 'sled' (Model III, c. 1983). Photo: Garrett Brown collection

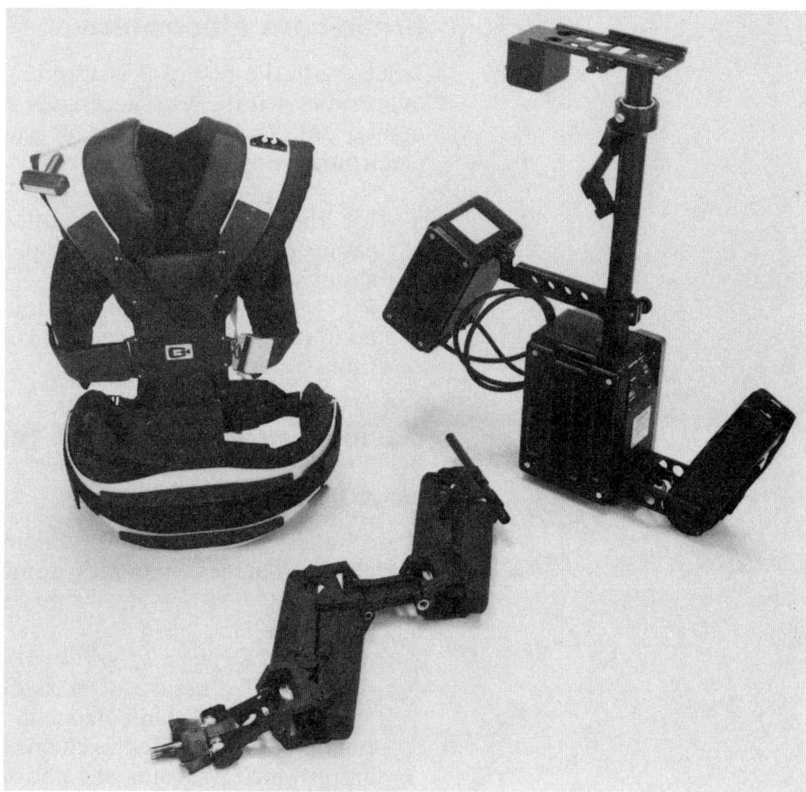

substantially counteracts the weight of the camera system with its spring-loaded links. It consists of a pair of articulated parallelograms, each of which acts as a spring shock-absorption system, connected to each other by an elbow hinge. The arm absorbs and neutralizes the vertical and lateral bumps transmitted by the operator when walking, running, jumping or so forth. It is the heart of the Steadicam system and uses titanium springs, which are lightweight and highly resistant to stress.

3 The *Telescoping Support Post*. This post, which can be lengthened or shortened, has the camera mounting platform on top and the Electronics Module, battery housing and monitor on the lower end. It is connected to the arm by means of a low-friction, free-floating *gimbal*. The gimbal is designed to rotate up to 360° on all three axes and to withstand the forces generated by the moving equipment. The power supply (12–15 volt, 3.5 amp/hour nickel-cadmium battery pack) plugs into the lower portion of the post.

4 The *Monitor*. Like a viewfinder, the monitor shows what the camera sees. It allows the operator, who cannot look through the camera viewfinder, to follow and control the action and his or her own movements. The screen has a filter with an anti-reflective coating that eliminates reflections on its face, including those from direct sunlight. The monitor can be pivoted around the post or slid up or down the full length of it. In this way, the entire system can be turned upside down to convert to the 'Low Mode' configuration, in which the camera can be held just a few inches above the ground.

Steadicam Electronics

Just as with the rest of the system, the Steadicam electronics evolved over time, with each successive model, to provide better performance and to give operators greater control of the device. The electronic components consist of:

- for the CP-35 model: (monitor separate above built-in Arri camera) camera motor and amplifier, monitor high-voltage supply and battery
- for Model I: included monitor, power supply, battery and adaptor card slot for plug-in cards to adapt to various video and film cameras.[7]

Basic principles used in the Steadicam

How it works

The Steadicam's structure (Figure 2.8) uses three fundamental principles to achieve its extraordinary characteristics of balance and stability:

1 *Shifting the centre of gravity of the camera*
The so-called centre of mass or centre of gravity is the point at which an object is in balance in all three dimensions. If the operator could apply force exclusively at the camera's centre of mass an unwanted transfer of rotation would be limited. This is impos-

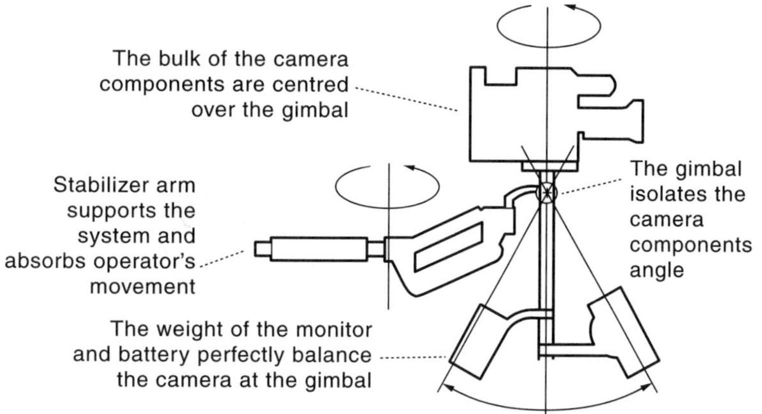

Figure 2.8 The basic principles used in the Steadicam

sible, however, because a camera's centre of gravity is too deep inside the machine for the operator to use it to advantage. Instead, the operator's manipulations inevitably cause the camera to undergo rotation. By placing the camera at one end of the post and the battery and monitor at the other end, once the rig is balanced, the Steadicam system has its centre of gravity in the post just below the gimbal. The camera rests at the level of the horizon and the operator can manipulate the rig without adding unwanted rotation. In short, the principal characteristic of the Steadicam system is that it stabilizes the camera by using balance, isolation and inertia. The job of the operator using the Steadicam is not to remove instability, but to shoot without adding any.

2 *Spreading the camera mass*
The worst enemy of image steadiness is camera rotation. The Steadicam fights this rotational instability by increasing the camera's inertia. By having the camera mounted on one end of the post and the monitor and batteries on the other, the Steadicam structure spreads the camera's mass and increases its moment of inertia[8] sufficiently to counteract the rapid and involuntary rotational movements transmitted to the camera. The operator can easily give the camera any rotational movements required, thanks to the positioning of the gimbal at the centre of gravity of the entire system.

3 *Camera isolation*
The Steadicam isolates the camera from all but the largest movements of the operator by means of the stabilizer arm and gimbal. The gimbal prevents unwanted effects from the angular movements of the operator (and allows the camera to be aimed with the lightest possible touch), and the arm's two-spring system absorbs the up-and-down jerks caused by the operator's movements through exploiting the high inertia of the rig (camera and electronics) and the flexibility of its support (the arm). The structure also isolates the camera from unwanted forward and lateral movements owing to the flexibility of the arm's 'joints'.

The potential of the Steadicam

The camera system is attached to the support arm by means of a free-floating gimbal. In this manner, the camera operator is able to pan or

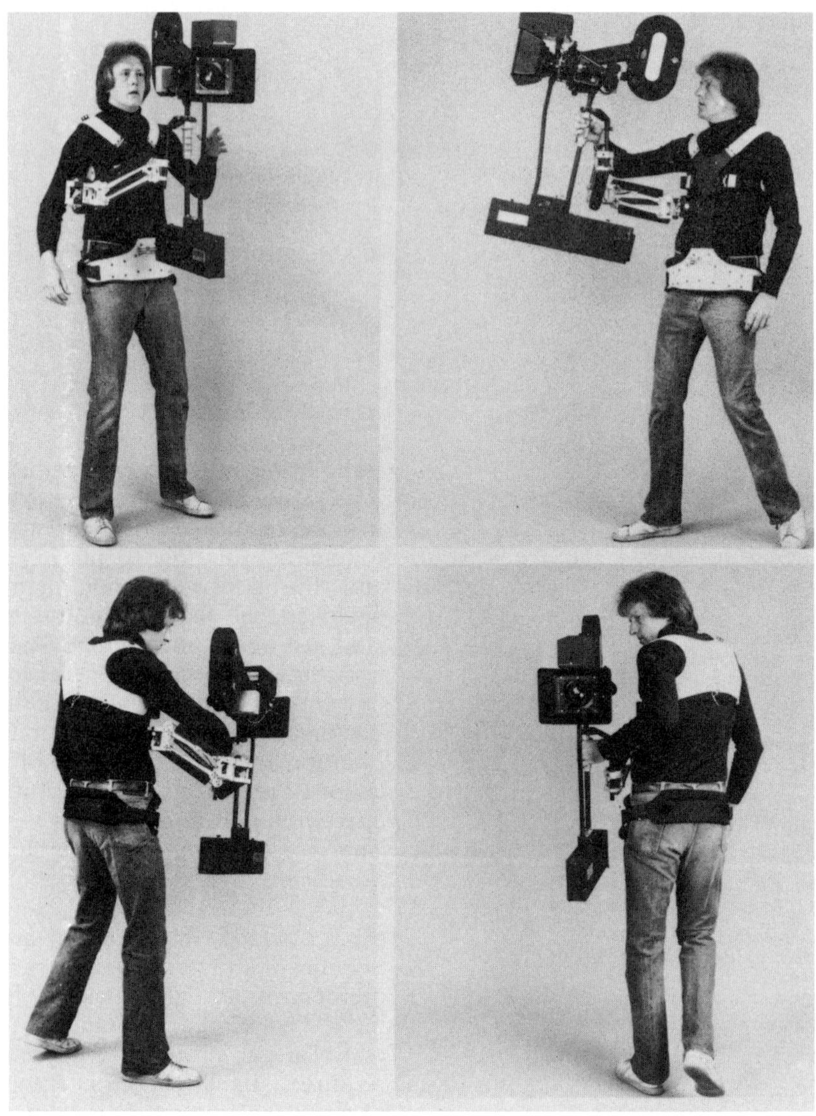

Figure 2.9 Garrett Brown demonstrates the amazing manoeuvrability of his invention in four poses showing the one-handed operating positions with the 'Brown Stabilizer', c. 1975. By the time it was sold in 1976 it had been renamed 'Steadicam'. Photo: Garrett Brown collection

> tilt the camera at will, and move it up or down, or side to side, in a free-floating manner.
>
> For instance, the camera operator can boom up or down nearly three feet, he can pan a full 360° or tilt up or down without limit ... and he can accomplish all this while he himself is in motion.[9]

The Steadicam can be used for a great number of different shots, thanks to the movements it can make and the positions it can be placed in (Figure 2.9):

- High-mode and low-mode are the two main configurations of the Steadicam, which make it possible to shoot from a maximum height of above the operator's head to a minimum height of just below the operator's knees.
- Don Juan and Missionary are the two main positions for the

operator. The first allows him to walk holding the rig facing in front of him; the second to walk forward shooting with the rig facing behind him.

- The operator can adjust his position with respect to the frame, according to what is necessary for making the shot, without altering it in any way since he can move himself around the camera at will.
- The Steadicam can make all the classic camera moves:
  - *horizontal pan* (easily, since it is done with respect to the vertical axis, which coincides with the post)
  - *vertical tilt* (the camera moves up or down along a vertical axis, more control is needed with regard to balance)
  - *whip pan* (very fast, can be done both by rotating the camera rapidly through its own vertical axis – the post – or by the operator moving together with the rig)
  - *roll* (the camera moves sideways around the horizontal axis, passing through the camera parallel to the direction from which light enters the camera lens)
  - *booming*: since the Steadicam was designed to remain balanced (thanks to the increase in inertia created by moving the centre of gravity out of the camera and spreading the masses), it is perfect for booming up and down, and this movement can be done without affecting camera angle. On the other hand, movements that involve the other axes need greater control to avoid deviations during execution.
- Furthermore, the place where the arm is attached to the vest can be switched from right to left as needed. It is important for an operator to learn equal control of the rig on both sides.
- The usefulness of the Steadicam is further increased by combining it with other devices and forms of transport, such as cranes and various types of vehicle, which increase its range, speed or scope of movement, while preserving the Steadicam's image stabilizing properties.
- Objective vehicle/subjective vehicle: when the Steadicam is mounted on a vehicle it can shoot from the point of view of the 'vehicle' to the subject, recreating, simulating or negating the movements of the vehicle and viewing as either an onlooker or the 'narrator' would; or it can include part of the vehicle in the frame, such as in shots from within a car, train, boat, etc., which incidentally remove the vehicle's inherent motion in order to see more as the human eye does. The Steadicam also has the ability to simulate the motion of a vehicle, such as a plane or boat, while shooting on an essentially static set. This is done by rolling, vibrating or booming the Steadicam during the shot to give the correct illusion of motion (Figure 2.10).

The great variety of shots that can be obtained with the Steadicam

Because of how it is made, the Steadicam can obtain a great variety of shots. It is good for going down narrow alleys, scraping along walls and going through doors, precisely because the operator no longer

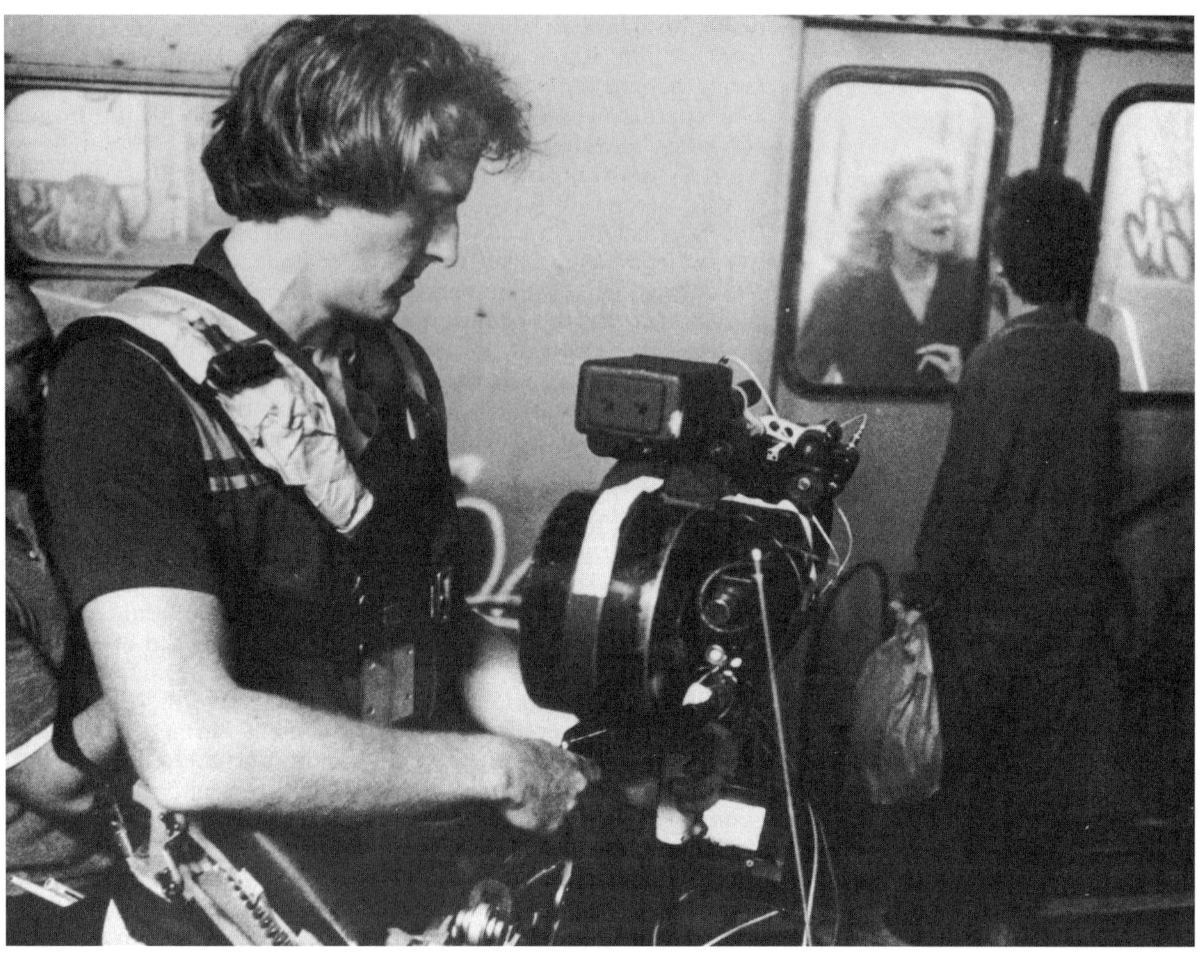

Figure 2.10 *Fame*. After a hair-raising run down four flights of steps to this New York subway platform toting the Arri BL, Garrett concentrates on a 'lock-off' end frame. Note the ancient, patched-with-tape Steadicam vest and the 'quick-release' handle that allows the operator to escape in an emergency (Garrett has only needed it twice in 20 years). Photo: Garrett Brown collection

has an eye glued to the viewfinder but is looking at a monitor with the equipment held a short distance away.[10]

> *The Fugitive*. Chase scene in drainage tunnels.
> *The Sheltering Sky*. Kit and her guide race through the alleys and passageways of Maadid looking for a doctor.

It moves well over rough ground, slopes and along trails through thick vegetation:

> *Casualties of War*. Steadicam operator Larry McConkey: 'I shot a number of scenes where the squad was marching over bridges, through villages, along mountain trails, tracking shots that would change, for example, from two then three soldiers in frame, and then down along the line of men to someone else and so forth ...'.[11]

It is good for long sequences when the tracks for a dolly cannot be set up or the scene cannot have interruptions:

> *Raising Cain*. Long walk of two policemen and a doctor who leave an office, go down two corridors, take an elevator and then climb two flights of stairs on their way to the Police Department headquarters.

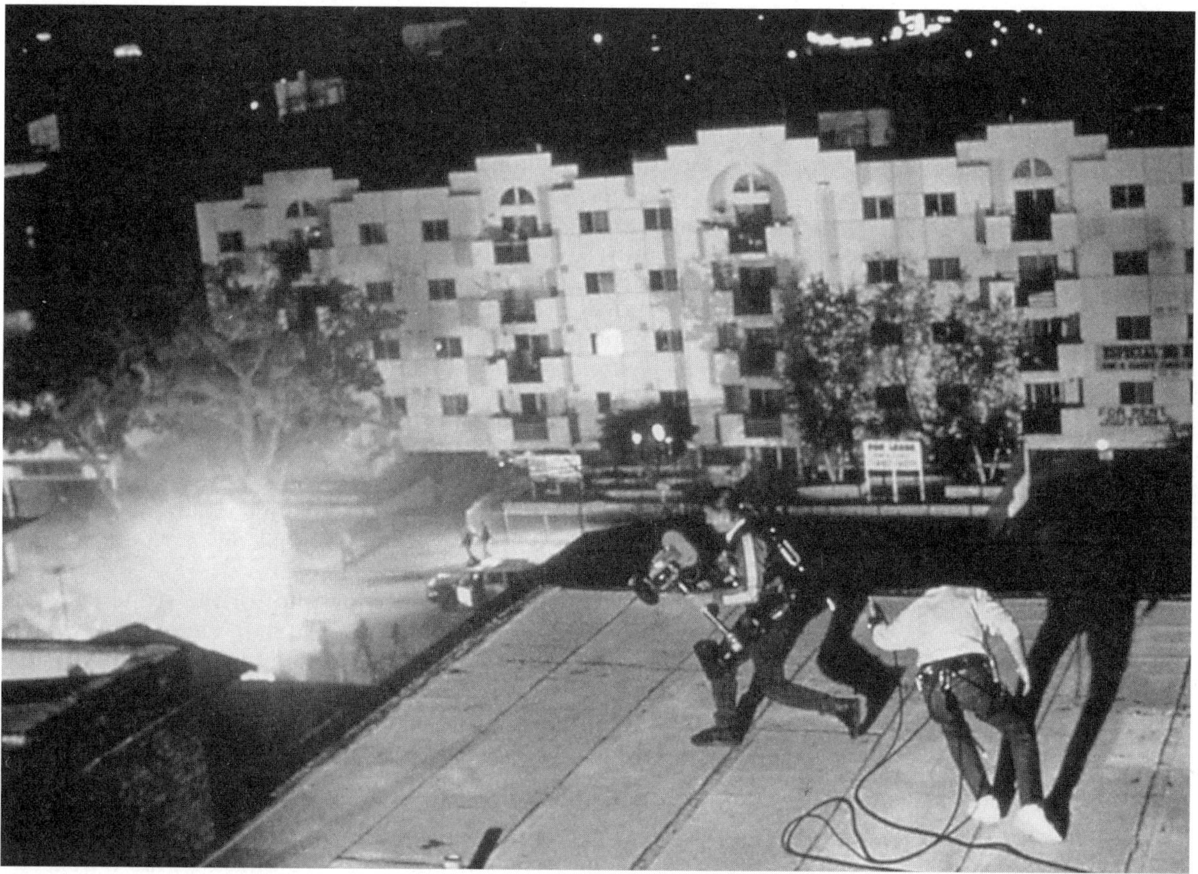

Figure 2.11 *Strange Days*. The operator and his assistant with the Steadicam while, attached to a safety line, they follow Lane's flight at high speed, simulating the gaze of the accomplice, which will then be experienced by the moviegoer as his own observation point. Photo: Mondadori Press

The Bonfire of the Vanities. The walk at the beginning is a 5-minute scene shot by Steadicam.
Snake Eyes. The entire opening scene as the main character makes his way to the place where the boxing match is held, almost 12 minutes long.

The Steadicam is also used:

- When no other set-up will work to get shots with a lot of effect but undisturbed by camera jarring:
  Strange Days. The robbers' flight, seen from the point of view of one of them who begins to run as soon as he gets out of the car at the restaurant they plan to rob ... hallways ... stairs ... roof of the building and free fall (much of the scene is uninterrupted and shot by Steadicam) (Figure 2.11).
- For moving through crowded spaces:
- *La mort en direct*. Romy Schneider's race through the flea-market.
- To isolate the camera from any vehicle on which it is mounted, i.e. car, motorcycle, horse, helicopter ...
- For any dolly shot: forward, backward, sideways, diagonal, circular ... the operator can walk ahead and shoot behind him.
- To simulate the effect of the zoom, as it can perform exaggerated movements towards and away from the subject.

- To shoot at an extremely low height, with the rig turned upside down:
  Mamba. The shot from the snake's point of view
  Wolfen. The shot from the wolf's point of view
  The Shining. Wendy drags Jack's unconscious body by its feet over the floor of the hotel kitchen; the camera is just a few inches above the ground.
- To take shots from the point of view of any person, animal or object that is very close to the ground:
  Evil Dead II. The point of view of the hero's cut-off hand as it moves around the house.
- To shoot a point of view shot of any person or object:
  The Untouchables. The murder of the policeman, Malone, from the point of view of the murderer who, spying from outside the house, finds an open window, creeps in and moves through the house as the camera shows it to us
  Strange Days. The murderer goes to kill the prostitute in a hotel room and his route is one long point of view shot (opening the door, the room, the balcony ... until he finds the girl)[12]
  Casualties of War. Point of view shot of the scene in which a group of American soldiers arrive in a Vietnamese village, break into a hut and find a girl hiding there: 'Soldiers came into the village at night searching from one hooch to another until they find a woman to kidnap. We moved down the village set and we'd slide off to the right of this little street into one hooch, look into it, back out, slide across the street to another one, back out and so on. Laurie Sahen, the gaffer, was holding a red spotlight, flicking it on and off as if it were a flash-light that I was holding. We had to agree on exactly what I was looking at. I would first look at a woman in the back, then I would pan down to 'look' at the child at her feet, then Laurie would flick off the light and we would move on. In other words, the camera and the light were coordinated'.[13]
- To simulate flight or fast motion in a point of view shot:
  Birdy. Dream/vision of the hero flying through in the alleyways around the houses
  Runaway. Subjective view of a superfast bullet that runs down its victim. Sequence showing the murder of a mathematician in an alley in New York realized with a fast zigzagging by the Steadicam through traffic
  Bram Stoker's Dracula. Point of view shots of the bat and the wolfman
  The Return of the Jedi. The flying motorbikes chase Princess Leia and Luke Skywalker through the woods.
- To shoot situations in which a set cannot be built:
  Marathon Man, *Kramer vs. Kramer*. Both have scenes shot on the streets of New York
  Cliffhanger. The main character must cross a rope bridge and the operator precedes him (Figure 2.12).
- For stationary takes and linking shots: the Steadicam is used in many films to shoot small movements that reframe the subject, follow gestures, close in on characters or environments:

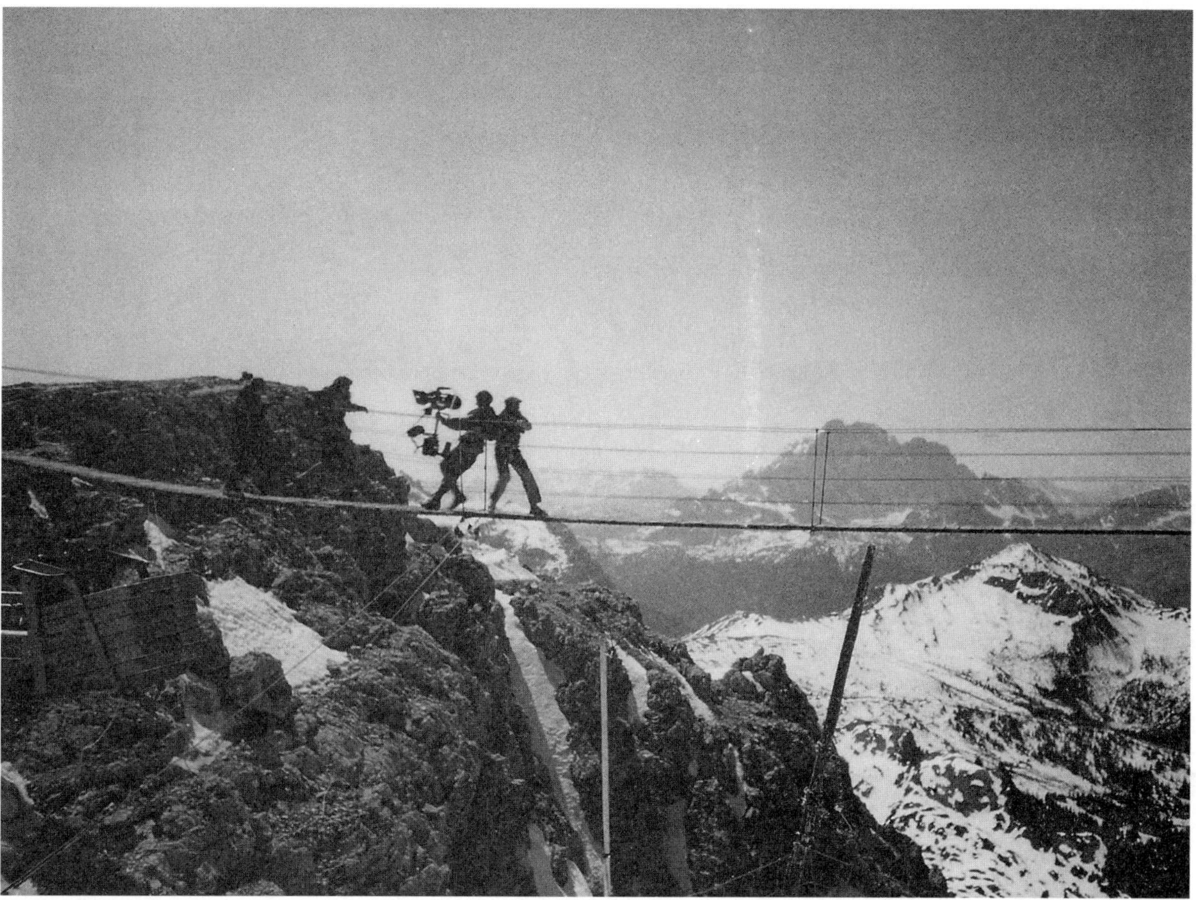

Figure 2.12 *Cliffhanger*. Photo: Nicola Pecorini collection

Coup de tourchon. The Steadicam is used continually for dolly shots and pan shots to accompany the actor, to introduce spaces.

- To circle freely and repeatedly around someone:

  The Crow. Sequence in which the policeman, having lost sight of the disoriented boy (the crow), stands still in the middle of the street whilst the camera circles around him three times

  Rocky. The hero has reached the top of the stairs and the camera makes a half circle behind him.

- To shoot unpredictable reactions, with child or animal actors:

  Fried Green Tomatoes at the Whistle Stop Café. Scene with bees, the girl is followed as she goes to get the honey.[14]

- To maintain the horizon level at sea while simulating the motion of the waves:

  Bitter Moon. 'The Steadicam was used because all the action takes place on board a cruise ship and it was necessary to show the movement of the ship.'[15A] 'The Steadicam is extremely useful for shooting on boats. The horizon remains as level as you want it, and the viewers get a tremendously realistic view of the boat rising and falling in the foreground.'[15B]

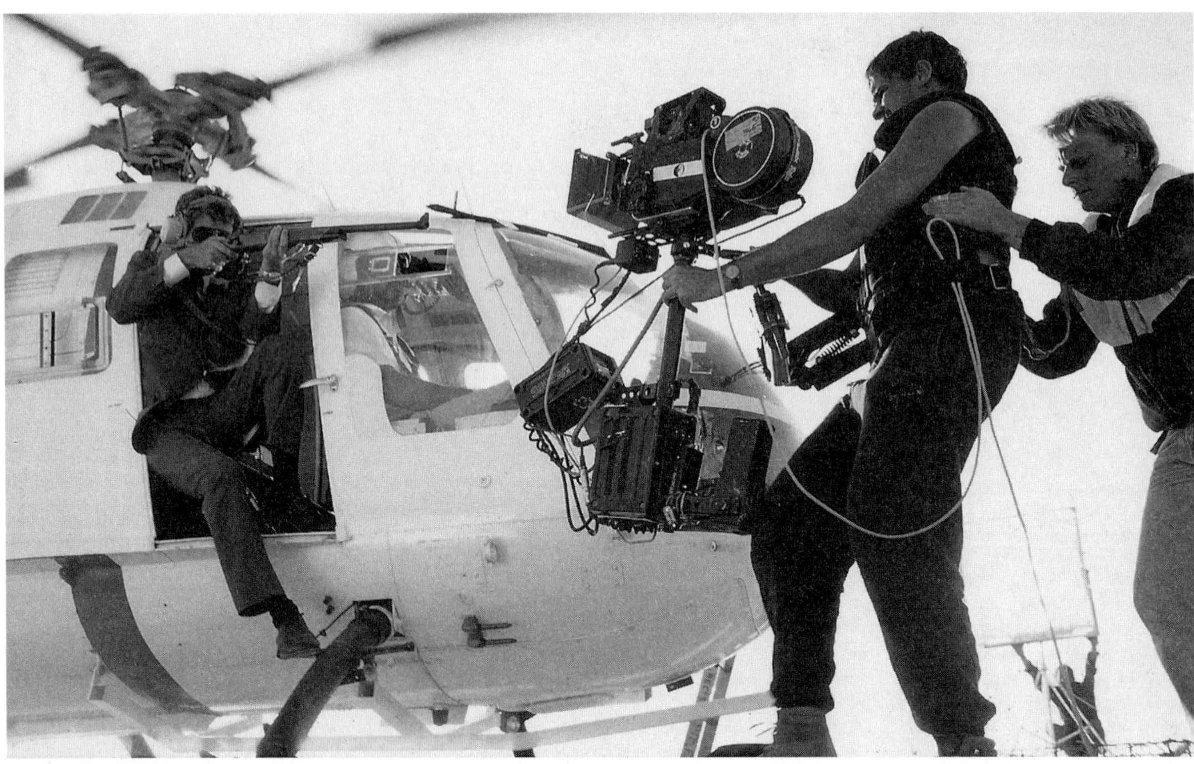

Figure 2.13 *Isthar*. Photo: Nicola Pecorini collection

- The Steadicam can also be used in the opposite sense, to create effects of unsteadiness:

  The Twilight Zone – the Movie. 'Terror at 20 000 feet' episode. The action takes place entirely on an airplane built in the studio; to create the effect of the storm: 'I asked Garrett to make his machine an unsteady camera and that's how we got the look of an airplane caught in a storm: transforming the swaying of the camera into a splendid sensation of seasickness'.[16]

  On the other hand, it is not a good idea to use the Steadicam for those really traumatic shots that put the operator and the equipment at risk, such as those taken from violently moving vehicles (Figure 2.13).

Early use of the Steadicam in the movie industry

Bound for Glory

The first movie in which the Steadicam was used was *Bound for Glory*, directed by Hal Ashby (Figure 2.14). The film is based on the life of Woody Guthrie, the singer and songwriter who left his home and family to seek his fortune and spent various periods of his life mingling with the enormous number of migrant agricultural workers heading to the West Coast to find work during the Depression. Haskell Wexler, the Director of Photography, was the first to use the newly invented Steadicam, employing it in a number of shots. Here is Garrett Brown's description of the longest one:

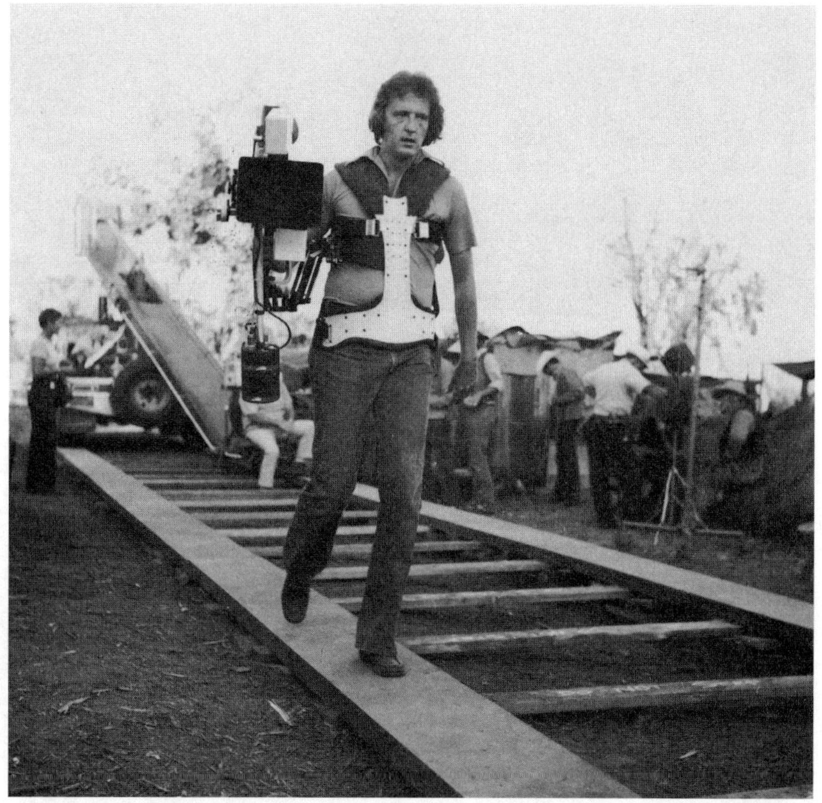

Figure 2.14 *Bound for Glory*. Old and new technology: Chapman Titan crane meets Steadicam prototype on the set of *Bound for Glory* in 1975. Brown would soon begin his first feature shot standing high on the Titan's platform. Photo: Garrett Brown collection

> Early in 1975, we were engaged to shoot *Bound for Glory*. Haskell was DP and had persuaded the late Hal Ashby to try an extravagant, time-consuming, expensive megashot with complete reliance on our contraption. We had only one throated magazine. I had never been on a feature set until I arrived in Stockton, CA and entered Ashby's enormous migrant worker camp with 900 extras. Neither had I seen a Chapman Titan Crane in person, prior to being put up on the platform 30 feet in the air, hands shaking violently, with Don Thorin, the regular operator, who said, 'Look, that's funny the camera isn't shaking'.
>
> I got two rehearsals, and we broke for lunch, during which I had a beer and Don calmed me down a bit. Then we made just three four-minute takes. As the crane boomed down besides David Carradine, I got off and 'walked' with him across the huge camp and most of the way back, dodging kids and crowds and tent ropes and vehicles.
>
> In the end, I was numb with fatigue and nerves, and the whole crew flowed away to resume the regular work without a backward glance.
>
> It was two nights later that I finally saw our amazing shot and received a standing ovation from the large crowd in the screening room ...[17]

Throughout the entire four-minute scene, the camera follows the action discreetly, but nonetheless from close up, and the effect is that of participation and interest without the camera being too conspicuous.

> .. the audience is instantly transformed from a third-party voyeuristic perspective to a participatory point of view.

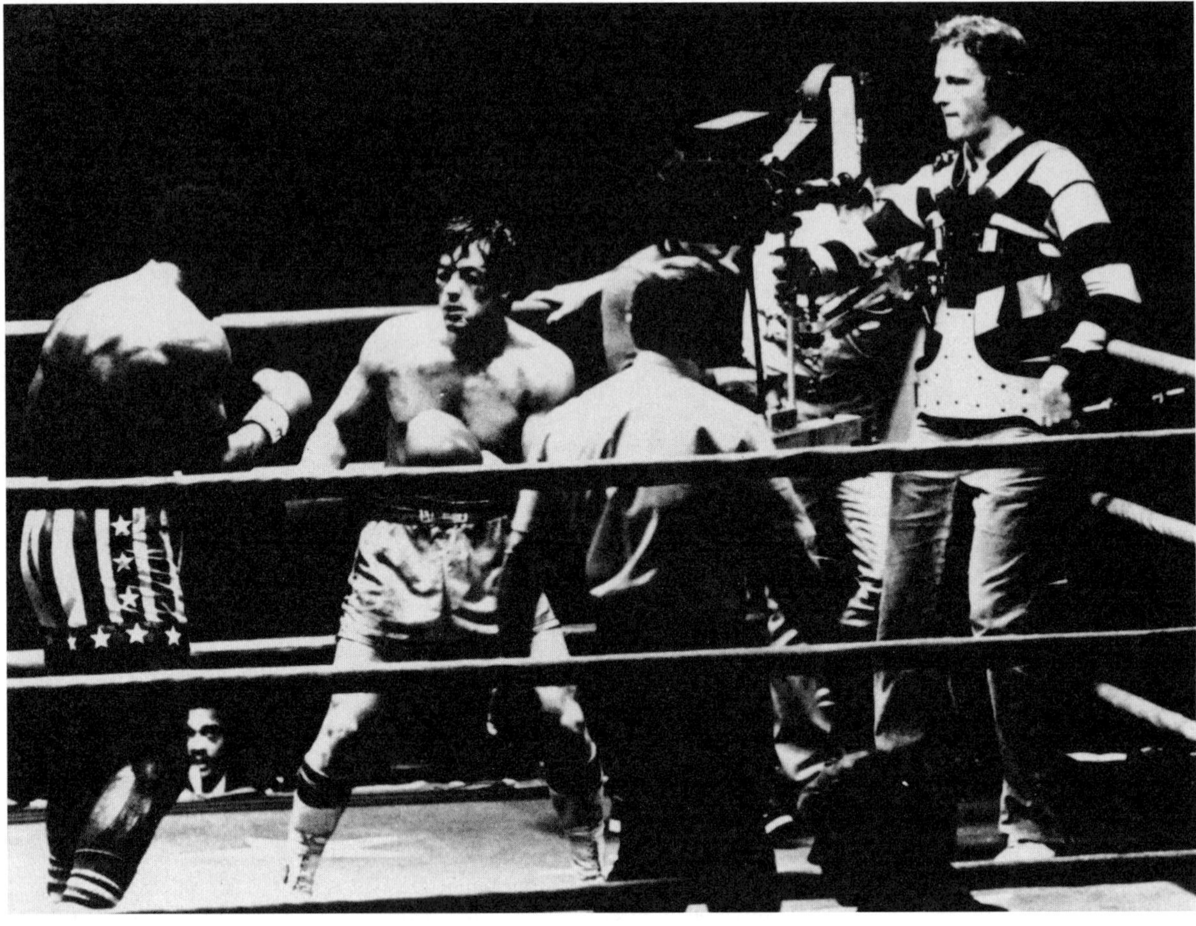

Figure 2.15 *Rocky*. Stallone's Rocky battles with Apollo Creed as Garrett Brown circles warily in the ring with the prototype of the CP-35. Photo: Garrett Brown collection

> I think every camera operator has dreamed about the visual impact of walking off a dolly with a camera in a scene like this. There are times when it is better to hand-hold a camera or to ride a dolly track. But there are other times when there is nothing like the smooth gliding motion you get with the Steadicam.[18]

In another scene, which takes place the morning after Woody has met a woman in a bar, the shot opens by showing us the woman asleep. The Steadicam then travels around the bed, moves over her face next to the night stand, goes backward through the door to discover Woody sitting at a table writing and moves around him until the scene stops on his hands.

Rocky

During the filming of *Bound for Glory* Garrett Brown was called to work on the movie *Rocky*, directed by John Avildsen (Figure 2.15). It is the story of a boxer, Rocky, a perennial loser, who commits himself to fighting the heavyweight champion. Rocky has practically no chance of winning, but through his love for his girl and the help of a good trainer he earns self-respect and, in his match with the champion, the result is a split decision.

The film was shot entirely in real settings, with no studio reconstructions. As James Crabe, the Director of Photography recalls, this caused some problems with lighting and camera moves because of the limited dimensions of Rocky's house and the enormous size of the arena where the boxing match takes place. The fight scenes were shot with three cameras running simultaneously, one of which was a Steadicam used to obtain an effect of greater closeness to the actors and to achieve greater mobility around the set. 'Of course, where it comes to camera movement, the film will be remembered mainly for the Steadicam shots, which were quite spectacular'.[19]

The Steadicam and its operator can be ferried about by any means: in *Rocky*, Garrett Brown filmed part of the fight scene while sitting on a cart that was being pushed around the ring:

> My only problem was keeping the camera running in the cold. The two CP batteries weren't strong enough, particularly after a dent in the centrepost started rubbing against the internal motor shaft. We made the well known Art Museum steps shots with Ralf [Bode, the original Director of Photography who photographed the locations scenes in Philadelphia] running along beside me carrying two automobile batteries to jump start the Arri ... Shooting began again with Sly bashing sides of beef in a cold locker, and moved on to the LA Coliseum for the fight sequences. We pioneered a new look for fight footage, and incidentally devised a method of recording the video on a portable Akai ¼" recorder.[20]

Marathon Man

After *Rocky*, Garrett Brown was called to work on *Marathon Man* that, to a large extent, was filmed in New York (Figure 2.16). In this

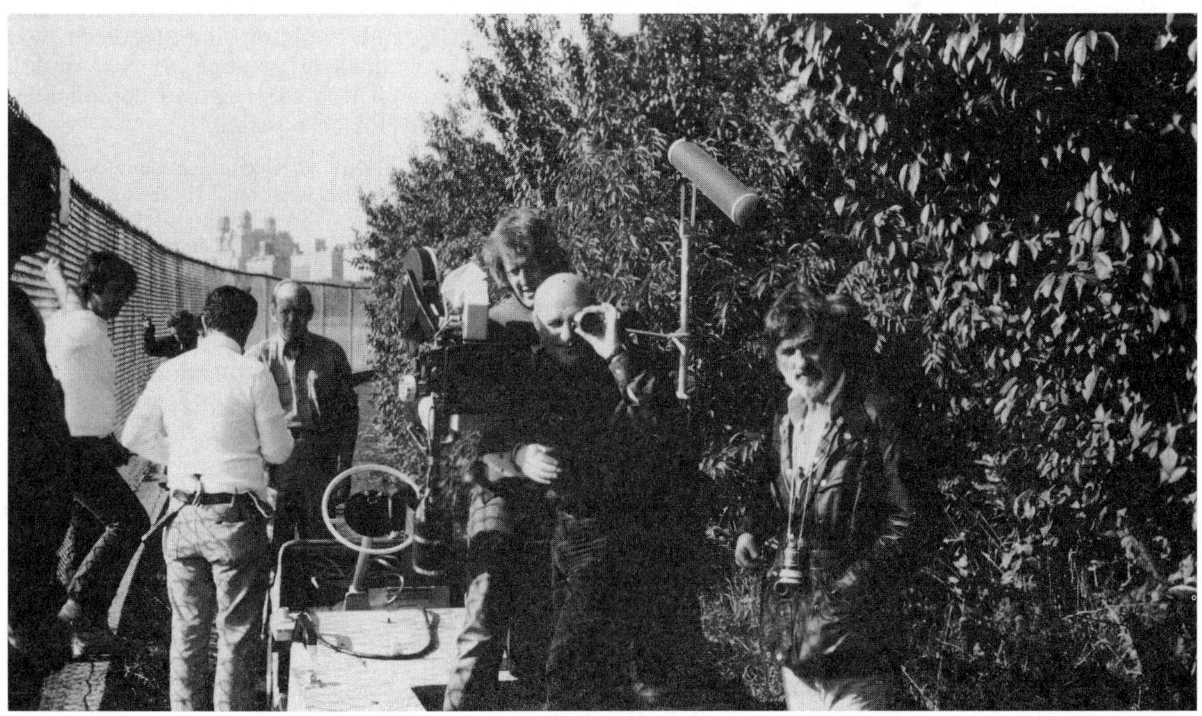

Figure 2.16 *Marathon Man*. John Schlesinger, director, lines up the first-ever Steadicam golf-cart shot so Garrett Brown can endlessly chase Dustin Hoffman around the Central Park Reservoir. DP Conrad Hall is on the right. Photo: Garrett Brown collection

movie, a young, shy, Jewish man, following the murder of his brother, finds himself involved with ex-Nazis who are selling diamonds in New York. The Steadicam, with its particular structure adaptable to any, or almost any, situation, made it possible to shoot scenes in the diamond merchant district in downtown New York without affecting the 'spontaneity' of the street, because of the relative ease with which the camera operator was able to carry it into the crowd and follow the characters. Garrett Brown remembers:

> I began work with Conrad Hall on *Marathon Man*, on the streets of New York. We had a large crew and an enormous budget, and every tool known to man on the grip truck, so when I was used, it was because there wasn't any other known way of getting the shot.
>
> The new by-wire servo focus control arrived from CP, so my assistant had to stay with me as I jogged miles around the track in Central Park, keeping up with Dustin, outdistancing the AD's, until we stopped exhausted, to wait for the unit to catch up ...[21]

The Shining

With *The Shining*, the Steadicam really made a name for itself. Stanley Kubrick had seen a demo reel made by Garrett Brown and, enthusiastic, decided to call Brown for his new movie: 'Demo reel on hand-held mystery stabilizer was spectacular and you can count on me as a customer. It should revolutionize the way films are shot ...'.[22]

The movie tells the story of a man, a writer, his slow descent into madness and his relationship with his wife and son in a situation of complete isolation. The Steadicam is used abundantly and skilfully. John Alcott, the Director of Photography for the film, felt that 'Kubrick chose the Steadicam precisely because of its mobility and ability to maintain a steady image even while running and fluctuating in space'.[23] Furthermore, in Alcott's opinion, the Steadicam was the most appropriate means for illustrating such a large hotel, making it possible to travel through it with long and complicated dolly shots which otherwise would not be possible.

> The kitchen set was a maze in itself with all that equipment. When one travels through the kitchen in the first sequence there are twistings and turnings in and out amongst the ovens and the kitchen furniture – a kind of backtracking. I don't think you could find a dolly that could do that. The Steadicam was an ideal piece of equipment in that instance ...[24]

The Steadicam was also used to advantage for a series of frames beginning in an 'impossible', uncomfortable position, making it possible to continue more easily and end with a precision that the dolly could not have achieved. For the shots of the boy on the tricycle, Brown worked on a wheelchair (already used by Kubrick in *A Clockwork Orange*) for better control in the slower sequences.

It is interesting that Brown himself found, in Kubrick, the director most capable of understanding the potentials of his invention: 'Kubrick would use the Steadicam as it was intended to be used, as a tool which can help get the lens where it's wanted in space and time without the classic limitation of the dolly and crane'.[25]

For the lighting, Alcott had to create a light set that would not interfere with an extended and liberal use of the Steadicam. To this

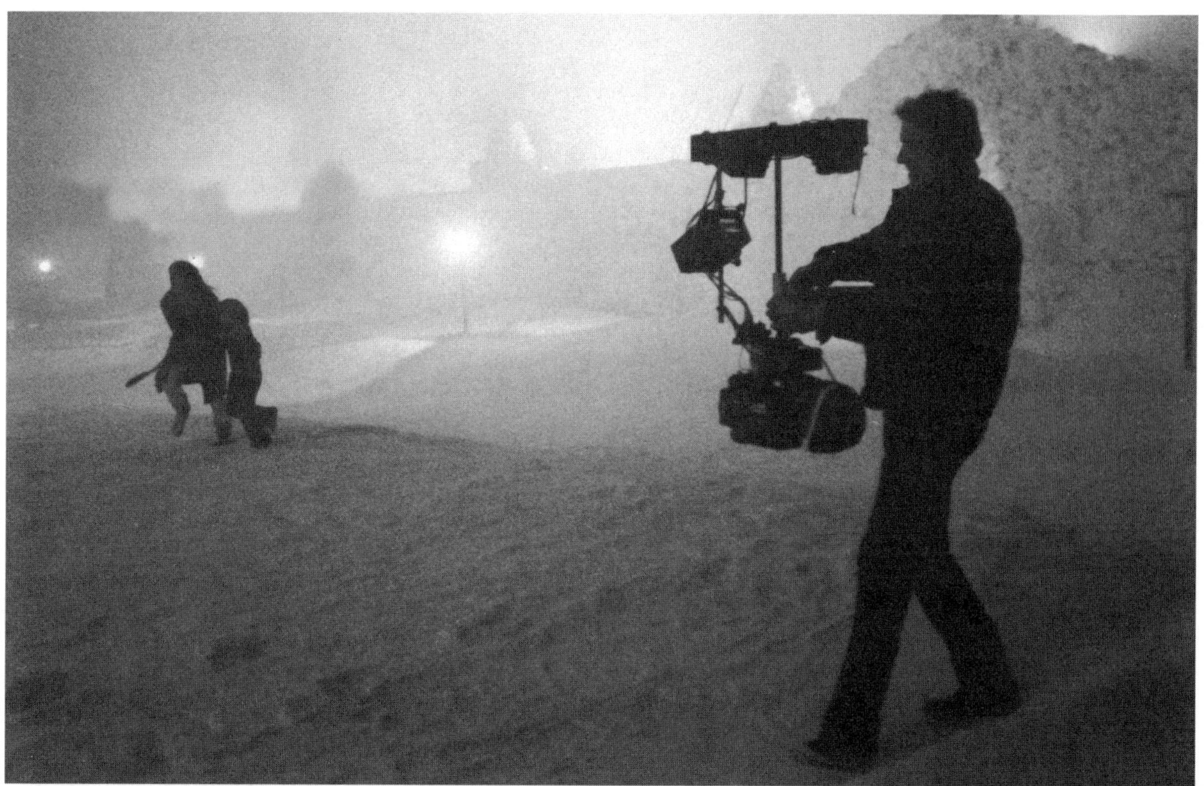

Figure 2.17 *The Shining.* Shelley Duval and Danny Lloyd flee Jack Nicholson's character on the 'snowy' back lot at Elstree Studios, UK. The Steadicam is the low-mode Model II prototype (invented for *The Shining*). The 'snow' is 900 tons of dairy salt; the fog is oil smoke. Note the first use of the 'two-handed technique', which had to be invented and perfected in order to achieve the precision Kubrick demanded. Photo: Garrett Brown collection

end, he eliminated any possibility of light coming from the pavement and strengthened the hotel's lighting system, changing the bulbs of the chandeliers in the hallways, and connected the entire system to a control panel. This allowed him to turn up or lower the lighting as the Steadicam passed on its long dolly shots. 'I could change the light settings of the chandeliers as the Steadicam was travelling about the set by simply talking to the control room. This happened in several instances and it was a great help.'[26]

In the maze, the Steadicam embodies the instrument that witnesses Jack's mad chase and Danny's daring flight: 'One set in particular, the giant hedge image, could not have been photographed as Kubrick intended by any other means'[27] (Figure 2.17).

This is a sequence shot under extremely difficult conditions, as the 'snow' consisted of a layer of noxious salt about 30 cm deep.[28] The Steadicam allowed the director to build up a situation of suspense and record it with dolly shots that anticipated or followed the characters without leaving physical signs of the camera's passage.

It was during this movie that Garrett Brown developed the two-hand method for Steadicam shooting, in which the operator manoeuvres the Steadicam with each hand serving a different purpose: control and grip. This was also the film in which he first experimented with using the Steadicam in low mode configuration (Figure 2.18), as in the shot in which Wendy drags Jack's inert body to the walk-in refrigerator.

Although there were some dissenting voices, such as Jean Rouch who felt that the use of the Steadicam conditioned the realism and

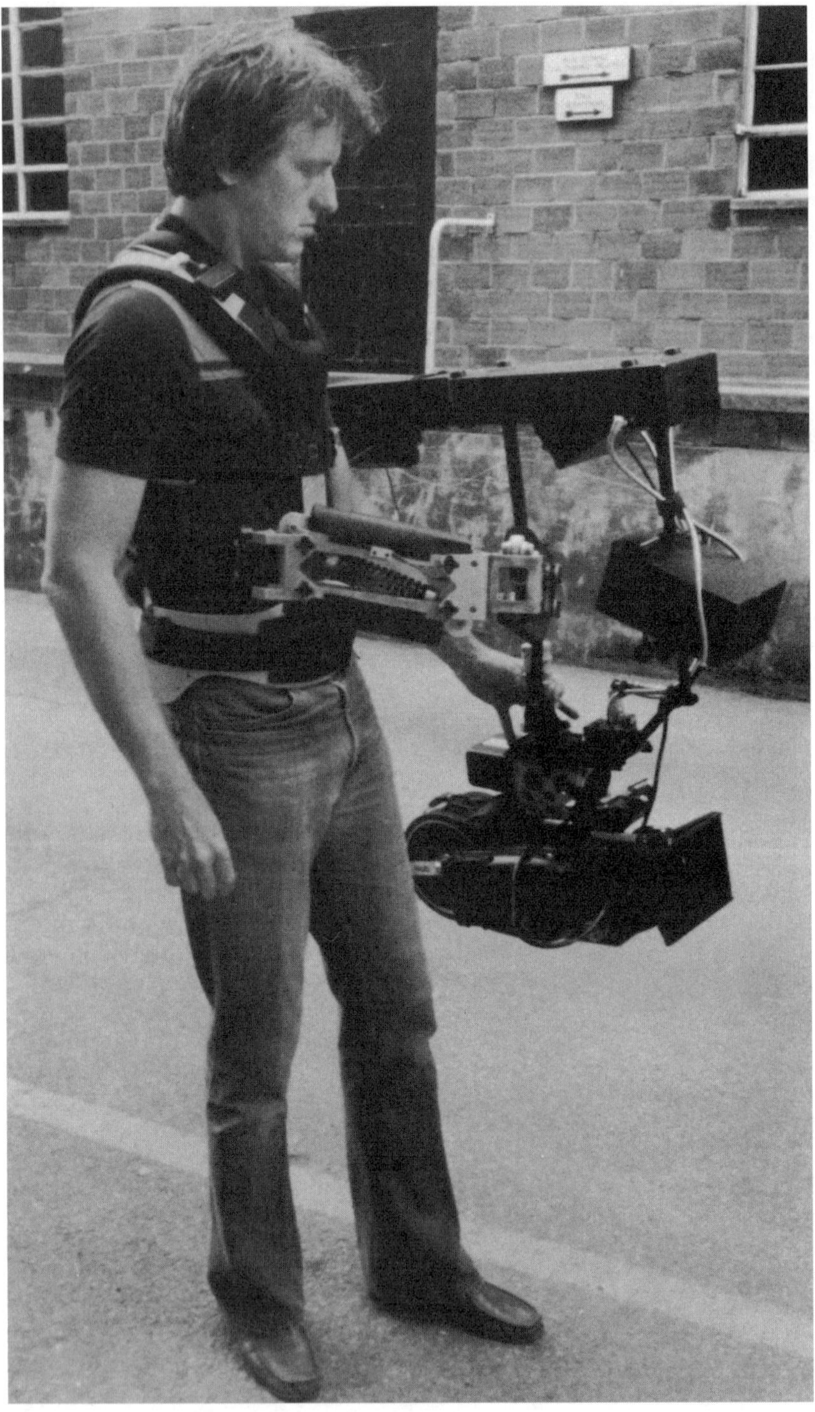

Figure 2.18 *The Shining*. Garrett Brown, on the back lot at Elstree Studios beginning a year on *The Shining*, shows off a series of 'firsts': first low-mode rig; first use of the Arri 'BL' sound camera on a feature; first use of the new Model II prototype. Photo: Garrett Brown collection

naturalness of the hotel shots and that Kubrick should have built larger sets so that the camera could travel freely,[29] the photography of *The Shining* won the admiration of the vast majority of critics and moviegoers.

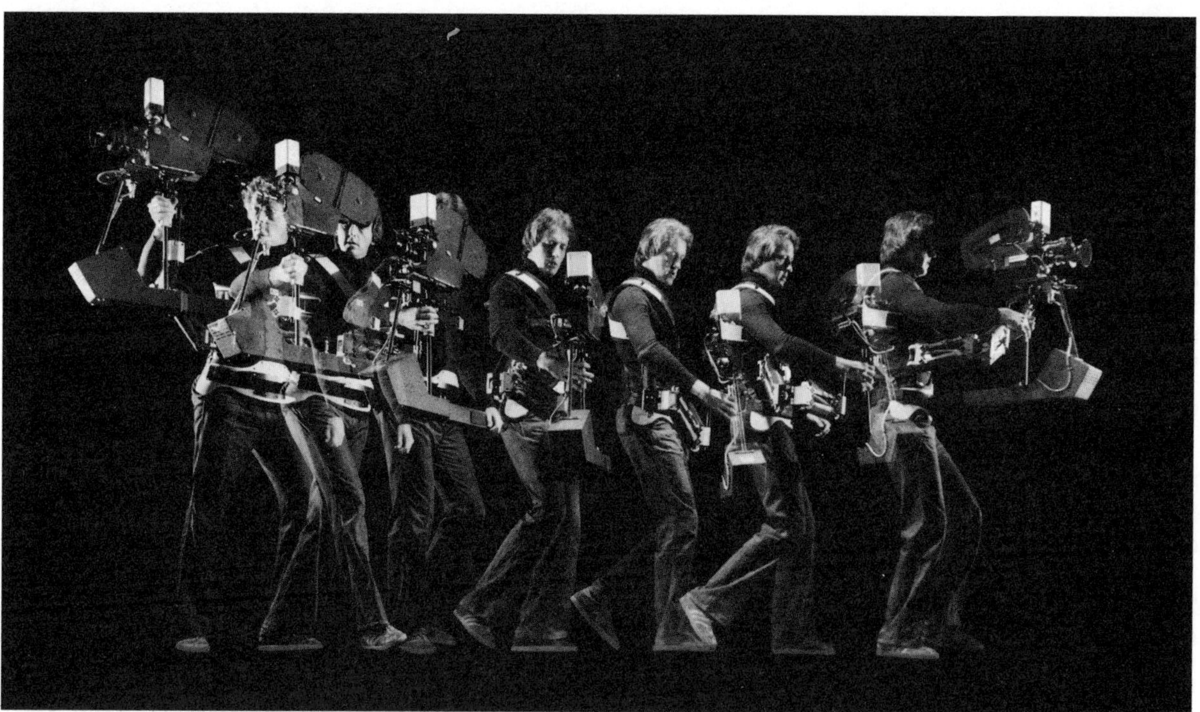

Figure 2.19 'Strobe' shot of Garrett showing a series of operating positions using the Universal Model I Steadicam. Photo: Garrett Brown collection

Using the Steadicam

Since 1976 the Steadicam has become an indispensable tool used in many action and adventure movies as well as horror movies (Figure 2.19). In addition, precisely because it can also be used for stationary shots, it is often employed in other kinds of movies and is chosen when costs must be kept down and/or building a set is problematical.

The Steadicam, however, is expensive and difficult to use well. Its cost is due to the intricate mechanics and the sophisticated materials of which it is made.[30] The difficulties are due to the fact that the operator needs specialized technical knowledge and physical ability superior to that normally required of a camera operator: agility, balance, strength and precision are the basis of making good shots with the Steadicam (Table 2.1).

The Steadicam configuration: high mode and low mode

The Steadicam can be used in two main ways: high mode and low mode. High mode is the standard position in which the camera, supported by the post, is nominally at eye-level. Low mode is the opposite of high mode (Figure 2.20). The camera is mounted upside down on the sled, below the gimbal, and the electronics, monitor, batteries and sled are above the gimbal. This configuration is made possible by means of a low mode cage or a low mode bracket, and this new arrangement of components must be rebalanced, both statically and dynamically.

Table 2.1 Basic procedures. There are four basic procedures involved in using the Steadicam correctly

1 Adjusting the vest
The vest must be adjusted to fit the operator's body; since it is the primary connection between operator and camera, through the articulated arm and the gimbal. Good adjustment takes into account the wearer's build and the weight of the rig. The vest must fit snugly and still allow the operator to breathe, preferably with the diaphragm. Its length must also be adjusted to ensure that the operator has freedom of movement at hip level.

2 Adjusting the arm
The arm is adjusted before the rig is attached to it so that it rests approximately in the centre of its up-and-down range and does not pull away from the operator. The adjustments involve both the spring strength of the arm and its attachment to the vest socket plate. The correct angle of lift is achieved by adjustments to the socket block and the mating portion of the arm. The arm height (lift capacity) is adjusted to the load of the camera and accessories.

3 Balancing the rig
The various components must be balanced to allow correct distribution of weight, since this affects the static and dynamic performance of the Steadicam and, consequently, the results that can be obtained. In short, an arrangement is required in which the various components are in balance with respect to the centre of gravity of the system.

Static balance
The Steadicam must be balanced so that it remains vertical by making it slightly bottom-heavy, so the sled (monitor, electronics module and battery pack) hangs approximately upright and level with the horizon.

Dynamic balance
The Steadicam must be balanced to ensure that the rig will stay vertical and not 'precess' when the camera is panned, by properly distributing the weight of the components of the rig with respect to the centre of gravity and its vertical axis (in this case, the post), so that the centrifugal forces acting on the components cancel each other out.

Trim
Trim refers to balancing the rig so that it seeks a certain attitude and thus helps maintain the operator's chosen reference points with regard to framing. With the newer Steadicams, the operator can adjust the trim continuously with wireless remote control motors in the camera mounting stage.

4 Walking correctly
To walk correctly with the Steadicam, the operator must start from the correct standing posture: straight and leaning slightly back to offset the weight of the rig. If the camera moves away from the operator, he/she should not bend the legs or lean forward; the camera can be brought to its correct position by using the pelvis and leaning slightly further back. Furthermore, the operator must always keep in mind that, after a pause, there may be a need to move again to follow the action. Therefore the weight is kept almost all on one foot so that there is no weight shift needed before taking a step, which the camera would record.

Handling the Steadicam
Each of the operator's hands has a distinct function requiring a different grip: the hand which supports and guides the rig grips the arm more strongly, allowing it also to boom the camera up and down; the hand that performs pan and tilt movements operates directly at the Steadicam's centre of gravity (the most sensitive point) and consequently uses a light grip, except when more control is needed during acceleration, deceleration or rapid panning.

Missionary
The operator holds the Steadicam alongside his body while shooting ahead.

Don Juan
The operator holds the Steadicam to one side with the camera shooting behind him

Switch
The change from one shooting position to another is called the Switch. It allows the operator to adapt the Steadicam to the various cinematographic requirements while shooting, by changing his position relative to the camera while still maintaining the frame.

The Steadicam can be used in two main ways:

High mode, standard position in which the camera, supported by the post, is nominally at eye-level
Low mode is the opposite of high mode. The camera is mounted upside down on the sled, below the gimbal, and the electronics, monitor, batteries and sled are above the gimbal.

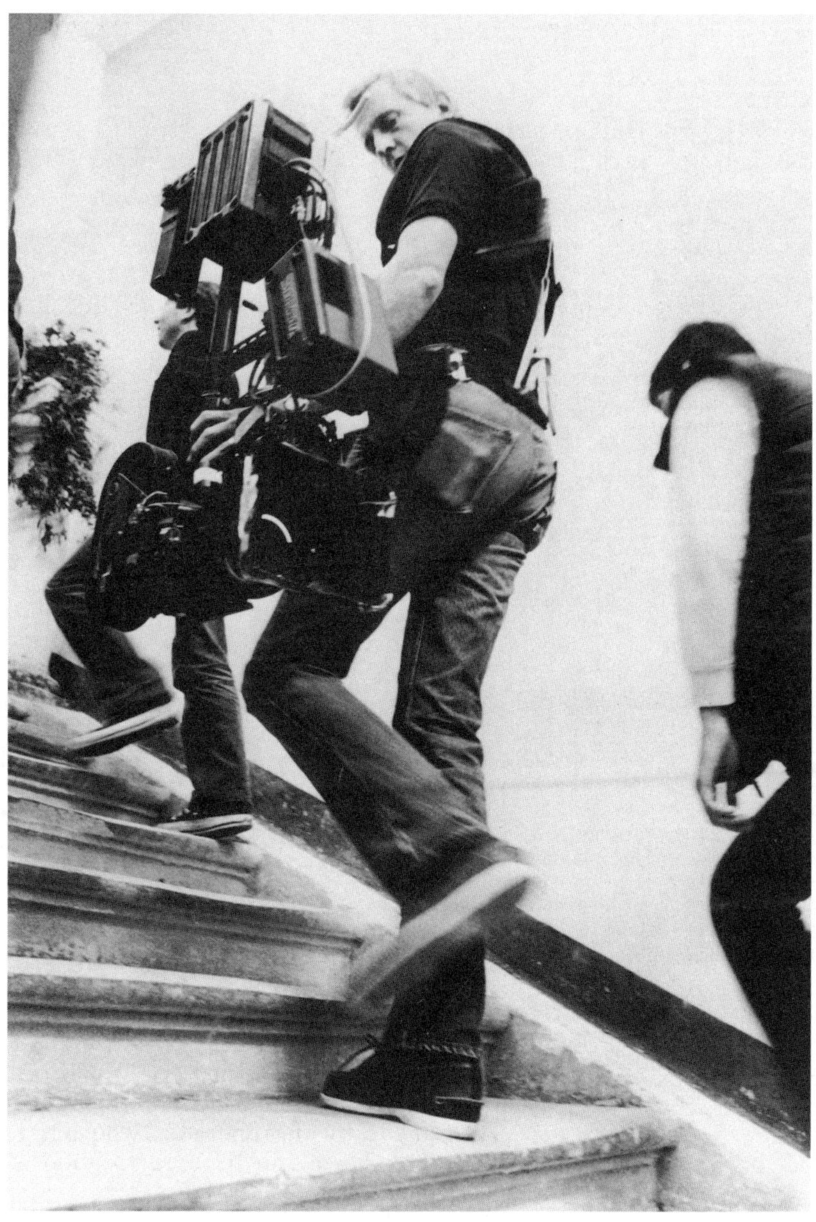

Figure 2.20 Garrett Brown demonstrates a low-mode stairs shot for the students at the first Italian workshop in L'Aquila in the mid-1980s. Photo: Garrett Brown collection

Operating in low mode is generally more difficult than in high mode. One reason is that the camera bodies are wider and generally longer than the bottom of most Steadicams. In addition, the operator must hold the rig further from the body and push it further away when making changes and, consequently, it is heavier and takes more effort to use.[31]

The extension of the post can be increased in order to reach more extreme positions: extreme high mode and extreme low mode (with the camera almost on the ground).

It is important to be able to judge whether it is really necessary to shoot in low mode, because at times it is necessary for only a

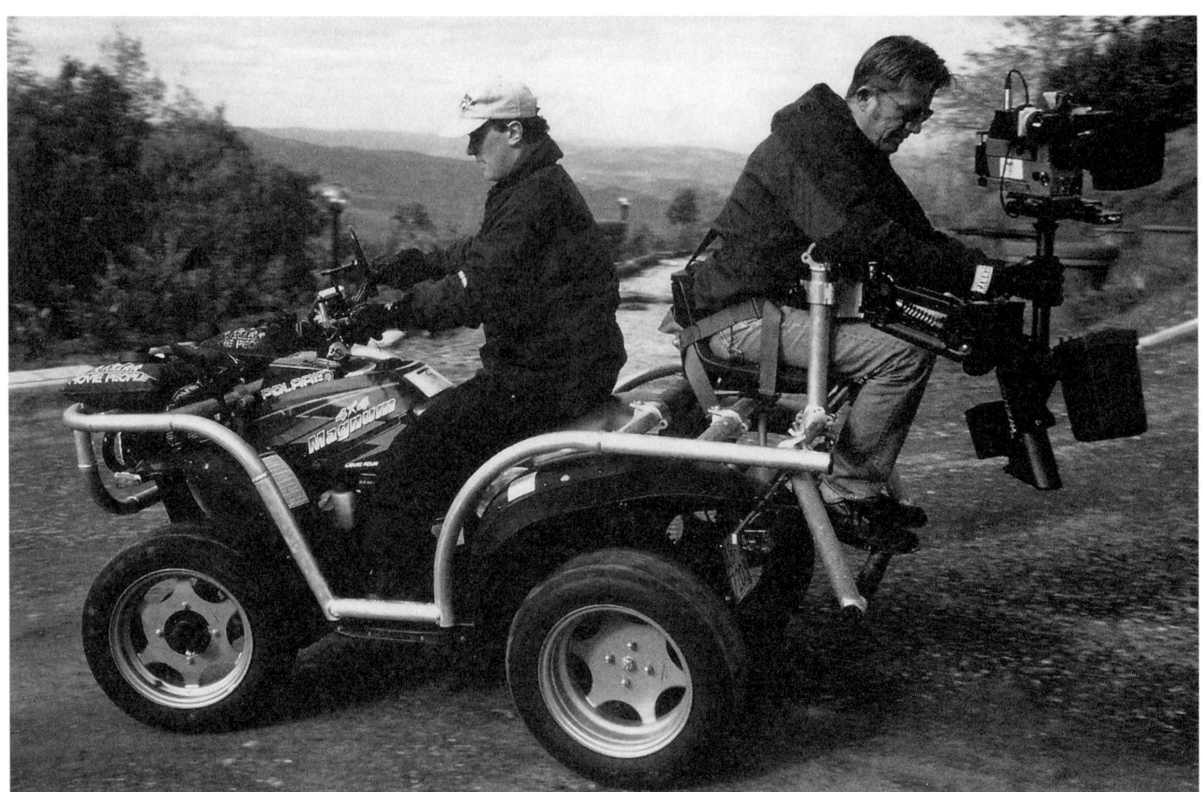

Figure 2.21 Hard mount on quad runner. Driver, Mario Maronati; Steadicam operator, Gene Taylor; location, Montalcino workshop, Tuscany, 1998. Photo: Elisabetta Cartoni collection

minimal portion of the sequence. It is a good idea to have the accessories for using the Steadicam in low mode always on hand.

The mounted Steadicam : hard mount and soft mount

The Steadicam can be soft-mounted, worn by the operator who is carried by a vehicle, or it can be hard-mounted, when the arm is attached directly to the vehicle (Figure 2.21). The choice must be made by the operator, who has to decide in which situations the Steadicam can be used to good effect without being worn on the body.

It is important to note that hard-mount operating is limited by the range of travel of the arm links, so an excessively bumpy ride risks exceeding this range and damaging or breaking apart the arm. Consequently, if the surface is very uneven it is better to wear the Steadicam so that the operator's legs can help absorb the shocks.

The Steadicam can be used with any kind of vehicle (moving platform, dolly, crane, wheelchair, etc.). In this instance, the operator does not bear the weight of the equipment and can concentrate on perfecting the frame. However, in order to achieve such freedom, the operator is in the hands of the vehicle driver and is no longer in total command of the tool.

Two convenient accessories are available to help transform a sturdy surface into a mount:

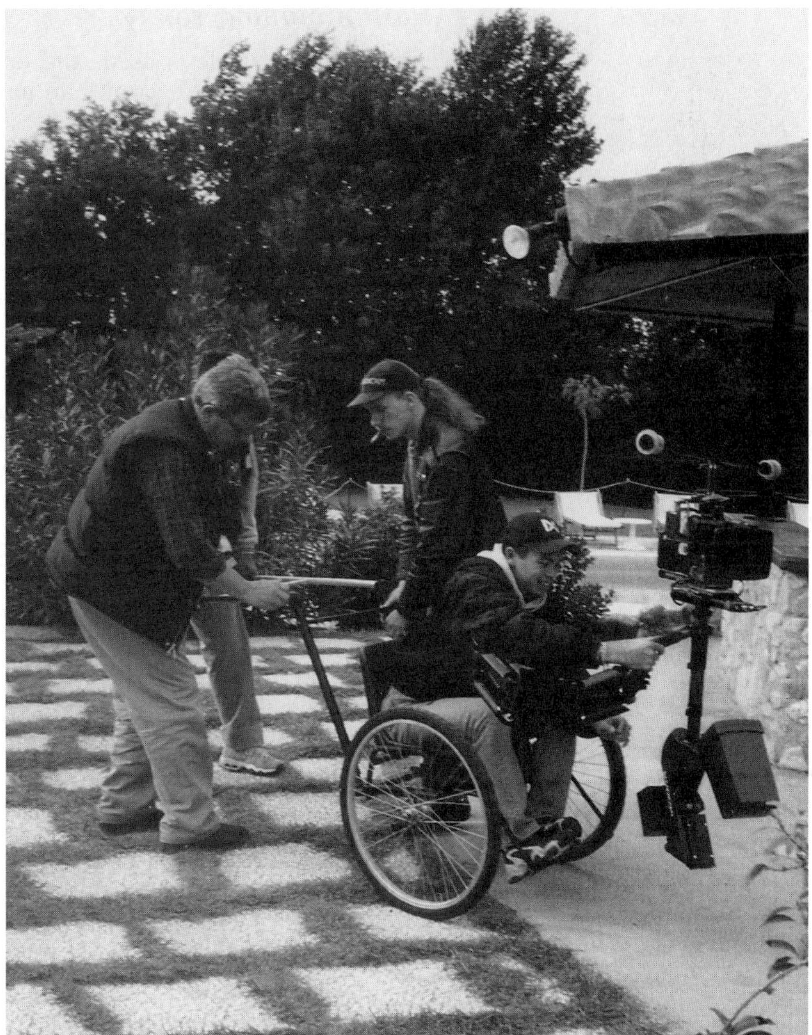

Figure 2.22 'Rickshaw'. Location, Perugia workshop, Umbria, 1998. Photo: Serena Ferrara collection

- *Wheelchair mount*: formerly used with wheelchairs and then with dollies and vehicles, this device attaches the Steadicam to a wheelchair arm or similar surface (Figure 2.22).
- *Garfield adapter*: this adapter threads into any standard Mitchell mount dolly, tripod or highhat, providing a base for the wheelchair mount.[32]

Soft mounting safety

- *Standing soft mount*: the operator must have something to hold on to with one hand while operating the Steadicam with the other. There should be a railing at about waist height to lean against and it is also a good idea to have a grip hanging on to the operator.
- *Sitting soft mount*: the operator must avoid sitting for long periods of time. The vest can dig into the operator's legs, cutting off circulation and damaging the nerves in the thigh.

Hard mounting safety

Whenever a vehicle is used, and especially when its speed exceeds walking pace, safety becomes an important issue.

The operator must travel the route in advance without the Steadicam in order to assess the surface it offers and to calculate the correct and safe speeds for the various segments.

- Excessive acceleration is hard on the operator as *g*-forces can pull the Steadicam out of the hands.
- Bounces of over 1 foot as, for example, caused by an unexpected wave during a boat shot, can exceed the range of the arm, causing the pins to break.
- The vehicle on which the operator rides can flip over or collide with other vehicles. The operator, leaning out to get the shot, will take the brunt of the impact.
- All vehicles must be in communication, and the driver must listen to the operator. The operator should avoid vehicles that have a tendency to turn over, and must decide whether it is better to be secured to the vehicle or to be held by an assistant, thus allowing instant escape.[33]

Shooting with the Steadicam

Preparing and programming the shot

1 Evaluate whether a shot can be achieved and whether it can be carried out safely.
2 Is the Steadicam the right tool?
3 Study the scene, plan the take:
   - a take is programmed mentally, the operator must know exactly what is needed:

> You have to do it in your head in advance, because it will be too heavy to react instinctively. (Larry McConkey, Steadicam International Workshop, Perugia, Italy, October 1998)

4 The route: the operator must choose reference points:
   - the operator and the camera should form a whole; the operator must be aware of the size of the equipment and must locate or even bump into possible obstacles in order to commit them to memory
   - the operator must be sure of his moves and arrival point
   - at the end of each move the operator must immediately get into position for the next one.

5 The operator must calculate the distance to be maintained from the actors (which may also help the assistant keep the shot in focus):
   - keep checking the edges of the frame for slight motions, etc.

6 If the sequence requires the camera to follow the actors for a long time, the actors should do something that gives a reason for the action and which can also facilitate or motivate possible changes of frame. An example is the scene in *Raising Cain* in which the action of the doctor going the wrong way gives Larry McConkey the chance to widen the field.

7 If the shot involves the use of a vehicle the operator should:
   - decide if a soft mount or a hard mount is better
   - decide whether it is necessary to be secured to the vehicle
   - be able to communicate perfectly with the driver of the vehicle
   - try the route first to evaluate the camera response to the road surface, the extension of the arm during possible bumps, the speed of the vehicle and the centrifugal and centripetal force, all of which can determine how dangerous the shot will be
   - know when it is necessary to refuse to do a shot if it is too risky. It is very important to remember always that a shot may be very tiring, difficult and uncomfortable, but it must not be dangerous. The operator must always feel at ease and confident with the requirements of the shot.

8 Attention to clothing:
   - choose the clothes best suited to the temperatures on the set
   - if the shot includes reflecting surfaces (such as glass windows), both the operator and the assistant should wear black. The operator should be as invisible as possible.

9 Something may break; the operator must always inspect the equipment for loose connections and remain vigilant.

10 It is important to know when to take rest breaks.

> You must be comfortable. (Jerry Holway)[34]

> ... one can consistently crank out frames that are virtually indistinguishable from dolly or tripod. Ironically the greatest aspiration and reward for a serious operator becomes, by default, the indetectability of one's work. (Ted Churchill)[35]

Some of the most basic techniques and rules of operating according to Garrett Brown are:

- Lights in frame

> Keep looking! Use your own eyes and identify what each dangerous light actually looks like on your screen as you dip it into frame during rehearsals. Programme yourself to watch for them as you shoot.

- In order to maintain focus when you precede an actor at high speed through narrow corridors:

> I have all these tricks. I made the job easier just by mounting a simple car antenna with a flag extended out under the lens, so the actor could have a mark to help him maintain the distance.[36]

> My style is oriented towards rehearsing and trying to learn the ground like a dancer ... I like doing multiple takes because, like a dancer, you find yourself continually improving ... beginning to really make a movie out of a long difficult shot, until you can master the smallest nuance.[37]

The long take

Larry McConkey, famed for his long takes with the Steadicam, says (in an interview with the author, Perugia, Italy, October 1998):

> There are many adjustments that can be made to the Steadicam to make it work best for any particular situation, but in a long unbroken

shot you can only go for the best compromise: no one configuration will do everything well. I work hard to avoid any gratuitous movements with the camera, breaking down each shot into a series of clearly articulated ideas. I normally work this out with a viewfinder, setting precise marks for both the camera and the actors, and figuring out the most elegant way to move between them. The actual execution then becomes a simple matter of moving the Steadicam from one predefined point in space to the next. In a long shot this may involve hundreds of separate ideas – an intricate choreography that must be exactly memorized – so before each take I do a previsualization of the entire shot, much like an acrobatic pilot mentally rehearses a routine before an air show.

Larry McConkey shot the long take in the movie *GoodFellas*:

> The two main characters get out of the car, cross the street, go between the people standing in line, enter the door, go down the stairs. Ray tips the man at the entrance, they turn right, go down a series of hallways meeting various people ... they get to the kitchen, cross it going between plates and cooks, making a series of zigzags until they get to the dining room, the owner greets them and has the waiter bring them a table and put it right in front of the stage.

Larry McConkey says: 'What makes this such an effective shot is how appropriate it is for the story, and how the actors accommodate the limitations of the camera'. The director walked through the shot with the DP, Michael Ballhaus, and Larry following the actors:

> We followed them down steps, along the hallway, and into the kitchen, made a circle and back out into the hallway, and finally into the dining room. I immediately thought that this shot could get boring ... there was no scripted dialogue until the end ... why would we [the audience] want to follow them for such a long time – just to see where they ended up? So I started walking through with my viewfinder imagining how an audience might react.
>
> In shooting long shots like this, I am constantly asking myself, on behalf of the audience, am I interested in what is happening right now? I search for a series of ideas that will take the audience on a vicarious trip, from moment to moment, always discovering new things. I try not to call attention to what the camera is doing, but rather to set up a situation that makes the audience want the camera to do something, and then satisfy that wish. I then respond on an emotional level to what is happening in front of my camera. It is both technical and instinctual. I depend on the actors to guide my attention and on the background artists and the physical set to influence their actions. Once you decide not to depend on editing for the manipulation of space and time there is no other way to control the flow of ideas. If there is a long physical space to cross, some ideas may have to be invented to fill the time required to cross it in a way that adds to the storytelling and character development of the scene ... it shouldn't be just 'noise' or 'shoe leather'.
>
> Early in the shot I needed some help negotiating the stairway. If the actors walked in a normal way, either they would disappear around the corner at the bottom of the stairs before I could catch up to them, or I would have literally to leap down the stairs causing the audience to be more concerned with the camera movement than the actors. I asked the First Assistant Director, Joe Reidy, for some help, and he placed a doorman at the bottom of the stairs; Ray could stop and talk to him for the instant of delay that I needed. In fact, Ray gave him a generous tip as a delaying tactic. I thought this action

nicely demonstrated both his status and a method by which that status was obtained; rather than confusing the scene, or offering unrelated details, our solution to a tactical problem resulted in a clearer definition of the drama. Perfect! Then halfway down the hallway I thought – it's starting to get boring – so again I asked Joe for help: 'can we have an extra or two here in the hallway for Ray to interact with?'. Joe moved a couple of extras into place and asked them to 'make out'. Ray improvised some dialogue with them, again consistent with his character and the scene. Now I was starting to get anxious about only seeing the back of his head, and so I asked him to wait until he was already passing by the couple before turning back to talk to them. That way I could see his face. He obliged and improvised another short bit of dialogue. Things were working out well. By the end of the hallway I was aching for a real change of pace, and I thought the answer would be to make the entrance into the kitchen a big surprise for the audience, so I planned to be very gentle with camera movement until just before getting there, turn the corner fast and suddenly reveal the frantic activity of the kitchen staff and the waiters. Joe choreographed some background crosses at the corner, separating me from Ray and Lorraine for just a moment and then I had a chance to catch up with them. Now the space got really tight, and again I had a problem keeping the actors in the shot. In fact, to keep Ray from disappearing around a corner this time I would have to be uncomfortably close to him ... really breathing down his neck. I knew this would send the wrong message to the audience. They wouldn't want to close in on him unless there was a reason for it. I couldn't think of a good reason, so I invented another piece of business for Ray – he said a greeting to one of the cooks behind the counter just *before* turning the corner. I panned off Ray to see the cook's response, and then panned back to Ray after turning the corner myself. His timing had to be perfect, but the audience is satisfied by the camera move, and it further elaborates on Ray's connection with the people behind the scenes in the club.

There are dozens of these little devices built into that shot. I wanted to link a series of ideas, each expressed by my reaction to the actors and the scene, by using a lot of little tricks to connect them all fluidly into a single unbroken shot, leading inevitably to a conclusion by the stage. So at the very beginning, at the very start of each take, I'm thinking about the stairs, the doorman, the couple in the hall, the kitchen, the *Maitre D*, the table, and my goal is to link these ideas so seductively that the audience feels I am just satisfying their desire to follow this couple through the club and sit at a table which is miraculously placed at the very front of the stage. In long shots, I manipulate the actors, the extras and the physical space, but I make sure it's in a way that helps to tell the story. Done right, it is what makes a great shot.[38]

Clothing

Clothing must be:

- *comfortable* – it must allow freedom of movement
- *functional with regard to temperature* – it must provide insulation in cold temperatures and should be removable in layers as the body heats up with exertion (Figure 2.23)
- *suited to the needs of the shot* – it must camouflage the operator as much as possible, with particular attention paid to reflections.

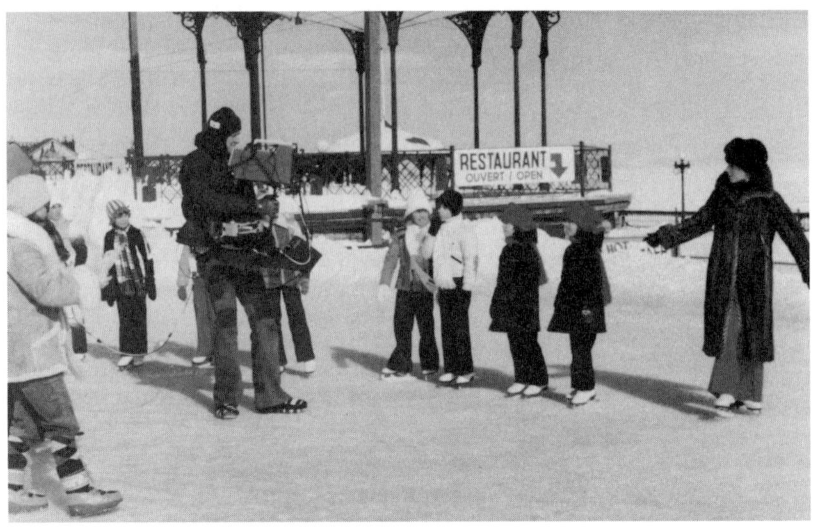

Figure 2.23 Garrett Brown shoots a TV special: 'Dorothy Hamill [on the right] at the Quebec Winter Carnival', in 1977, with the brand-new TK-76 on the Model I. Brown quickly learned how to keep Steadicam batteries alive at temperatures as low as –30°F (alcohol-fuelled hand warmers and insulated bags!). Photo: Garrett Brown collection

Physical training

It is very important for a Steadicam operator to be in good physical shape to ensure the necessary capacity and strength and, above all, to avoid the problems which may arise when great physical effort is made without a prior warm up. The best sports and exercises for an operator to choose are: swimming, dance, abdominal exercises, cycling to strengthen leg muscles and, above all, back extender and stretching exercises for the entire body.

Safety

The most important element of safety is to foresee all possible dangers, including the worst, and to have a system which allows the operator, if in danger, immediately to get free of the rig and away from the vehicle if one is being used.

In situations requiring the use of a vehicle, it is important to know the shot perfectly – place, action, actors, route, surface, the speed involved, whether it will be too long or too uncomfortable and if there is any possibility of interference with or reactions to other vehicles involved. With very complicated shots that require teamwork, the collaboration among drivers, assistants and operator must be well-planned, because improvised or careless collaboration can be dangerous. All hazards must be evaluated beforehand. The operator must feel confident at all times. He must also refuse to do shots that are too risky.

Limitations on use of the Steadicam

The Steadicam is not suitable for:

- Static shots of long focal lengths. It is possible, but not particularly enjoyable, for a Steadicam operator to hold a frame entirely still out to about 100 mm, but to do this only makes sense if it is at the beginning or end of a Steadicam move.

- Extremely violent action (this kind of thing is perfect for 'Shaky-cams' or 'Pogo-cams' that do not have to be rock-steady and that generally do not need viewfinding).
- Being mounted or being carried on things that regularly crash: e.g. skis, skates, horses, helicopters, vehicles in violent motion, etc.
- Any shots which can be easily and perfectly executed using a dolly.[39]

> Every now and then you get a brutally difficult running shot, which I don't encourage, frankly, because there are a lot of other ways to transport a camera. I love to ride on a western dolly and concentrate a little more on the operating.[40]

It should be remembered that there is other equipment available that is simpler and better suited to certain situations, precisely because its simplicity means that the specific requirements of situations involving bumps, etc., can be easily satisfied, i.e. 'Pogo-cams', 'Shaky-cams' and others.

Evolution of the Steadicam

The Steadicam has undergone extensive changes, while maintaining the same structural and functional principles. It has been modified, lightened and differentiated to provide a better technical and expressive response to the various requirements which have arisen during its use in many areas: film, television and sports (Table 2.2).

Garrett Brown, Jerry Holway and others, along with Cinema Products, have carried on a continuing dialogue with Steadicam operators over the years, soliciting comments and listening to a number of suggestions for possible changes born from the operators' personal experiences. Furthermore, in the course of the Steadicam

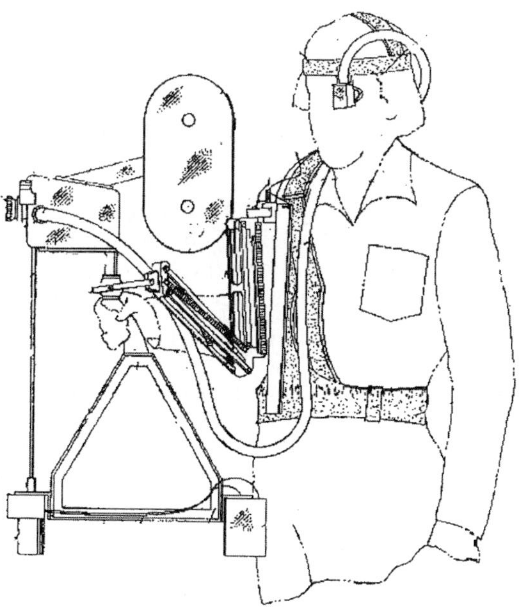

Figure 2.24 Patented Steadicam prototype

workshops that introduce the Steadicam, teach its use and give an in-depth look at its capabilities and the techniques involved, new ideas arise and are discussed, inspiring changes and new features, accessories and aids such as Antlers, the Bodycam, the Slavecam, etc.

The first modifications to the Steadicam arose from the direct experience of Garrett Brown, who experimented with this new tool in the first movies to make use of it: *Bound for Glory*, *Rocky*, etc. He immediately felt the need to make the device more versatile and easier to use. Each element was studied and changes were made that always aimed at developing its technical capacity according to the requirements of the shots to be made.

At the beginning, the camera was fixed in place, an integral part of the structure; later the attachment was changed so that the camera could be detached and used alone, making it possible to switch between a 35 or 16 mm camera and a video camera (Universal I).

The viewfinder in Garrett's prototype used a fibre optic bundle from the camera to the eye. Later, a video viewfinder was positioned above the camera. This was lowered to the sled on the Universal model, and finally given an approximately intermediate position on the post between the camera and the battery. During this time, it changed from being a black and white viewfinder to a three-inch 'green phosphor' screen, visible even in sunlight.

The arm evolved through five versions with springs and parallelogram links. The versions differed in their weight-bearing capacity, construction materials and in how they were adjusted. Thus it progressed from the early articulated arm, with a natural midpoint where the arm likes to 'float', to the recent isoelastic arm, characterized by the facts that it neutralizes the weight of the camera in any position in its vertical range, and that its lifting power can be hand-adjusted while holding the rig.

It must be emphasized that all elements that make up the rig have evolved including, besides those described above, the various electronic components, the cables, the materials and the accessories.

All the research done was aimed at improving the form and the capabilities, with a degree of specialization according to the model and the requirements of shooting, and always with particular attention paid to the quality and lightness of the materials. In this way, a number of models were born, for use by either professionals or amateurs.

Twenty-six years after the first version, the 'Ultra' was created, the latest model of the Steadicam which, as its name implies, gives maximum performance in all areas. Nevertheless, the Steadicam can always be further perfected and, for this reason, research never stops:

> In the future we will see the contribution of electronics and automation. That is the first step. As with the Master Film model, for example, and that little remote control knob that moves the stage forwards and backwards: that's the route to take. The other evolution will be in what it is equipped with and then there will be an evolution of the materials used. Consequently, less weight and better performance.[41]

Table 2.3 lists Steadicam features by model. It must be noted that weights can vary depending on optional equipment and accessories.

Table 2.2 Steadicam models and year of development

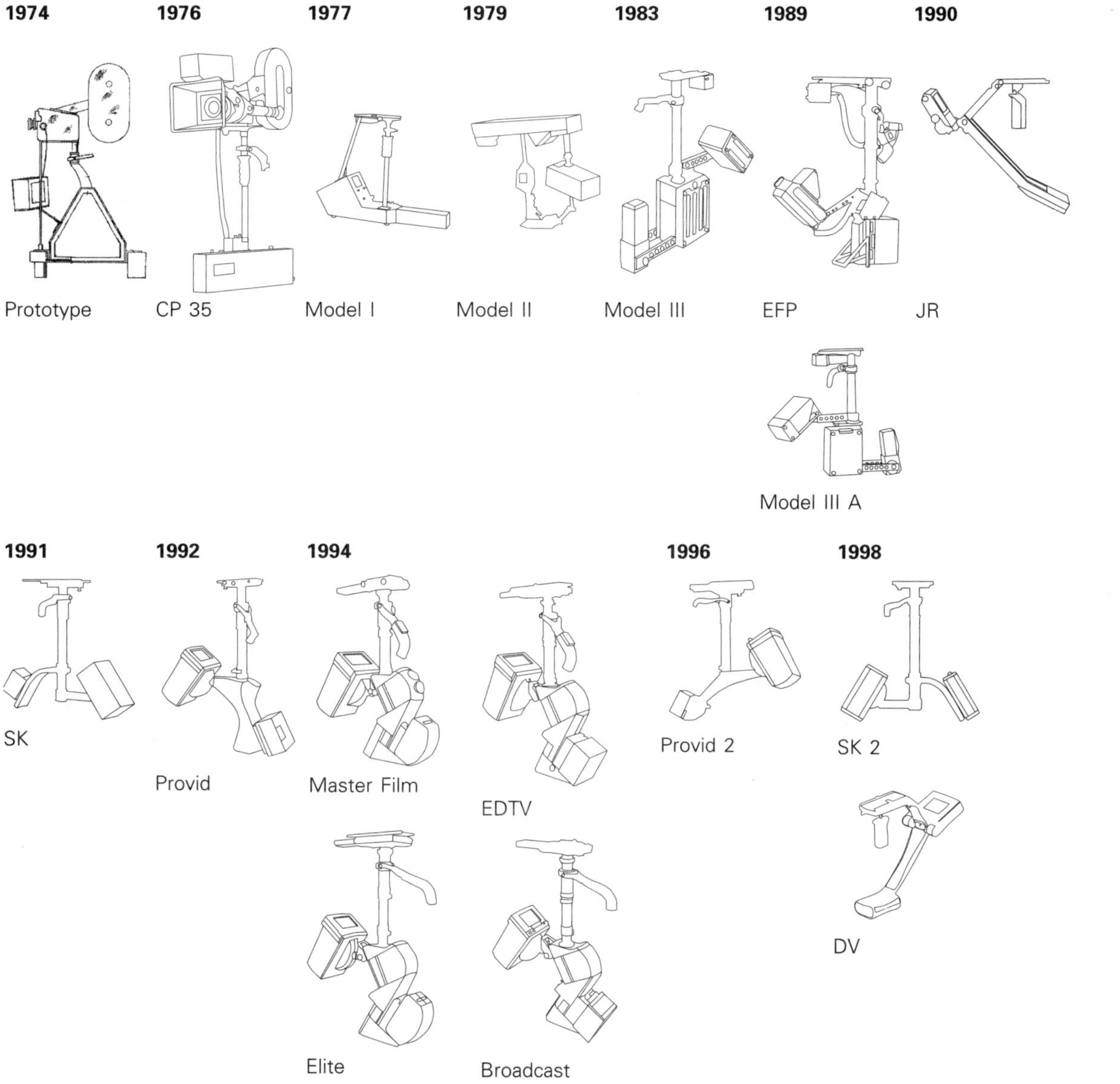

Year	Models
1974	Prototype
1976	CP 35
1977	Model I
1979	Model II
1983	Model III
1989	EFP; Model III A
1990	JR
1991	SK
1992	Provid
1994	Master Film; EDTV; Elite; Broadcast
1996	Provid 2
1998	SK 2; DV
1999	Mini
2000	Ultra

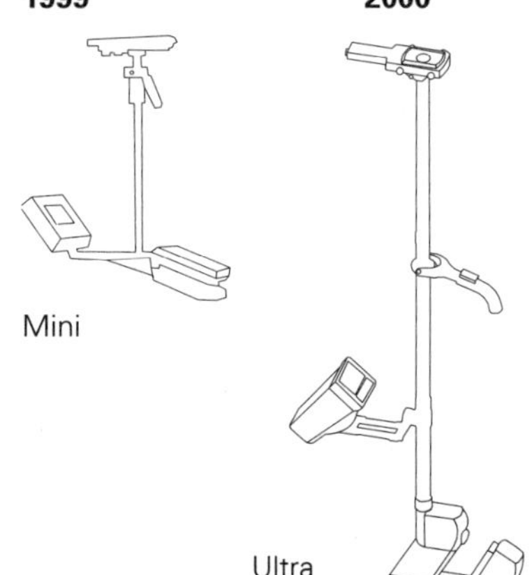

Every element of the Steadicam evolved from model to model but, for reasons of space, only the changes to the arm are described in full.

Evolution of the Steadicam arm: 'The arm itself was inspired by looking at old articulating lamps and imagining new ways for two arm sections to work together'. Changes were made over the years to the shape, the material from which it was made, its weight-bearing capacity and its response to the effects of movement. From model to model these changes were:

Steadicam models I and II had a single hinge and only a small weight range; Models III and EFP had arms with a double hinge that easily flipped to right- or left-side operation and had a greater weight range.The arm used in the Master Series has a different design that incorporates a large weight range and no-tool adjustment. One adjustable knob per arm segment permits fine-tuning the exact float point and the precise interaction of each arm segment in seconds while standing or walking with the camera floating (the SK arm is a slight variant of the Master Series design, with only one sprung section).

Table 2.3 Steadicam features (by model)

Year	*Weight*	*Name and model*	*Vest*	*Arm*	*Rig*
1974	23 lbs	**Prototype** Patented triangular configuration (but the invention is not limited to any particular shaft or frame)	Initially a brace that is sized and built to rest upon the shoulder of the cameraman to support all the equipment, later a non-adjustable vest of the current configuration, sized to fit Garrett Brown	Spring-loaded support arms: a pair of longitudinally juxtaposed support arms with a parallelogram configuration	Triangular configuration, the function of the frame is to expand and space the various portions of the expanded camera, to provide a system that is substantially balanced throughout with the handle positioned approximately at the centre of the moment of inertia of the expanded camera
1976	35 lbs	**Steadicam 35** A dedicated system	Plastic and nylon, normal configuration (padded close-fitting harness-like jacket) No quick-release	First Cinema Products arm: exoskeletal-type articulated support arm, which parallels the operator's arm in any position and almost completely counteracts the weight of the camera system with a carefully calibrated spring force	The CP 35 model has two posts. The main post holds the gimbal (to which the arm is attached) and the drive-shaft for the Arri camera which comes up the centre from the motor below to the camera above. The other support post is for a support brace
1977	Sled only 17.5 lbs	**New 'Universal Model' I.** Allows the camera to be removed from the system, and allows one Steadicam system to be used interchangeably with either a hand-held video camera, a hand-held 16 mm camera or a hand-held 35 mm camera	With velcro quick release	The exoskeletal-type articulated support arm parallels the operator's arm in any position, and almost completely counteracts the weight of the camera system with a carefully calibrated spring force. Non-adjustable; very light weight	Attached to the sled are two vertical members which support the camera mounting platform, one of which mounts the gimbal-handle (vertically adjustable)
1979	18.0 lbs	**Model II**	As Model I	Double-acting hinge system joint added. Adjustable spring tension with allen wrench to charge lift also added	As Model I, except front post is interrupted with rectangular tiltable mounting brace for raised monitor

Camera mounting stage	*Monitor*	*Batteries and electronics*	*Balance*	*Movies*
Simple connection to camera and camera motor drive shaft	The camera viewer is provided with a remote view-finding device, such as a flexible fibre coherent optic bundle extending between the reflex view-finding system of the camera body and the cameraman's eyes, or a video monitor affixed to the camera	Battery is positioned near one corner of the frame, the motor near another and the handle is affixed to a third corner of frame, to provide a unique expanded and balanced arrangement for the camera equipment	Pre-set	First films: *Bound for Glory* *Rocky* (part) *Marathon Man* (part)
Only mounts 35 Arri IIc camera	The 3" high intensity monitor is placed at eye level on the camera	Servo follow – focus system operated by an electronic remote control box either through a thin electric cable or by wireless transmission. The lower portion of the camera assembly, in a T-bar arrangement, contains the monitor power supply module, crystal-controlled camera drive motor and control circuitry, and the battery pack (silver-cadium) powering both the film and video system	Pre-set Side-to-side balance by swings battery	*Marathon Man* (end) *Rocky* (end) and many others
A universal model that allows the camera to be removed (it is adjustable back and forwards in order to maintain camera balance)	The 3" high intensity video monitor is mounted directly onto the sled at approximately a 45° upward angle (using a the same special green kinescope tube and sunlight-reflecting filter as on the CP	The sled-like assembly at the bottom of the system contains the video viewfinder, the electronics to run it and the battery pack to power both the camera and the viewing system. Also high-voltage power supply for the monitor	Handle/gimbal has a 2" movement; battery swings side-to-side. Camera dovetail mounting plate moves fore and aft. Inherently dynamically balanced design, but operators were unaware of the importance of this until much later	'Hundreds of movies, worldwide'
A universal model that allows the camera to be removed (it is adjustable back and forwards in order to maintain camera balance; as Model I)	The monitor is moved up on the 'front post' and can be tilted and rotated	The sled-like assembly at the bottom of the system contains the video viewfinder, the electronics to run it and the battery pack to power both the camera and the high-voltage power supply for the viewing system. Plus monitor high voltage power supply below.	Not dynamically balanced (far worse dynamic balance than Model I)	Debut on *The Shining*

Table 2.3 Steadicam Features (by model) – continued

Year	*Weight*	*Name and model*	*Vest*	*Arm*	*Rig*
1983/84	18.0 lbs	**Model III**	Added aircraft pin quick-release, leather straps	Has an articulated elbow; anodized, all black	Single central aluminium post acts as support and handle (operator's hand holds post just below gimbal – gimbal bearings in discrete housing – some operators added clamp-on handle for better grip; monitor support bracket mounted to post, electronics below surround post are rotatable for side-to-side balance
1989	15.0 lbs	**EFP:** Works well with video, 16 mm. and very light 35 mm camera (will not support the larger cameras)	Lighter vest construction (fabric) than Model II, velcro quick release	Double hinges are easily flipped to right- or left-side operation and have a large weight range	Single centre post, ultra-light electronics housing, Anton Bauer battery mount
1989	19 lbs	**Model III A**	Same as Model III	Same as Model III, with quick-release socket to change from left- to right-side operating	Same as Model III, but rotation eliminated from electronics, extra fore–aft adjustment added for dynamic balance, side-to-side vernier adjustment added to stage
1990	2 lbs	**JR** For handycams, especially the lighter ones Great for home video Very good for practicing broad rehearsals of shot	None	Instead of a suit and arm the bottom of the handle (the grip) is supported with one hand and the other hand is used to pan and tilt, barely touching the top (the guide). Between the grip and the guide is a miniature three-axes gimbal	Structurally JR is a camera platform, a gimballed handle, a flat screen monitor and two folding arms
1991	13.5 lbs	**SK** (more compact and less complex)	Same general design, smaller, no quick release, simple upright pin for arm-mounting socket (non-adjustable in angle for different operator body types)	Iso-elastic one-spring active one-section arm	Single centre post, detachable, invertable (for low mode) bracket that holds monitor and mounting for compact Anton Bauer battery
1992	15.8 lbs	**Provid**	Stronger than SK, adds primitive angle adjustment (via rotating cams) for different operator types	Iso-elastic two-section, two-spring arm	Discrete carbon-fibre housing, mounts invertable monitor and Anton Bauer battery mounting plate

Camera mounting stage	Monitor	Batteries and electronics	Balance	Movies
A universal model that allows the camera to be removed (it is adjustable back and forwards in order to maintain camera balance)	Slightly larger tube, tiltable and rotatable on its support bracket	Included: monitor high-voltage supply, adaptor plug for CP (and later Seitz) wireless focus system, sensor for on-screen level indicator, control panel with various power plugs, 12 V battery	All the lower components rotate side-to-side. Camera moves fore and aft (side-to-side vernier came later with Model IIIA	Debut on *One from the Heart*
A universal model that allows the camera to be removed (it is adjustable back and forwards in order to maintain camera balance)	Self-contained monitor originally LCD, later lightweight green screen	Simple battery connection and follow focus connection	Dynamically balanced with after-market accessory	Used worldwide
A universal model that allows the camera to be removed (it is adjustable back and forwards and side-to-side in order to maintain camera balance)	2.9" high intensity monochrome flat screen LCD monitor with sunlight-reflecting filter	Two discrete mounting compartments for c-batteries, wiring for camera video connection and 'obie' light connection	The camera platform is vernier – trimmable in all three axes, so is balanced.	
A universal model that allows the camera to be removed (it is adjustable back and forwards in order to maintain camera balance; also side-to-side vernier adjustment	Slightly larger than Model III	As Model III	First model dynamically balanceable from factory	Thousands
Compact, includes fore-aft adjust, side-to-side vernier	Self-contained green screen	Compact Anton Bauer battery, plugs top and bottom to facilitate reconnection when inverting for low/high mode switch	Dynamically balanced from factory	Mostly video
Similar to SK	Self-contained	Simple batteries only	Dynamic balance adjustable via extendable battery mount	Video

Table 2.3 Steadicam Features (by model) – continued

Year	*Weight*	*Name and model*	*Vest*	*Arm*	*Rig*
1994	 23.0 lbs 21.5 lbs 22.5 lbs 20.5 lbs	**Master Series** The most radically redesigned Steadicam Different models: **FILM** **ELITE** **EDTV** **Broadcast**	New connecting hardware and roller-blade type straps can be instantly loosened between takes and retightened for shooting. Fits small to large male or female operators. Industrial belting – leather, aluminium, nylon composites	New 'iso-elastic' Master arm; no-tools adjustment; lift-stays iso-elastic, which means even lift throughout arms vertical range. One adjustable knob per arm segment permits fine tuning the exact float point and the precise interaction of each arm segment in seconds while standing or walking with the camera floating	Sleek, streamlined and compact. 'Ultra-narrow' design, keeps the sled close to the operator's body to improve control and reduce fatigue
1996	15.8 lbs	**Provid 2**	Same as SK	Single section Provid-type arm	Single post, lighter carbon fibre housing below to hold invertable monitor and battery mount
1998	2.5 lbs	**DV** Specially designed for the digital video camcorders		Primitive 'lamp' type parallelogram arm – single active section	Folding plastic sections, stage above, monitor connection at the joint, battery compartment below
1998	14.5 lbs	**SK2**	Same as SK	Available with two-section arm	Discrete carbon fibre housing holds invertable monitor and battery mounting bracket
1999	9.5 lbs	**Mini**	Custom lightweight vest	An articulated iso-elastic arm that booms up and down smoothly and effortlessly	Single centre post, with gimbal/handle vertically adjustable, lightweight connection below for monitor and battery
2000	20–23.5 lbs	**ULTRA** Extraordinary possibilities: post length 28–71" continuous (time to configure post 1 minute)	Master vest (leather)	Master arm	Built-in telescoping 4-section hi-modulus carbon fibre post

Camera mounting stage	*Monitor*	*Batteries and electronics*	*Balance*	*Movies*
Motorized stage allows adjustment in tilt and roll at any time during the shot, via digital-wireless buttons on the gimbal or by the assistant via conventional wireless at various agreed points during the shot, without touching the camera	Wide screen is the largest available. The monitor pivots for viewing without affecting dynamic balance	Ultra-narrow sled design improves clearance, reduces fatigue, and puts monitor and battery at the correct dynamic position for the best viewing in high and low mode. Battery: minimum envelope single battery system (monitor and its power supply separate). Includes: adaptor plug for 24 V converter, power distribution panel, level sensor, 12 V battery, electronics module with video distribution amplifiers, level-sensor conditioning circuit board (bubble tamer), frame-line generator board, etc.	Stage motorized for *x*, *y* adjustment by wireless remote control (no need to touch stage – can be adjusted during shot	*Casino* (Garrett Brown first movie with Master)
Same as Provid	Light green screen	Battery connection, video connection to monitor, etc.	The sled is dynamically balanced by design	
With in-line screw fore–aft and side–side drives; dovetail mounting with quick release	4"; active matix colour monitor display with OCLI anti-glare coating	New built-in 12 V nicad battery pack, can be disconnected and removed or recharged in place	The sled is dynamically balanced by design	
Same as SK	Lightweight green screen, self-contained	Anton Bauer bracket, suggested for hytron NimH batteries	Inherently dynamically balanced	
SK-style, adjustable in two axes	Colour LCD, as in DV	Anton Bauer-type mounting plate	Dynamically adjustable by swinging battery and monitor brackets up and down	
Motorized, remote controlled by new wireless Link Corp transmitter and receiver	Monitor and built-in power supply separate – diagonal, self-contained	Same electronics module as Master, but 24 V battery, and built-in 12 V downconverter	Dynamic balance calculator facilitates battery position adjustment for perfect dynamic balance	*All the Pretty Horses* (Steadicam operator: J. Holway – first movie)

In the list below, weights are given for 'normal' equipment including appropriate battery/batteries:

1974	patent triangular	23 lbs
1976	Steadicam CP–35	35 lbs (the only unit listed with camera)
1977	Model I	17.5 lbs
1979	Model II	18.0 lbs
1983/84	Model III	18.0 lbs
1989	EFP	15.0 lbs
	Model IIIA	19.0 lbs
1990	JR	2.0 lbs
1991	SK	13.5 lbs
1992	Provid	15.8 lbs
1994	Masters Series:	
	Film	23.0 lbs
	Elite	21.5 lbs
	Edtv	22.5 lbs
	Broadcast	20.5 lbs
1996	Provid 2	15.8 lbs
1998	SK2	14.5 lbs
	DV	2.5 lbs
1999	Mini	9.5 lbs
2000	Ultra Cine	23.5 lbs

New tools developed from the idea of Steadicam

The Steadicam is an ingenious tool based on simple and fundamental principles of physics which are 'coordinated' by the operator's ability. Since Garrett Brown had the idea for this tool, he has seen similar ideas and tools emerge, entirely inspired by and copied from his and which, at times, even boasted of precedence over the Steadicam.

The history of the now defunct 'Panaglide' is a story of intrigue and competition, with the 'Panaglide' attempting and failing to disprove the Steadicam's priority. The 'Panaglide' was a clone of the Steadicam; however, it did not have the same capabilities, since it was copied based only on an external view of the Steadicam, without knowledge of the principle by which the articulated arm works.[42]

Ed DiGiulio, the President of Cinema Products, tells how Garrett Brown first proposed his invention to Panavision and how they did not want to sign the secrecy agreement regarding the invention before signing a contract. They did not trust its originality, nor did they realize its potential. Consequently, Garrett Brown took it to Cinema Products, where a solid collaboration was born with regard to both invention and production.

Besides the Panaglide, which was officially a product developed with the structure of the Steadicam and capable of generating the 'Steadicam effect' (see the interview in Chapter 4 with John Carpenter, *Halloween*), a number of products have appeared, at times at the amateur level, which copy or attempt to use the basic principles of the Steadicam but which differ in materials and performance. The 'Glidecam' is a typical example of these.

With the 'birth' of the Steadicam, Garrett Brown was creatively inspired by its effects and the results it obtained. He continued to design, with Jerry Holway and others, new tools which use the same physical principles or which integrate the Steadicam into a larger structure.

> The versatility and precision of the Steadicam operating has expanded greatly in the past few years because of our clearer knowledge of static and dynamic balance and other aspects of the Steadicam system. New devices, such as Buddycam, Slavecam, were the result of understanding how each part of the Steadicam system works and then wondering about the implications of that knowledge.[43]

In 1991 the 'Skyman' was born, a new vehicle for aerial Steadicam shots developed by Garrett Brown and Jerry Holway. It was designed to extend the capabilities of the Steadicam by providing a fast, reliable, low-tech 'flying carpet' for shots over inaccessible places such as rivers, canyons and so on. Skyman carries both hard mount Steadicam and operator. It consists of an ultralight aerial cablecar with foot-operated braking and 360° rotation.[44]

The 'Flyman' was invented in 1991. Here, the operator hangs directly below the crane. It is a 'hanging system' and should be supported by a special vest with a hook at the common centre of gravity of operator and Steadicam to operate while hanging upright.

Furthermore, with the commercialization of the Steadicam there has been a parallel exchange of experiences among the various operators who have studied the needs arising during filming and expressed their opinions and suggestions for changes. This has given rise to an extraordinary debate that first began thanks to the Steadicam Operators Association (SOA)[45] and the publication of the *Steadicam Letter*[46] and which still continues on the Internet.

Ever since it became well-known, the Steadicam has been copied and has inspired many amateur versions. At the professional level, there have been a series of accessories and changes proposed by the Steadicam operators, which have increased the 'Steadicam heritage'. In 1992, in response to some of these suggestions, George Paddock produced a variation on the sled, beginning the Pro®.

'Steadicam' is, of course, trademarked and, since 1976, Cinema Products has been the exclusive manufacturer. Aside from the early Panaglide (manufactured under licence to Garrett and Cinema Products), Steadicam was the only complete system of its type until, in 1993, there was the debut of the 'Pro', based on Garrett's expiring early patents. Paddock began by marketing just a monitor, and subsequently a battery holder. His associates sold a post and a top stage separately, and they could be combined to make a sled.

When in 1994–1995 Garrett Brown's original patents for the complete Steadicam and specific arm expired, Paddock began to openly sell the other components as well: gimbals, arms, vests, etc. The version he developed, based on the requirements expressed by many operators, became the alternative to the Steadicam, increasing the competition faced by Cinema Products. The latter, inspired by the same requests, did its own research and created the Master Series in 1994.

The various experiences and requirements reported by operators have stimulated the continued evolution of the Steadicam, inspiring changes in its structure and level of performance that have led to a diversification of models specifically suited to various requirements

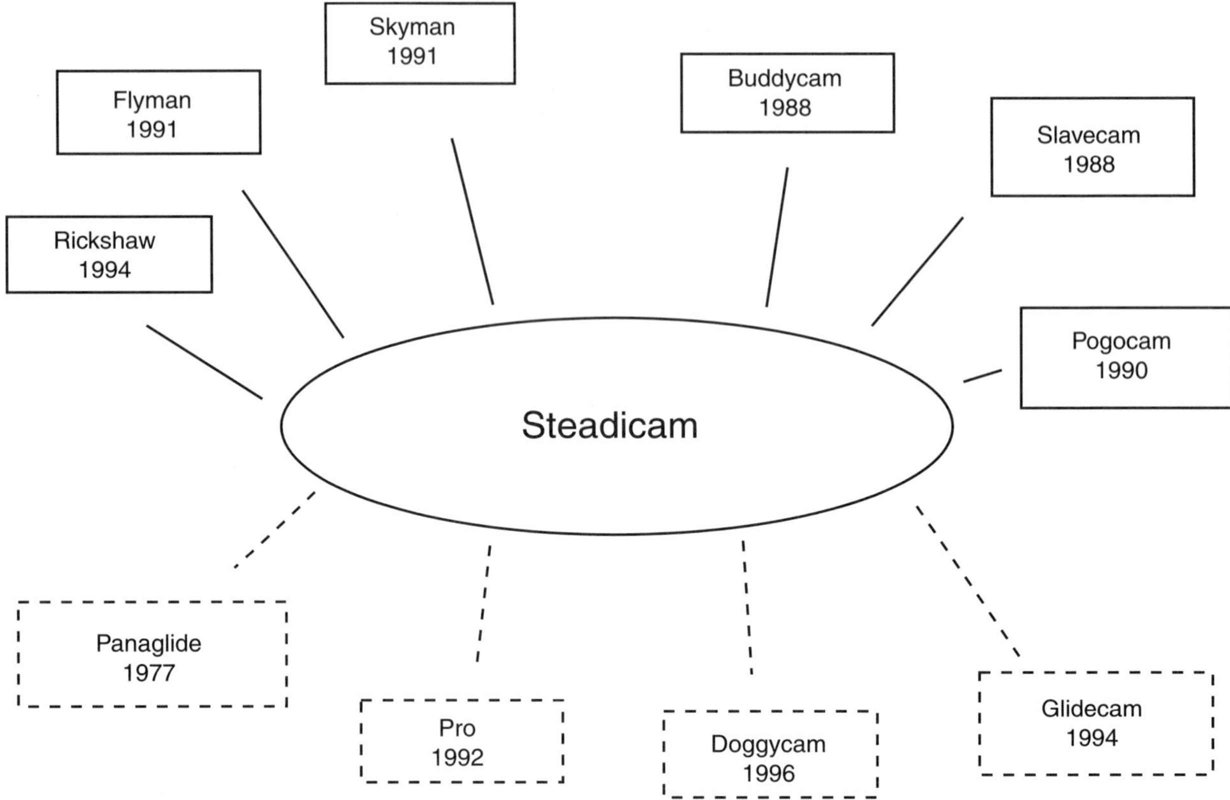

Figure 2.25 New tools born from the Steadicam idea

(e.g., lighter for video use) and, simultaneously, to the creation of an ever more perfect version which would give optimum performance in all areas (the Ultra). The Steadicam, therefore, is still evolving, though it continues to use the same basic principles.

The devices shown in Figure 2.25 all tend to reproduce the Steadicam effect and performance.

The Steadicam's accessories

There are two basic categories of Steadicam accessories: indispensable and optional, although in certain situations (such as strong wind) the optionals become indispensable (Figure 2.26).

Necessary accessories

As the Steadicam is a system that floats undisturbed 'in space' it is obviously impossible for the assistant to follow and focus the camera in the normal way. Thus it is necessary to have a system that can be operated by a remote electronic control box, either through a thin flexible electrical cable or by wireless transmission.

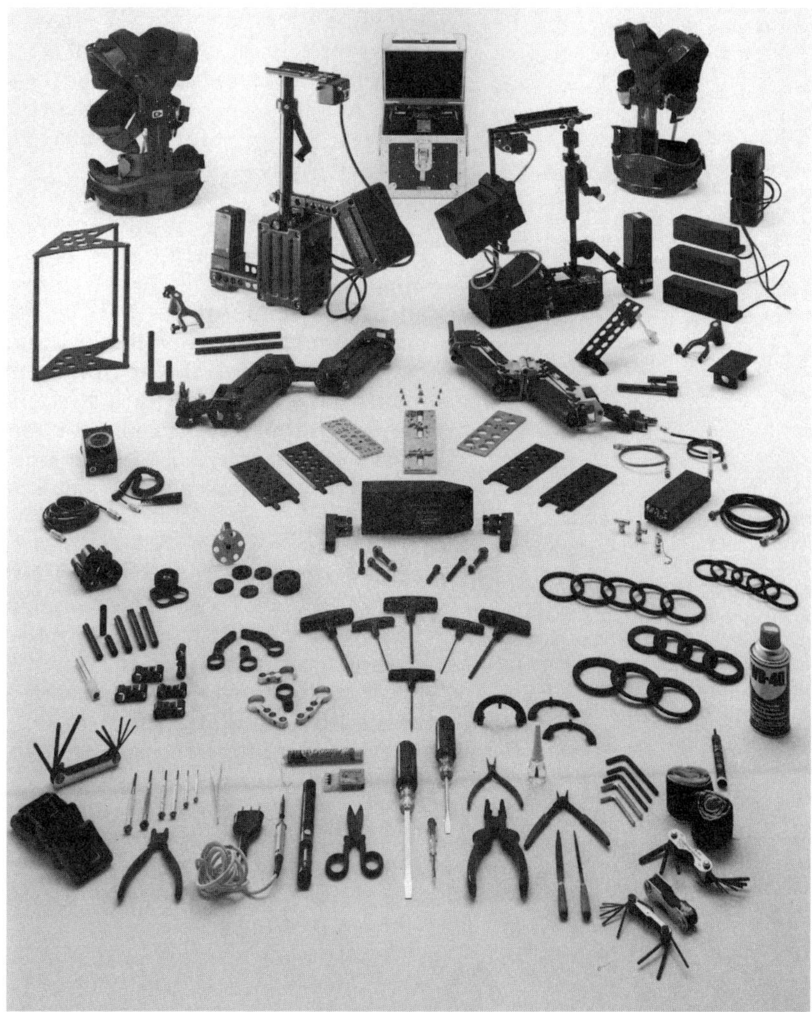

Figure 2.26 Nicola Pecorini's joke shot illustrating the back-up equipment needed by a professional Steadicam operator (extra everything). This display shows Nicola's large inventory of personal equipment as of 1985. Photo: Garrett Brown collection

Consequently, the Steadicam should be supplied with a follow focus device, usually consisting of a wireless transmitter (FM or microwave) that talks to a wireless receiver mounted on the Steadicam, which drives one or more servo motors connected to the lens via a series of gears. The unit is operated by the camera assistant (who is able to alter focus, iris or zoom). A video transmitter allows the director to see the shot on a monitor. It works in UHF, FM or microwave bandwidth. In order to receive the transmitted video image a reliable multichannel video receiver is necessary.[47]

It is important to have at hand a wide range of brackets and cables, which are needed to switch from high mode to low mode and to adapt the rig to the various situations which can arise.

Optional accessories

Among the optional accessories for the Steadicam are the Antlers and the Gyros, which increase the inertia and the stability of the system.

The Antlers, or 'Inertial Augmentation System', are a metal bar that supports an equal weight at either end. They can be attached above the camera, adding inertia to the rig by extending mass and thus making it easier to control, especially in windy situations. Antlers rely on the 'square law', which provides that positioning well-separated, small masses above all the other components will efficiently add a lot of inertia with very little extra weight.[48]

Gyroscopes use a different approach to increase the inertial response of the sled. Two brass or tungsten rotors spinning in opposite directions at 20 000 rpm inside a helium-filled can produce an astonishing stiffness.[49] They add faux 'inertia', and the correct positioning of a gyro will add stability to two axes so that they both become stiffer and the operator's unforced errors or slight misjudgements have less effect on the stability of the shot. With three gyros correctly mounted the operator can cover all three axes.[50] Each gyro works on a single axis so that one stabilizer actually affects two of the three axes that need to be controlled.

The Steadicam in fields other than cinema

The Steadicam's first real debut took place in 1974 in the field of advertising, when Garrett Brown was asked to shoot a commercial for 'Keds' (Figure 2.27), directed and shot by Haskell Wexler with whom he would later shoot *Bound for Glory*. The commercial used a series of running shots to follow a group of speedy children.

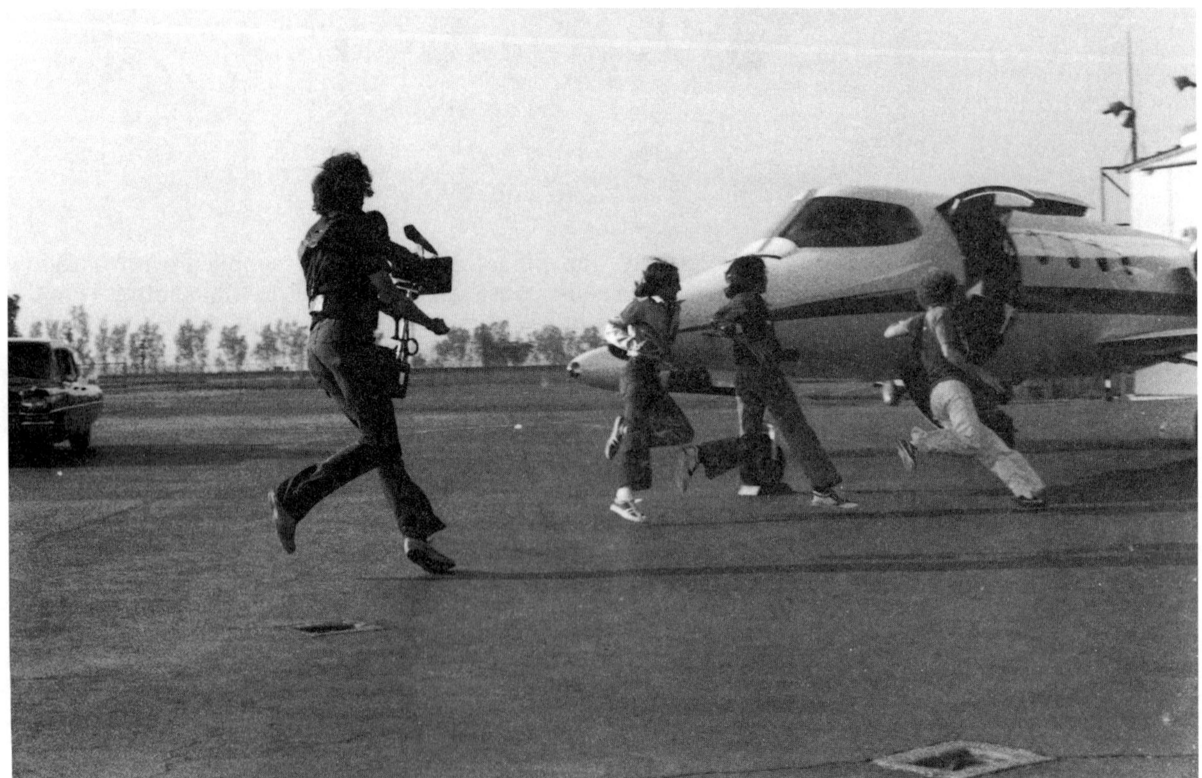

Figure 2.27 *Keds*. Production still from the very first Steadicam commercial, Haskell Wexler's *Keds* spot. The prototype weighed only 23 lbs and Garrett Brown was able to overtake even the fastest of the 13-year-old actors. Photo: Garrett Brown collection

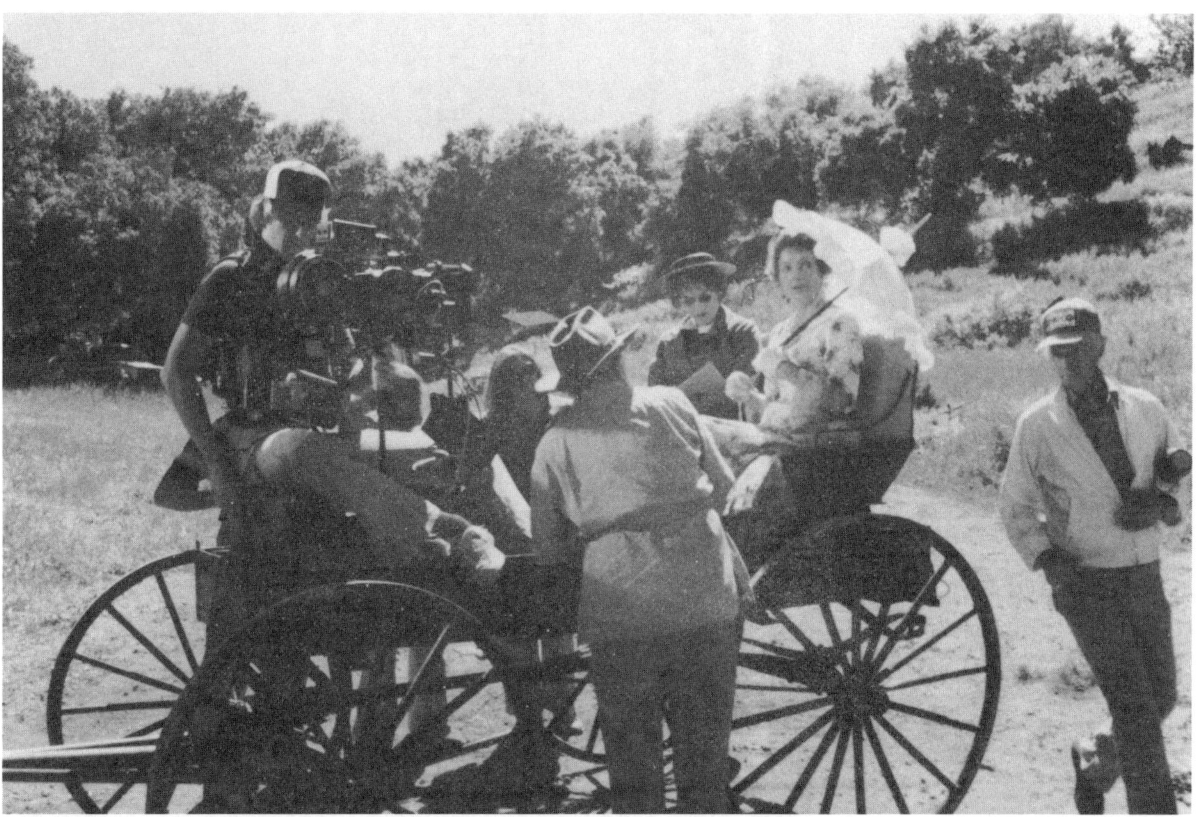

Figure 2.28 *Little House on the Prairie*. Garrett Brown flies the heavy Arriflex BL sound camera 'soft mounted' (wearing it!), sitting on a wagon to shoot a travelling dialogue two-shot. The late Ted Voightlander, veteran DP, is standing with his back to the camera. Photo: Garrett Brown collection

Later, during the time when the Steadicam was beginning to be used in movies, it also made its official entrance into the world of television. The Steadicam Universal Model was used with a RCA TK – 76 colour video to provide coverage for ABC-TV's telecast of the National Academy of Television Arts and Sciences 28th Annual Emmy Awards presentation in May 1976.[51] Some of the television shows that first employed the Steadicam are *Little House on the Prairie* (Figure 2.28), *The Miracle Worker*, and *60 Minutes*.

Thanks to its incredible potential, the Steadicam is unsurpassed when it comes to the requirements of transmitting sports events on television, such as a continuous presence on the field and the need to satisfy the public's curiosity and stimulate its interest (Figure 2.29).

The Steadicam can follow games from the sidelines and provide 'colour' shots of training, award ceremonies or players entering and exiting the locker rooms without architectural barriers being a problem.

Just as for sports, the nature of which is expressed in movement, the Steadicam takes on the role of omnipresent witness for musical events as well. It climbs onto the stage, moves around the performers and wholly involves the spectator with images perfectly meshed with the rhythm of the event (Figure 2.30). If at first its use was optional, it has now become a basic and necessary tool for filming a show or concert.

Television, therefore, which needs to be sure that it is capturing the attention of its viewers – who at times are not paying attention,

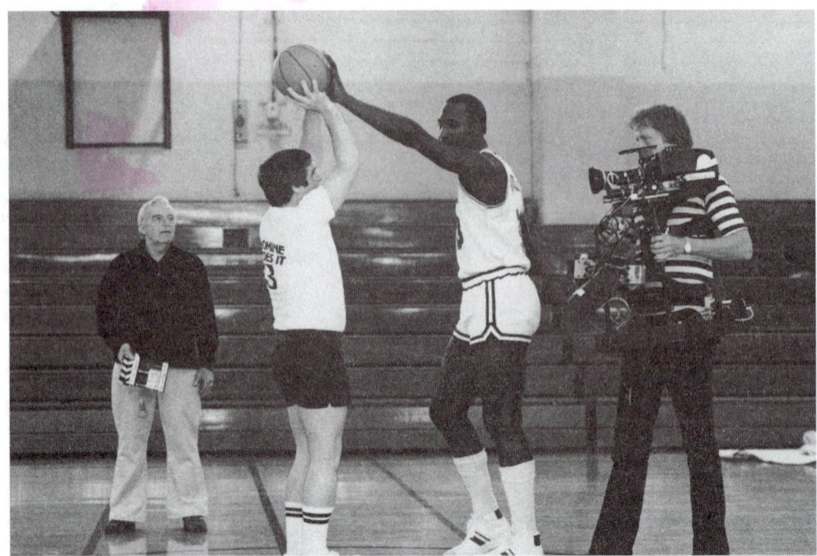

Figure 2.29 Garrett Brown prepares to film basketball star Moses Malone with the Model II, which was developed for use on *The Shining*. Photo: Garrett Brown collection

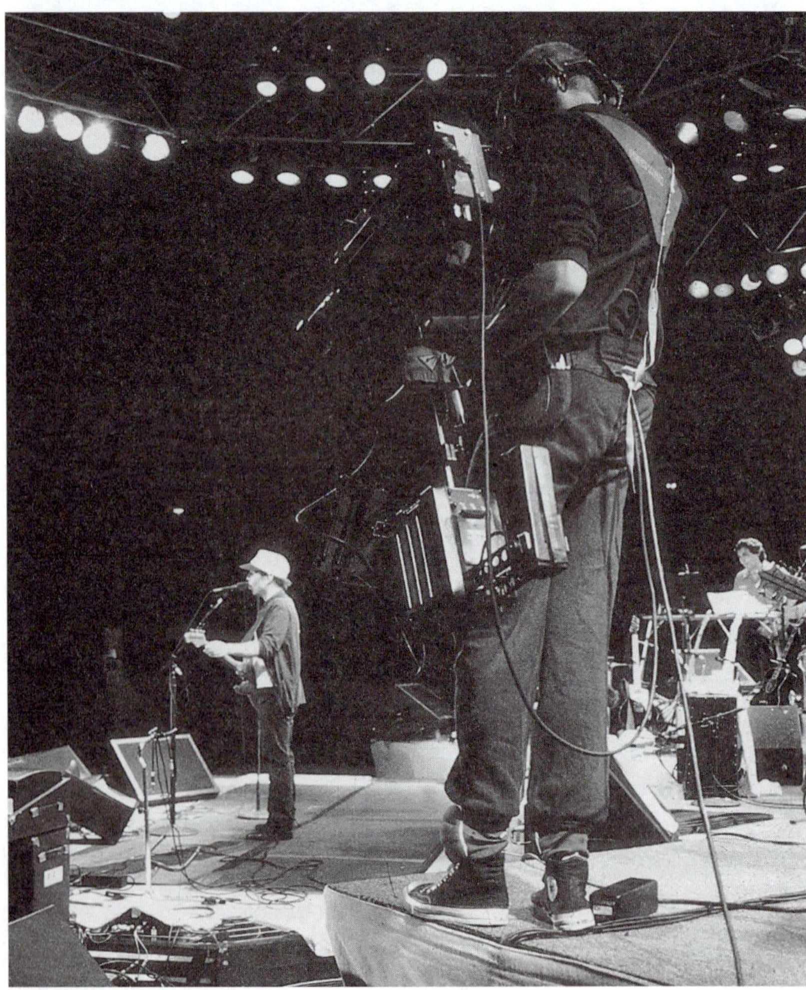

Figure 2.30 Simon and Garfunkel concert. Photo: Nicola Pecorini collection

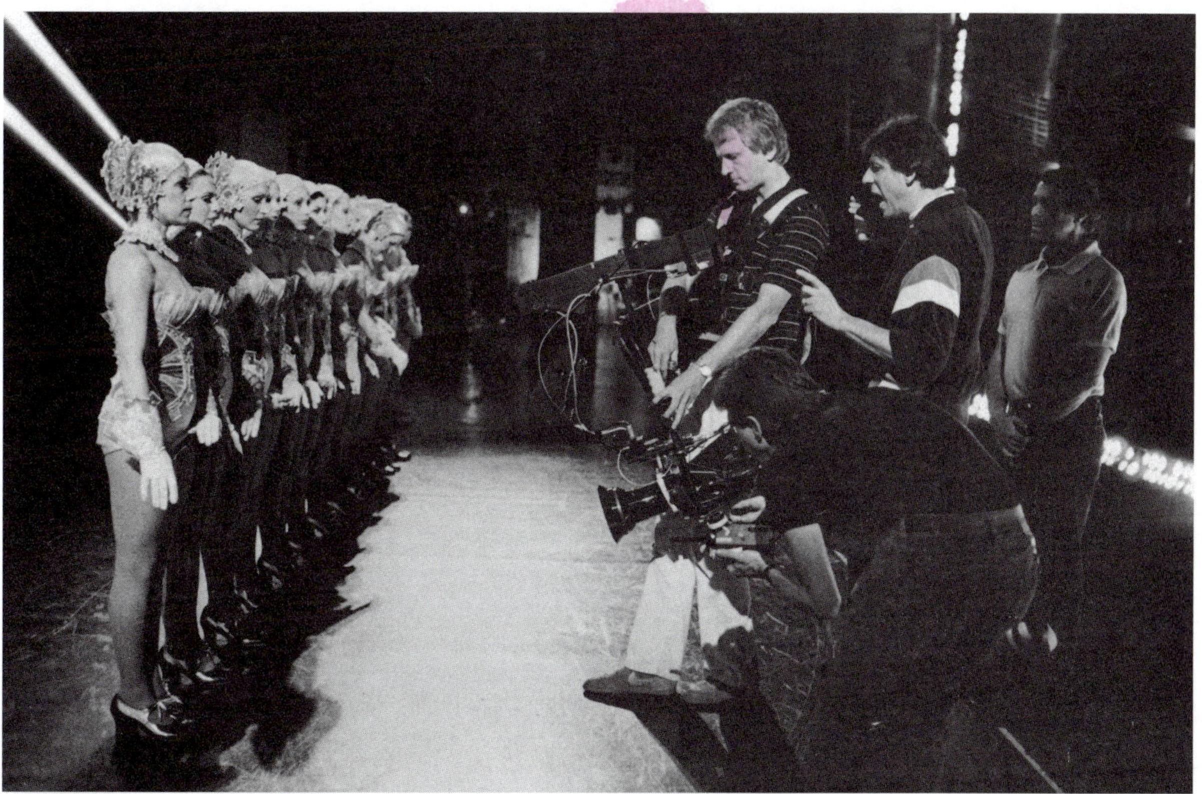

Figure 2.31 The Rockettes at Radio City Music Hall for *Annie* (Garrett Brown is shooting in low-mode). Photo: Garrett Brown collection

but who are very demanding and pitiless when they are – has adopted the Steadicam as a tool of unsurpassed scenic value and functional capability. The Steadicam, which can move continuously around performers always allowing them freedom of movement, while providing a steady and clear image on the screen, has made its role as television narrator and witness, and has become part of the 'tradition' of television production (concerts, ballet, shows) (Figure 2.31).

Many television drama series also make considerable use of the Steadicam. A good example is *ER*, which is essentially based on the constant presence of the Steadicam, following the characters as they go about their urgent work. A constant and assiduous witness, the Steadicam acquaints us with the characters, setting them in their work environment as it moves around them, breathing with them; the tension and urgency are underscored with tracking shots, circles and semicircles around the medical staff and their patients.

An example of how the Steadicam can interpret the language of sounds and 'music in movement' – as occurs in dance – can be found in the video of Carolyn Carlson, one of the most interesting contemporary choreographers and dancers, *The Water Cities*,[52] filmed in Venice. The video is a mental voyage through the artist's past and memories, set in the old *calles*. We enter the narrow and twisting streets as if we were entering the labyrinth of her personality; the movement and the spontaneous gesturing are registered by the Steadicam with great effectiveness. It almost seems itself to be dancing, alongside the dancers. The Steadicam makes it possible to

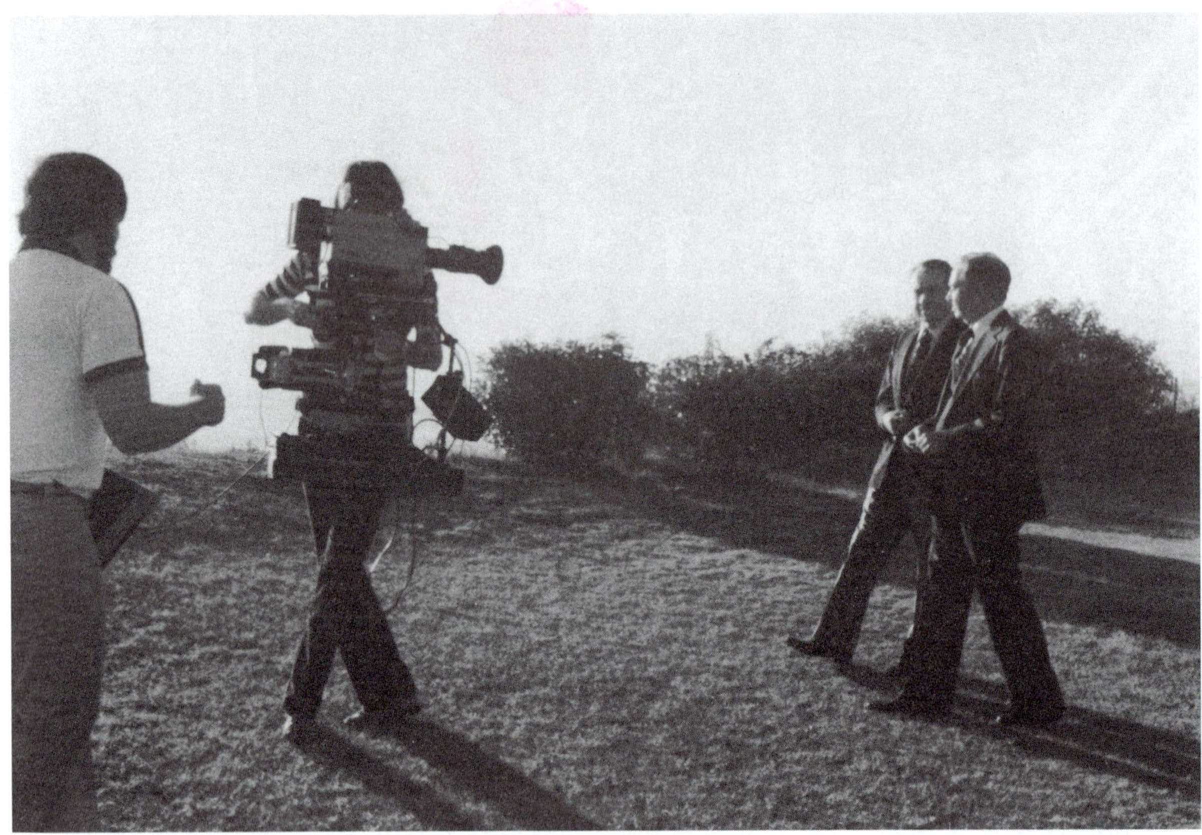

Figure 2.32 Garrett Brown precedes Richard Nixon and TV host Howard K. Smith for a TV special (*The American Presidency*) at Nixon's California home. Photo: Garrett Brown collection

comprehend the movement as it evolves and captures it moment by moment.

The potential of the Steadicam for filming television documentaries and news programmes was appreciated early. A perfect example of how the Steadicam could be used to advantage in this area was in the early 1980s, when Garrett Brown was called to shoot an episode of the television special *The American Presidency*, in which Howard K. Smith did a post-Watergate interview with Richard Nixon. This shoot was notable for two reasons. First, Nixon was the only person Garrett ever photographed who needed to stop walking in order to be able to speak; secondly, although Nixon had insisted that the interview should last only twenty minutes, at the last minute he decided that it could go on indefinitely, after which Garrett made a continuous shot with the Steadicam that lasted for an hour and forty minutes – a record that remained unbroken for many years (Figure 2.32).

The workshop experience

The Steadicam has limits. How these are defined depends a lot upon the operator. On a simple level, the physical structure of the Steadicam and its relationship to the operator does not allow the camera to get everywhere all the time. Part of what you will learn in this course is how to get the most out of the machine.

> Learning to operate Steadicam might be a lot like learning to ride a bicycle in the 1800s: It's an unfamiliar mechanical device that takes some determination to learn to use and trust.[53]

It is interesting to realize (only possible by direct participation) that although the simplicity and cleverness of this 'machine' are easily appreciated, the key mechanisms for interacting with it cannot be grasped until the operator has put it on and seen how it feels. It is necessary to acquire a 'consciousness' of the device or using it will feel unnatural and the correct position for holding it will continually be lost. The operator has to become one with the machine and, at the same time, has to know how to keep his/her distance; how to use it and to respect the camera's identity, because sometimes keeping it a little further away is what produces the best frame, action, sequence.

I was able to experience directly what it means to 'work' with the Steadicam at the workshop. It is a fantastic experience: exciting, engrossing and dynamic. You draw near the Steadicam almost sensually, you look at it from afar, you talk about it, you learn how to approach it and then, finally, comes the encounter: the first date, the first dance. Using the Steadicam is like leading a partner during a dance.

Garrett Brown explained to us how to hold and lift the Steadicam and how this is like 'holding' and 'leading' a ballerina without ever showing the effort involved in lifting her, continuing to move with the same agility, grace and elegance. It is a close relationship, involving complicity and also hard work, but if you maintain the right posture there is no undue effort on your part. It is a relationship of complicity precisely because the Steadicam is detached from you although you are wearing it; while the vest and the arm are uniting you, the gimbal and the support post are giving the camera its own identity. Through the handle and the grip you can take the Steadicam anywhere, rotating it on its own axis, lifting it and turning it. At the same time, the Steadicam is a unique tool because it is almost an extension of your own body, an encumbrance of which you must always be aware. You can do anything with it, but you must always be aware that you have a sort of 'aura' that envelops you and the device and, for this reason, you must always calculate your movements and the space in which you will move.

The workshop, which lasts five days, allows you to meet the best teachers (Garrett Brown led the one that I attended, with Larry McConkey, Jerry Holway, Floris Sijbesma, Harry Panagiotidis and Gene Taylor, all great and generous professionals, as the other teachers) and represents the best approach to the device because it acquaints you both theoretically and practically with the Steadicam's possibilities.

Beginning with a description of the tool through a series of exercises (that teach you to assemble and hold the rig in the correct position, to walk and to perform the various movements possible during shooting and so forth), you get a chance to experience all the most important situations that a Steadicam operator will encounter with his equipment.

Wearing the Steadicam is quite tiring (particularly in my case, as I am smaller than the average Steadicam operator and the rig weighs

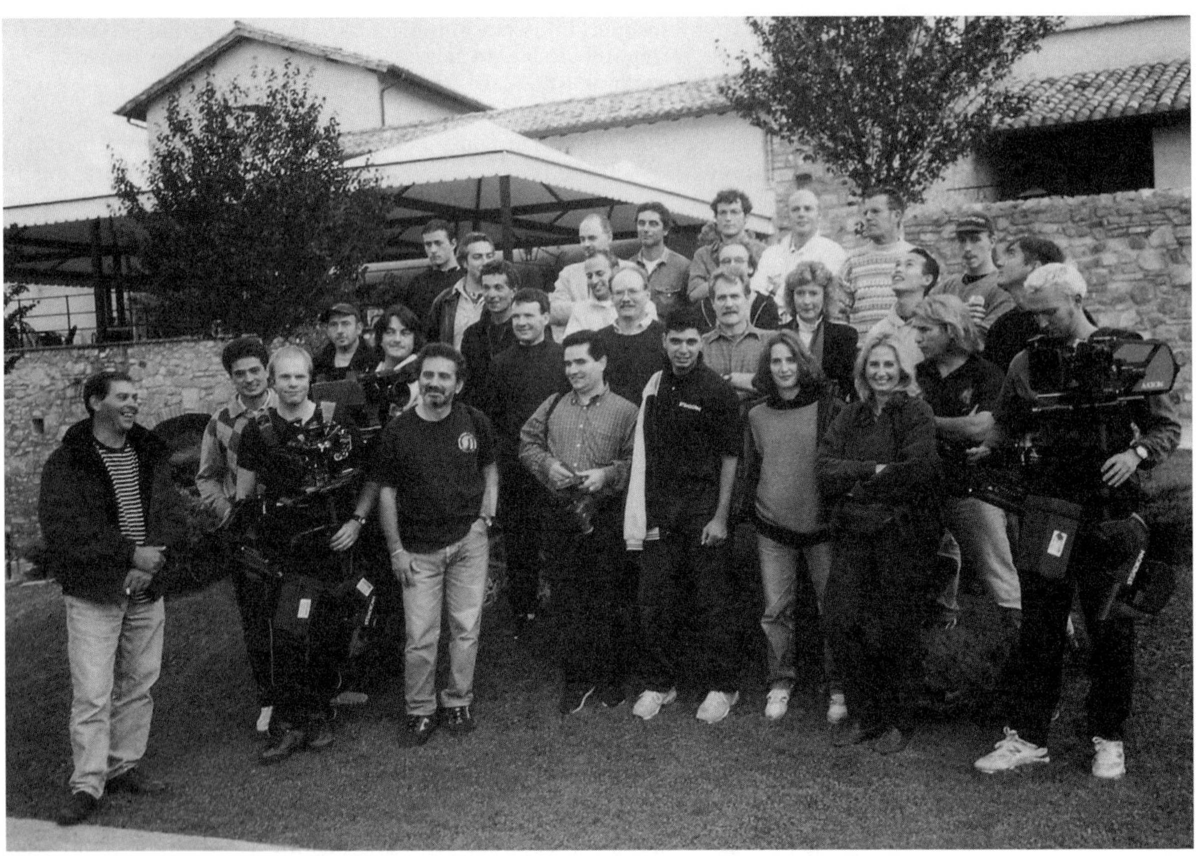

Figure 2.33 International Steadicam Workshop Group, Perugia, Italy, 1998. Photo: Serena Ferrara collection

almost as much as I do), especially when emotion, nerves and fear make you tense: weighed down by 25 kg of equipment, kept as close as possible to the body in order to feel the weight less, you cannot breathe and you think your experience will end right there. Instead, after a rather heavy impact (like that experienced by Wily Coyote when the boulder falls on him), you begin to understand, because you must for personal defence, that the 'trick' is the device itself: as apparently heavy and hard to tame as it is, it is actually a question of balance, both yours and the system's; and with incredible amazement and excitement you find yourself at the end of five days shooting a final 'test' in which you even run along behind the main character.

It is clear that a workshop is not everything; a number of encounters and much practice are necessary (better yet if with your own equipment) to gain good control. But what you realize, after a while, is that these professionals have taught you everything from the start and, if you make good use of that knowledge, you will have all the tools you need. And, thus, what was previously only an effect, a type of shot called Steadicam, is consolidated into a closer relationship with an instrument and its extraordinary potential. With the workshop experience your point of view regarding this tool changes: what you called the 'Steadicam effect' when watching a movie becomes also an awareness of its potential and a direct relationship between image and effect.

Wearing the Steadicam, the operator becomes something 'more', a new entity, united and separate; the Steadicam comes to resemble the mind's creativity, the fusion of what you see with your eyes and a viewfinder and what you imagine will be its best technical realization (Figure 2.33).

Notes

1 *Steadicam Operation Maintenance Manual Universal Model 3A*. (1990) Cinema Products.
2 Brown, G. (1988) Ancient history: The Brown Stabilizer. *Steadicam Letter*, 1 (3), December.
3 A parallelogram system.
4 Brown, G. (1988) Ancient history: The Brown Stabilizer. *Steadicam Letter*, 1 (3), December.
5 Garrett Brown, posted on Internet: www.steadicam-ops.com/resource or www.steadicam.com.
6 The CP 35 model had two posts. The main post held the gimbal (to which the arm was attached); the drive-shaft for the Arri camera came up the centre from the motor below to the camera above. The other support post was only for a support brace.
7 Model II: (monitor separate above base) included: monitor power-supply, card slot similar to Model I battery.
Model III: (monitor separate) included: monitor high-voltage supply, adaptor plug for CP (and later Seitz) wireless focus system, sensor for on-screen level indicator, control panel with various power plugs, 12 V battery.
Master Series: (monitor and its power supply separate) includes: adaptor plug for 24 V converter, power distribution panel, level sensor, 12 V battery, electronics module with video distribution amplifiers, level-sensor conditioning circuit board ('bubble tamer'), frame-line generator board, etc.
Ultra: (monitor and power supply separate) includes: same electronics module as Master, but 24 V battery and built-in 12 V downconverter.
8 The moment of inertia refers to the resistance of an object to rotation around its centre of mass. Increasing the distance between the centre of mass and the masses within an object gives a higher moment of inertia.
9 DiGiulio, E. (President, Cinema Products Corp.) (1976) Steadicam – 35 – A revolutionary new concept in camera stabilization. *American Cinematographer*, July, p. 787.
10 '... since there are no geared-head handles in the way and no need for an operator's eye on the viewfinder, one can pass the camera within an inch of a wall or door frames ...'. Brown, G. (1980) The Steadicam and 'The Shining'. *American Cinematographer*, August, 61 (8), pp. 786–9, 826–7, 850–4.
11 'McConkey on Thailand': interview with Larry McConkey who worked for three months in Thailand on B. De Palma's film *Casualties of War*, 1988. *Steadicam Letter*, December, 1 (3), p. 4.
12 See Conclusions, Chapter 3.
13 'McConkey on Thailand'. *Steadicam Letter*, December, 1 (3), p. 5.
14 'On *Fried Green Tomatoes*, Bob Ulland shot the bee scene because "no one was sure how it was going to go". He was able to come up on Masterson, moving at her speed where she stood engulfed in bees. "By using the Steadicam we were able to stay with her wherever she went and get out quickly if we had to".' Comer, B. (1993) Steadicam hits its stride. *American Cinematographer*, 74 (2), February, p. 73.
15A Nicola Pecorini on Roman Polanski's *Bitter Moon*, Comer, B. (1993)

Steadicam hits its stride. *American Cinematographer*, 74 (2), February, p. 77.

15B Brown, G. (1982) *Using the Steadicam*, from the notes for the seminar 'Una città per il cinema' Aquila, Italy.

16 Chell, D. (1987) Intervista con Allen Daviau. *Le mille luci di Hollywood,* Milano, IHT Gruppo Ed, pp. 12–42.

17 Brown. G. (1989) The Iron Age. *Steadicam Letter*, 1 (4), March, p. 5.

18 Fisher, B. (1993) Haskell Wexler, ASC: innovation with integrity. *American Cinematographer*, 74 (2), pp. 44–52.

19 Crabe, J. (1977) The photography of '*Rocky*'. *American Cinematographer*, 58 (2), February, pp. 184–5, 205–21.

20 Brown, G. (1989) The Iron Age, *Steadicam Letter*, 1 (4), March, p. 6.

21 Brown, G. (1989) The Iron Age, *Steadicam Letter*, (1) (4), March, p. 6.

22 Kubrick's response to Garrett Brown by telex, 1974.

23 Ligthman, H. (1980) Photographing '*The Shining*': an interview with John Alcott. *American Cinematographer*, 61 (8), pp. 780–5, 840–5.

24 Ligthman, H. (1980) *op. cit.*

25 Brown, G. (1980) The Steadicam and '*The Shining*'. *American Cinematographer*, August, 61 (8), pp. 786–9, 826–7, 850–4.

26 Ligthman, H. (1980) *op. cit.*

27 Brown, G. (1980) *op. cit.*

28 Brown, G. (1980) *op. cit.* 'Two feet of dendritic salt and Styrofoam snow encrusted in the pine boughs. The quartz outdoor-type lights were turned on and a dense oil-smoke was pumped in for eight hours a day. I was hot, corrosive and in a spot in which to break'.

29 'Rouch saw in the Steadicam, and in particular in the use that Kubrick made of it in *The Shining*, the symptom of an illness of the image which isn't born out of the physical contact between the person who creates it and the one who provokes it; it is sick, maybe perfect, but created by a mechanical or electronic instrument such as, in this case, the Steadicam.' Grisolia, R. (1987) La Steadicam imprigiona corpo e mente. *Cinema Nuovo*, 36 (3), p. 15.

30 The price of the Steadicam varies according to the model; the Steadicam Ultra Cine costs, for example, approximately US$59 500 (as of September 2000).

31 Holway, J. (1998) *The Steadicam Workshop Workbook*, Philadelphia, PA.

32 Ruffell, B. (1998) *Steadicam: A Resource Manual.* Submitted in completion of the 700 level major project for the Bachelor of Broadcasting Communications at the New Zealand Broadcasting School.

33 Holway, J. (1998) *The Steadicam Workshop Workbook*, Philadelphia, PA.

34 Holway, J. (1998) *The Steadicam Workshop Workbook*, Philadelphia, PA.

35 Churchill, T. (1983) Steadicam: an operator's perspective part II. *American Cinematographer*, May, 64 (5), pp. 35–47.

36 Brown, G. (1993) Forgotten techniques. *Steadicam Letter*, 4 (1), July.

37 Dellario, F. (1997) Interview with Garrett Brown. *Filmcrew*, 16, p. 15.

38 Steadicam International Workshop (1998). Perugia, Italy.

39 Holway, J. (1998) *The Steadicam Workshop Workbook*, Philadelphia, PA

40 Dellario, F. Interview with Garrett Brown (1997) *Filmcrew*.

41 Franco, A. (1999) Un'intervista stabile e dinamica. *Millecanali*, 277, March, pp. 98–102.

42 See Brown. G. (1989) The contraption war. *Steadicam Letter*, 2 (1), June.

43 Holway, J. (1991) Physics is your friend. *Steadicam Letter*, 3 (3), December.

44 Brown, G. (1991) Skyman. *Steadicam Letter*, 3 (2), April.

45 Steadicam Operators Association, Inc. is a membership support and

referral organization for professional Steadicam operators founded by Garrett Brown and Nicola Pecorini in 1988.

46 Publication of the *Steadicam Letter* ceased in July 1995.

47 Ruffell, B. (1998) *Steadicam: A Resource Manual.* Bachelor of Broadcasting Communications, New Zealand Broadcasting School.

48 Holway, J. (1998) *The Steadicam Workshop Workbook*, Philadelphia, PA

49 Holway, J. (1998) *The Steadicam Workshop Workbook*, Philadelphia, PA.

50 Ruffell, B. (1998) *Steadicam: A Resource Manual.* Bachelor of Broadcasting Communications, New Zealand Broadcasting School.

51 In fact, a video camera can be mounted on the device. The Steadicam Universal Model was first used with a RCA TK–76 colour video to provide coverage for ABC-TV's Telecast of the National Academy of Television Arts and Sciences, 28th Annual Emmy Awards presentation in May 1976. Among the first television shows to use the Steadicam were *Little House on the Prairie*, *The Miracle Worker* and *60 Minutes*.

52 Carlson, C. (1988) *Le città d'acqua*. Music by René Aubry (55 minutes).

53 Holway, J. (1998) *The Steadicam Workshop Workbook*, Philadelphia, PA.

Part Two

Semiotics and Narrative

3

The Steadicam as a creator of effects and as a narrator

Following the description of the structure and technical capabilities of the Steadicam, it is interesting to analyse the relationships that are created between this means and the principal forms of narrative dynamics. Basing the analysis on the Steadicam's capacity to capture, while in motion itself, the motion of characters or objects, it is possible to identify a series of visual and narrative effects that give a movie a new 'construction'.

The camera and points of view

The first element to consider is vision: this is realized by the choice of the point of view, the dynamics of the 'narrative view' and the way in which the visual subject is portrayed.

The point of view is literally the point from which we are looking and thus it represents the choice, the selection of what is visible and presented in the frame, and the way in which that is shown (distance, angle, lens etc.).

Besides its physical attributes, the point of view also has an ideological component, since choosing is a mental process tied to the knowledge and ideology of the person making the choice. Thus, the narrator approaches the visual subject by deciding how it will be viewed: he can conduct a neutral, objective narration, he can insist on and stress a certain political stance. He can express himself in a myriad of ways; it will all nonetheless be filtered by his eyes as he views the subject and by the physical means with which he expresses his vision: the camera. The narrative gaze expresses itself by using the camera – its 'intelligent' eye on the world – and, at the same time, it is willing to lend its role as narrator to the characters who, in turn, express their points of view, thus enriching the narration. The narration is built up from the interplay of gazes and points of view, which express the various choices the author made with regard to telling, showing and making known his mental designs.

A film is, above all, a look at things, a gaze, and that is how it must be studied. Often, the gaze moves from one thing to another in order to understand better what it is seeing, focusing on details or looking at the surroundings. A camera films movement, from a fixed spot and while moving. Looking, moving and shooting blend together in the process of choosing, describing and narrating inherent in a film. The camera movement allows the viewer to be present with the character and to follow him on stage; it makes it possible to feel the three-dimensionality of space and contributes to the story's rhythm.

When it is the choice of movement that prevails, there remains still to be chosen the exactly appropriate manner, speed, path and style of movement. Moving through and across space, besides describing something and making it known, may also create a certain amount of tension. The vision is, in fact, mostly a surprise, since what is shown is tied to the discovery that the camera makes as it is moved. The viewer is guided by what is shown to him, in other words, that which is chosen for him; he is called to attention, as if someone is talking and from a sitting position gets up and says 'Look, I wanted to show you this ...'. The person gets up and moves toward an object, thus catching the viewer's attention, which then follows the movement and focuses on the object.

The same thing happens with the camera: the identification that suddenly occurs with the camera is necessary and, at any rate, spontaneous: since the camera is our eyes, we see that which is shown to us as if it were 'our seeing' – 'the viewer cannot do otherwise than to identify himself also with the camera which has looked before he did at that which he is presently seeing and whose position (frame) determines the vanishing point.'[1] To move or to stand still means, in any case, taking a position.

The fixed camera, for its part, performs a double underlining: one through the choice of field and another through the way in which the elements speak of themselves.

Moving offers the possibility of seeing better, of emphasizing: the camera shows certain details and invites the viewer to notice them, or else it moves away from them and allows the framing elements alone to dictate the importance the viewer is to give them.

As far as technique is concerned, we have seen that since the need to film in motion arose, various tools and mechanical means have been invented to allow the camera to do just that – to permit the narrator to move his point of view and construct the cinematographic story. Though they became lighter and more varied over time, the most important tools have always been the same ones available today; what has changed is the technical result, which has continued to be perfected. The invention of the Steadicam completes the process of pursuing various ways of filming with the camera 'on the shoulder', by uniting as much as possible the operator's body and the tool with which he is filming.[2]

Actually, the Steadicam provides us with a somewhat novel perspective, first of all because the Steadicam is less likely to present the usual 'eye-level' lens-height of the hand-held camera. In addition, a Steadicam operator may compose with more objectivity because of being a small distance away from the monitor, allowing a superior comprehension of the image in the context of a larger peripheral grasp of the space and the camera's motion within it. In comparison, a camera operator whose vision is monopolized by the huge image in the viewfinder will have a more 'immersed' perspective. Furthermore, the hand-held camera gives a mostly monocular vision, as the operator must have an eye glued to the viewfinder and exclude what the other eye sees. With the monitor, the vision is more detached both physically, because the monitor is located low down on the Steadicam post (the distance created by the articulated arm) and psychologically, since instead of full immersion there is a certain distance that gives the right parameters, also with respect to the situation of which it is a part.[3]

Subjective vision

From the beginnings of cinema, and especially when its realm grew to include the possibility of expressing a narrative discourse, filmmakers have attempted to reproduce subjective vision, distorting and emphasizing if necessary the visual process, such as shooting out-of-focus to render the vision of a drunk, as in F.W. Murnau's *Last Laugh* (*Der Letzte Mann*), 1924, or the point of view of a driver in A. Gance's *La Roue*, 1924. Besides telling the story from an external viewpoint on the visual level, filmmakers wanted to show, and consequently to make the viewer 'feel', what the character feels, inviting the viewer to identify with the character and enriching the narration with the depth of the first-person viewpoint.[4]

In order to reproduce subjective vision, filmmakers attempted to make the point of view of the character coincide technically with the optical view of the camera (the lens functions as the eye). The subjective – insofar as it is a vision seemingly devoid of a personality (except by reflection) – was increasingly perfected, creating various keys for interpretation and analysis.

In what we think of as 'classical' cinema, films that consistently respect the canons regarding construction and communication of information to viewers, subjective vision must convey the qualitative and connotative characteristics of the subject the camera is impersonating as, for example, in *Jaws*, when the underwater vision of the future victims is revealed later to be the shark's view.

In addition to the physical correspondence of lens and character's eye, a psychological correspondence may be created, giving us the point of view of the subject filtered by the camera but guided by his or her mood. For example, the sequence in *Birdy*[5] in which the main character imagines he is flying is done using a 'mental' view.

Often we find subjective visions which change into objective visions, or which deny their subjectivity by revealing that the vision belongs to the camera and not to the character, as in the sequence in *Ransom*[6] in which the character who is the brains behind the kidnapping enters the house where the child is being held. False point of view shots are frequently used, especially in 'thriller' and 'action' movies, for their ability to command attention and create nervousness when it is assumed that they are the point of view of a certain character who is then brought into the scene, revealing that it was not, after all, his or her viewpoint.

With regard to subjective vision, it is interesting to recall the analysis made of it by Braningan,[7] who defined the various ways it may be expressed: 'open', when we see only the vision, but not to whom it belongs; 'multiple', when we are given more than one viewpoint of the same object; 'delayed', when the moviegoer understands whose point of view he is seeing only after some time, in order to create tension and arouse curiosity; 'false', when it is constructed as a point of view but turns out to be something else.

The quality of movement in a point of view shot

The most important characteristic of the point of view shot as 'someone's view' is, however, still the discovery of space by going through it and doing so in such a way that nothing that is seen has been anticipated. Here what is off-screen comes into play, along with 'the new'; thus one of the basic principles of filming – choosing what to show and keeping the rest out of sight – turns out to continually change and to surprise us.

In point of view shots the unexpected is naturally stressed and, in certain kinds of film, is emphasized even more particularly by the effect of suspense and surprise combined, such as in the sequence in *The Untouchables* in which Malone is killed and the Steadicam shoots from the killer's point of view.[8]

The scene begins with an exterior night shot, someone on the street is checking an address written on a matchbox cover, the house is Malone's, the man goes away but someone else comes into view. He goes towards the house and peeks through one of Malone's windows, the Steadicam point of view starts: the camera looks through the window, the bathroom is empty, it moves along the wall, passes two windows, from which the dining room can be seen, then along the wall again to the kitchen window through which Malone can be seen pouring himself a drink. The person whose point of view we are seeing makes a noise and Malone looks towards the window (in other words, at the camera), the camera draws back, Malone leaves the room, the camera runs again along the wall from the outside, showing us the various empty rooms, it gets to the bathroom window, the killer's hand comes into view (a device which underscores the fact that it is a point of view shot), the camera goes in through the window and moves slowly down the hallway and shows us the various rooms again from the inside. It turns to check where Malone is and shows us the empty dining room and then the kitchen, it goes towards the door, moving slowly for fear of finding him outside it, then it turns around and looks towards the other end of the hallway, discovering Malone in the last room with his back turned, winding up his gramophone. The camera moves quickly up the hallway as if to surprise him and, when it nears Malone, he turns around.

The entire sequence is charged with tension, created both through our awareness of the fate which awaits the hero and the use of the point of view of the intruder. The Steadicam focuses our attention and moves with precision and tension, just like a slimy and nervous killer who has furtively entered someone's home. Usually nothing in a visual process is that charged with tension, unless there is a reason to be afraid, which may also be imagined: during normal walking or standing, etc., vision is selective and total at the same time.

Technically, to transpose a subject's view onto the screen a filmmaker will make the movement of the subject's head and eyes from right to left coincide with a slow horizontal pan shot, a slow crossing and exploring the surroundings, or a slow forward dolly, while continuing to use the camera as an 'eye', so that what is seen on the screen corresponds to the view through the lens. To heighten the effect, various techniques are used (fogging, shaking) that reveal the condition of the character whose viewpoint we are seeing, as in D. W. Griffith's first point of views; *The Maltese Falcon*, John Huston, 1941, a drugged character; *Notorious*, 1946, the character seeing things upside down after having been drunk; *A Fistful of Dollars*, Sergio Leone, 1964, a drunk; *Leon*, Luc Besson, 1994, a wounded man; *Snake Eyes*, Brian de Palma, 1998, the unfocused vision of the lead character who has lost her glasses.[9] However, unexpectedness, perfection, lack of shaking or jerking (except for objective reasons) are characteristics of our vision that some people feel can be obtained even without the Steadicam, with a skilfully used hand-held camera.[10]

What is unique about the Steadicam as a tool for reproducing our vision is the continual balancing that gives it the same stability as our head on our body, for which we can be likened to a good tripod with a stable and movable 'pan head'.[11] So, all movements that it would not be possible to film with a hand-held camera (even if held in a stable manner) because they are more violent and more subject to vibration, such as running or horseback riding, can be perfectly reproduced with the Steadicam, thanks to its ability to 'shock-absorb' the jerks and bounces.

The most important characteristic of the Steadicam is the quality of movement it gives: movement which is not perceived through its defects, but rather through its perfection. On the contrary, the hand-held camera is often used to emphasize instability, dynamism, struggles, as for example, in *The Duellists*, *The Strawberry Statement*, *The Conformist* and *Saving Private Ryan*.[12]

When we look at something, we are not aware of our vision because it is spontaneous and instinctive, inherent in the human organism. We are unaware of it unless something goes wrong – problems such as nearsightedness or double vision, which make it more difficult to see. Only when our sight is not perfect do we realize by comparison how perfectly our visual process works.

This can also occur when vision is transposed onto the screen, where the fact that a person is looking at something is underlined by those devices (lack of focus, etc.) mentioned above. Seeing movement through a Steadicam, when it is used by a professional, is very much like seeing it ourselves. There is a paradox here, since the Steadicam lacks mechanical defects linked to the recording of movement and therefore moves in a manner which is even too fluid: it can be recognized precisely because of that perfection. If the Steadicam is not used by a very capable operator,[13] a vague sense of dizziness is created because of the perception of the push that generates the movement (even if it is very slow and carefully calculated). In some films it is possible to see that the movement is done with a Steadicam, since it is coupled with an effect of moving closer or further away, characterized by a certain 'velocity' of execution.[14]

In addition, two errors often made by incompetent Steadicam operators, poor control of the roll axis and lack of rigour in keeping the camera's height consistent and its path straight whilst moving, produce images that give that 'floating' sensation which the Steadicam's inventor deplores.

These characteristics can be emphasized for narrative purposes as, for example, when one needs to convey a feeling of anguish and fear. However, they can be completely eliminated, making it almost impossible to identify the means used for making the shot.

The Steadicam, despite having quite specific technical characteristics, has therefore come to be seen as a potential 'skeleton-key', good for any occasion, with the risk of it being abused,[15] as has happened in the past with other cinematographic devices. The zoom, for example, is an invention that was certainly over-used in the B movies of the 1970s and 1980s.

The Steadicam is often used to give an uninterrupted view of characters who climb stairs, open doors, cross large rooms, go down narrow hallways and so on. Examples include the initial sequence of *The Bonfire of the Vanities* with B. Willis who arrives, gets into the elevator and goes up; the chase scenes in *The Fugitive*; the walk through the market in *La Mort en Direct*; and the race down the alleys to look for a doctor in *The Sheltering Sky*. The possibility of following what is happening without cuts makes the scene more spectacular and effective, as in the beginning sequence of *Strange Days*, a Steadicam point of view shot of a thief running from his pursuers who falls from a building (see Chapter 2).

Seeing 'the impossible' is tightly linked to the viewer's capacity to be aware of it and to the need to fulfil the expectations of an increasingly spoiled public. In other words, the viewer loves the trick when it is shown, but does not like being shown how it is done. Or, at the very least, the viewer studies the techniques and then watches the film to appreciate them.[16]

The interest in the story and the spectacle created by the movie's 'effects' blend together in certain proportions according to the director's expressive capacity. A film that is based exclusively on special effects and spectacularity endures only the short time that is necessary for those techniques and effects to become outdated,[17] while a film with a good, solid story, which also makes use of special effects, such as *2001 Space Odyssey*, will last 'forever'. All the movies which use camera motion in the classic cinematographic sense have enriched the history of cinema and, even if they can seem dated whether for technical or for socio-historical reasons, they stay 'alive' precisely because they tell stories well. 'What matters is the organic development of an idea and the technical instruments are there in fact to contribute to realizing it. First comes imagination, then you worry about details.'[18] 'Technique has to enrich the action.'[19]

Besides making it possible to shoot chases and people climbing stairs, the structure of the Steadicam, when it is used in low mode, makes it possible to shoot very close to the ground (as in the scene in *The Shining* in which Wendy drags Jack's body into the kitchen) – the Steadicam is at about knee-level so that it is possible to represent the point of view of something low down: a child, animal or object. An example of this is the point of view shot of the snake in *Mamba* (M. Orfini, 1988). The technical basis of this film is its ability to render the movement and sight of an animal, in this case a snake that slithers quickly or slowly over any surface. The camera recreates the movement and sight of the snake by using a particular lens:

the fish-eye, which gives a larger field of vision and makes use of the Steadicam's capacity to go just about anywhere smoothly.

Another example of an animal point of view shot is in *An American Werewolf in London*, in the scenes showing the lead character, transformed into a werewolf, running through forests and subway tunnels. These are point of view shots made with the Steadicam turned upside down. The same device is used in *Wolfen*, also shot with the Steadicam, to give the point of view of the wolves as they watch and then attack the man (here, the effect is heightened by having the image sun-struck, showing the action as the wolves see it). With the creation of the Steadicam and the discovery of its capacity to reproduce so well the subjective viewpoint of an animal or an 'alien', the use of this device has become practically mandatory in any film with such subject matter: e.g. *An American Werewolf in London*, John Landis, 1981; *Wolfen*, Michael Wadleigh, 1981; *The Thing*, John Carpenter, 1982; *Aliens*, J. Cameron, 1986; *Wolf*, M. Nichols, 1994; *Anaconda*, L. Llosa, 1997, etc.

Structural evolution in Steadicam use from the earliest movies to the present

In the twenty years since it was invented, the Steadicam has been used on a myriad of films. It has been perfected and is now accepted like any other irreplaceable cinematographic tool. In my analysis, taking into account the subjects discussed in Chapter 2, I have tried to illustrate the evolution of an innovative and 'problem-solving' technical device that also offers new possibilities at the narrative level, a tool which has its roots in classic movie history and solves the problems encountered with the hand-held camera while maintaining the same spirit and intention.

The Steadicam moves confidently, describing the action without anchoring the characters, going everywhere. It proves itself capable of leading the narrative play. Its role changes from creator of effects to narrative voice, in other words, the person who performs the narration, even if the limits of the roles are not well defined. Thus, following movies that used the Steadicam as a device for creating more spectacular effects and to 'fill-up' any gaps in the narrative, came other movies in which the Steadicam plays a role more useful to the narrative depth of the story, and then came movies in which the Steadicam is the actual narrator, a gaze among the many gazes, actively participating in the construction of the story.

Today the Steadicam is used in 90 per cent of movies, more or less obviously. The main reason for this is the fact that the Steadicam frequently offers a quicker and better solution (and sometimes the only solution) to objective technical problems such as set building, rough terrain to be crossed, power supply needs and so on. Thus, where its use is not necessary for narrative purposes, it is dictated by economic reasons.

Although a great deal of time is needed to prepare a perfect sequence (because the action to be coordinated lasts longer and is also less predictable, since the camera movement depends on the operator's steps), shooting with the Steadicam is still more economical than setting up a series of cranes and dollies in settings such as:

- a forest – *The Return of the Jedi* or *The Emerald Forest*
- Central Park, New York – *Marathon Man*
- a crowded marketplace – *The Sheltering Sky*, *La Mort en Direct*
- a rope bridge – *Indiana Jones and the Temple of Doom.*

The expressive capabilities of the Steadicam and the different functions it could perform were evident, however, even in the first years of its existence. For this reason, I have considered the movies that were the first to make use of the Steadicam: the first experiences with it. These works have already been mentioned in Chapter 2 and are discussed here to show how the unlimited possibilities offered by the Steadicam emerge from their cinematographic and narrative structure.

- *Bound for Glory*, Hal Ashby, 1976
- *Rocky*, John G. Avildsen, 1976
- *Marathon Man*, John Schlesinger, 1976

and later movies in which this device is used with greater awareness and experience:

- *The Shining,* Stanley Kubrick, 1980
- *Coup de torchon*, Bertrand Tavernier, 1981.

At the time of movies such as *Bound for Glory* – with its famous shot of David Carradine moving through the crowd (see Chapter 2) – and *Rocky*, the Steadicam was an experimental tool. In the sequences showing Rocky in training, as he jogs through the streets of Philadelphia and runs up the steps, followed by the Steadicam that captures his feet as he reaches the top, and in the boxing sequences, the Steadicam's close-up frames involve the viewer emotionally (the fight is seen from much closer and the viewer is caught by the dynamics of the match) and also show the point of view of Rocky as he fights (see Figure 2.15). These sequences demonstrated the Steadicam's capacity for illustrating subjective vision, which would be put to greater use in the following years.

In *Marathon Man* the Steadicam was used to show the main character, Dustin Hoffman, as he trains in Central Park (New York), capturing to good effect both the actual running and the character's exhaustion; for the scenes in which Hoffman attempts to run away (literally) from his pursuers; and to follow Sir Lawrence Olivier making his way among the crowd on 57th Street in New York's diamond district. Shot by Garrett Brown, this 'self-effacingly smooth walking-shot', as he calls it, is still his favourite. He recalls (personal communication, February 2000):

> We travelled like a ghost among 150 fake Hassids and a thousand real ones (in fact we couldn't tell them apart, and kept deferring to the fake extras, and insulting the real ones with directions), and since we wanted to be invisible, I had caused a three-armed sweater to be made to cover also the Steadicam arm, and I covered the camera with a garment bag with a hole for the lens ... so there we were ... only in NY could a three-armed man walking a floating whirring garment bag through a crowd be invisible!

The Steadicam is also used in this movie for several point of view shots, such as when Hoffman approaches the woman who intrigues him, or when he is jogging and tries to outrun another jogger and we see his view of their race. This marks the appearance of a new way of using the Steadicam: to capture what the character sees. Clearly, the next step is to use it for point of view shots as done with the hand-held camera, examples of which can be found as far back as the beginnings of movie history (for example as utilized by D. W. Griffith, A. Gance and F. W. Murnau).

Unlike the hand-held camera, however, the Steadicam first found acceptance as a tool that could make the viewer identify more closely with the screen images: its more fluid vision corresponds more adequately to the way we see things. In *The Shining*, this 'seeing' no longer coincides only with a character in the story but also shows up as a gaze from above that does not belong to anyone present on screen and to which the Steadicam gives a potential for expressing tension and suspense that exalts its own characteristics.

The Shining tells the story of a writer who decides to spend the winter, together with his wife and child, as a caretaker at a resort hotel in the Rocky Mountains. The oppressive isolation causes him to go insane, just as had happened to a former caretaker who, in the same context of solitude, had murdered his family. In this film the Steadicam is used both as a neutral narrative voice, as it describes what happens and follows the characters in the story, and as an object that is 'alive' in its own right, a separate entity that moves in a quasi-mental space. It fluctuates, thanks to its properties, between the physical reality of the flight (as in the escape through the labyrinth) and the unreality of a gaze that knows something, a gaze which, in its turn, has the gift of the 'shining', which knows what might happen and allows itself to delay some things (such as the hallway sequence in which the Steadicam does not follow Danny around the corner). Here also, therefore, the intention in using the Steadicam is to record movement, but there is also the intention to create suspense, to enter the realm of the undefined, which becomes embodied in the gaze of the storyteller.

The French movie *Coup de torchon* makes significant use of the Steadicam as a witness to the actions of the main character and to the development of the catharsis. The Steadicam follows and anticipates the action with an unsettling and nervous rhythm, showing its capacity for concurring with the characters' moods and determining the distinguishing traits of the narration.

As is true of other cinematographic devices, it is hard to distinguish clearly between the role of the Steadicam as a creator of effects and that in which it is a projector of the narrative voice since, with movies made by authors of a certain level and artistic culture, the means are no longer noticed for what they are; instead, they are used imaginatively and creatively, as are all other technical elements (lights, sound, etc.), to achieve an overall effect of plot 'construction'.

Although we look for the origin of a gaze and identify a narrative voice which acts in a certain way, it is wrong in these cases to break up the overall effect of a sequence into too many microelements, because we risk losing the essence of what is being described.

As in fiction, the narrative voice can be evident, hidden, multiform, etc., but no matter how many acrobatic acts the writer performs, he cannot give us a story without someone or something to narrate it. In movies, however, contrary to literature, the visual part is real, material, because it is a form of total representation. Thus in a movie image there is a narrative level that shows the events and the characters and has an active function in the story, and a descriptive level that serves as a backdrop and positions everything in its context. Thus, at the movies we see; when we read, we imagine. In literature, any image, no matter how precisely described, is always mediated by the reader's mental elaboration and representation; with movies, this elaboration is made easier by the actual existence and solidity of the image. Here it is the camera that tells the story, in other words, it is the gaze. Thus, even if we describe frames in which the choice of what to show is as neutral as possible (trying to completely avoid any characterization of the choice), as 'objective',[20] they are still frames caught by the camera and shown to the public when the movie is projected, one part that stands for the whole, a choice of one thing instead of another.

It is always the camera (which, in the primary identification coincides with the viewer) that shows us something and 'tells' us what happens: even if it records events passively, it will always choose a point of view. Thus in the tacit agreement of movie make-believe, of getting personally involved in the story, this narrative voice – even if, as in literature, it can be ignored by the viewer who, completely absorbed by the story, forgets who is showing it to him and who has constructed it – can nonetheless remain a perceptible entity, as it can materialize more concretely in the narrative gaze.

> The camera which records the play of a movie actor can simply because of the position which it occupies, or again, with simple movements, intervene and modify the perception that the viewer has of the actor's performance. It can even, and it has often been done, emphasize something, force the viewer's eye, and, neither more nor less, direct it.[21]

In every movie text there is, therefore, a narrative voice that tells the story, showing and making us feel what happens. If the narrator is outside the story, it is called extradiegetic and if, in telling the story, it chooses to have its role taken on by a character it is called a homodiegetic narrator. At this point the internal narrator can be assisted by the use of point of view shots so that the story is seen through his or her eyes (in this regard, Jost talks about 'ocularization', by which he means seeing through the eyes of the character).[22]

The transmission of sight through the filter of the character's eyes does not necessarily imply that all knowledge passes through. There is a tight and reciprocal relationship between that which is shown (the movie), who shows it (the narrator, who uses the camera to do so) and who receives it (the viewer), which is particularly conditioned by the receiver's participation in decoding the message and knowing how to 'read' everything that is contained within and behind the image. The viewers receive various pieces of information that they knit together or keep on 'standby' to be used later to reconstruct the story. The narrator, for his part, chooses the manner of telling – which point of view and information to transmit.[23]

As we have seen, a discussion of the point of view involves, obviously, both the physical point from which we are looking and the origin of the gaze, as well as the ideology that lies behind everything that is shown. In this way, all images are potentially point of view shots, since they can correspond to the point of view of a character that we will only see later or, at the ultimate level of point of view, to the point of view of the narrator of the film.

The gaze of the narrative voice

> In movies, the gaze is not just the passive reception of something, it is a language which structures the world, a seeing understood as an autonomous cognitive process.
>
> Movies pose the problem of the gaze as a creative and cognitive relationship between a subject and an object which do not exist separately, but which sense each other only within this gaze. There is a subjectivity of the gaze as there is a subjectivity of language ... to study movies means to study the forms of vision as a form of subjectivity.[24]

The camera represents the 'gaze among the gazes', in other words, it represents the gaze of the narrative voice. In movies, this gaze uses two dimensions, visual and audible, which are further divided on the basis of what can be seen and read in the image and what can be heard and understood on the soundtrack.

The narrative voice, which by definition produces the narrative discourse, is realized through the camera – its status, however, is decided on the basis of its narrative level and its relationship with the story. Thus, within the same movie, although there exists a gaze among the gazes which represents the main axis of the narration, it is possible to encounter other 'gazes'. And it is at the narrative level that we can distinguish the various exchanges of information which show us the voice that produced them.

> It may happen that – in the encounter with a narrative structure – the subject gaze is 'fractured' into a network of internal gazes, that is to say, it may happen that this encounter constructs the movie as a 'system of gazes' in which the internal configuration of the subject gaze can fade extensively, until it almost disappears, as we have already seen, maintaining however the function of 'time–space axis' that we have called the representation gaze.
>
> This fracturing – associated with taking on a narrative function – is the first thing that happens when the gaze is anchored to one or more characters ... not all the system of gazes underlying the movie finishes in the network of internal gazes ... A substantial portion of non-anchored gaze is left over, the gaze of the speaking voice which – to a greater or lesser extent – becomes a gaze among the gazes, becomes woven into the network, gives birth to a relay of gazes in which it too takes on the role of 'conductor' (in the physical sense) of the action and makes the diegetic material dynamic.[25]

The Steadicam, with its manner of narrating, is easily accepted by the viewer even when its use is evident, because it helps create tension and suspense; in addition, the use of point of view shots as an exchange of gazes creates even greater ambiguity and effect. In particular, the use of the Steadicam amplifies these effects because of its dynamic qualities and its capacity to 'get inside' situations. It actually inserts itself physically, moving within spaces fluidly and uninterruptedly, as well as psychologically, since the way in which it narrates creates certain expectations. Moving, discovering, can inspire curiosity, fear, tension; it can also mean an interior voyage, a search.

What happens to Jack Torrance, the main character in *The Shining*, during the entire movie is a slow and progressive descent into madness, which makes itself felt almost in a material dimension, through which the Steadicam moves.

In *Casino*, Scorsese uses the Steadicam as a quick, attentive 'illustrative gaze' that is involved in the story, moving from a playing table to a character who has just been named. As if it were running on slightly different time, it anticipates or follows the information that the off-screen narrator provides. It involves the audience in the story almost without allowing time to think. The viewer finds himself behind the croupier as he goes to get the money – the walk down the hall, the guards, the room where the money is counted, the money, the total indifference of the others, leaving the room, same walk, the salon. The camera allows the character to leave the Casino but, until then, it has followed him, circled him, allowed itself to enter the room before him or to be the recipient of the other characters' greetings instead of him; then it looks around and connects back to the character. This way of narrating with the Steadicam makes it possible to maintain a tight rhythm that serves the purposes of the story. The short pans from a person to an object, from a detail to a larger view, break up the way of looking, as if there were more than one view of the situation, all blending together in order to show as much as possible while involving the public and capturing its attention.

The Steadicam as a narrative voice

The Shining (Stanley Kubrick, 1980, USA) and *Coup de torchon* (Bertrand Tavernier, 1981, France) are two movies in which the function of the Steadicam as the narrative voice is quite clear. What these movies have in common is above all the effect of tension created by the use of the Steadicam. This tension is not always justified, and it takes the form of the nervousness contained in the camera movement, which is sometimes perceptible and at other times less so.

The Shining enters into the heart of its drama a little at a time, thanks to the Steadicam which, with its characteristic of 'suspended' shooting, leads us into a dimension of time and space inhabited by insanity and memory.

In *Coup de torchon*, the emphasis is above all on the 'anxious, nervous' characteristics that the narrative gaze takes on: from the beginning the movie communicates to the viewer a sense of uneasiness and uncertainty, because of the way the movement is shot with Steadicam pans and dollies that anticipate, stay with and follow the actors, devoid of solidity or fixed points. All this culminates in the explosion of a tension tied to the progressive mental decay of the main character, a rundown police officer who leads a mediocre, squalid and often cowardly life, yet is convinced he has the right and the duty to 'clean up' everything that is rotten in society.[26A]

What is interesting in these two movies is the role as the narrative voice that the Steadicam takes on. In fact, not only does it follow the events and testify to what happens, but it also actively conducts the narration; its narrative gaze presents itself as independent, superior and capable of tying together events, anticipating them and abandoning them exactly because it knows the story and chooses how to tell it to us.

We have already seen how, in *The Shining*, there are revelations of this gaze, particularly in certain sequences such as that of Danny in the hallway, when the camera does not follow him immediately when he exits the scene but lingers on the empty hallway and allows viewers a perception of its narrative methods. In *Coup de torchon* the narrative voice underlines its role with continual anticipations or by lingering on events which continue even 'without it'. It is as if it wished to underline that things go on anyway, that it is important to keep a certain distance and yet, at the same time, it tries to discover what will happen next, which creates a sense of unease.

In these two movies the Steadicam relates to events like an omniscient narrator, especially in the French movie where the camera moves continuously, demonstrating the independence of the narrative voice and its domination of everything. The Steadicam moves through the space and time of the story with the awareness of what is happening and what will happen and, on that basis, it chooses how to involve the viewer in the action.

Thus, there are moments of absolute identification and tension when the use of the point of view hands over the responsibility for the view of the story to a character, used as a filter with regard to 'knowledge' and as eyes with regard to identifying the point of view. In this way, the role of the Steadicam as narrator becomes blended with that of creator of effects, since in point of view (subjective viewpoint) it is precisely the movement forwards, 'to discover', that best describes a person's or animal's vision.

Any technical means can be used to take on the role of narrator; its function as narrator ends, however, when its movement is interrupted and it must turn the narration over to other means (for example, after a dolly shot it is impossible to climb stairs, enter a room, close a door). The Steadicam, however, ties the camera to the operator's body, allowing him to climb on to different vehicles, climb down from or up onto a dolly, without any interruption at the narrative level. Examples of this can be seen in *The Bonfire of the Vanities*, the initial sequence; *Carlito's Way*, when the Steadicam gets on the subway with the character during the final chase; *Raising Cain*, the long walk taken by the two police detectives and the doctor (who has to provide information about the father of the killer), entirely seen either from behind or ahead in one long Steadicam shot, starting from the police station, going down the hall, getting into the elevator, going down a couple of floors, getting out of the elevator and going down two flights of stairs.

Since a movie unites image and sound, it can show one thing and say something totally different, it can create a gap between what it shows and what it says or it can make them coincide, but all this will still be a narration, the telling of a story. The narrative voice will thus necessarily be the camera, as it is the physical means by which we see the story that is being told. Although the narrator can choose other temporary narrators, the mechanical means will still be the camera and the way it is used will have an effect, lesser or greater, on the narrator's intentions and his desire to communicate certain emotions, tensions, attentions and so on.

The Steadicam is technically a tool, like a dolly or the hand-held camera itself, and consequently it will be used like any other tool to realize various camera moves. At the same time, precisely because of the myriad possibilities inherent in any action, it can take a greater lead with regard to the narrative play and take on the role of narrator in a more knowledgeable way than is possible with other means. It becomes an instrument instead of merely a tool.

While it remains a choice for the author to make, the technique is suitable for determining effects that enter the realm of the narrative, from mechanical to emotional. The Steadicam can show an image of itself which is almost a materialization of the narrative gaze. A good example of this can be found in Tavernier's *La Mort en direct*, in the flea market sequence: this gaze walks around (and lets us physically feel it and see it) among the crowd and follows and looks for the actors with an insistence and relentlessness which correspond to the sight of someone who is physically in those places and going after what he wants. In this sequence, Romy Schneider and Harvey Keitel walk around the market followed by the driver, who loses sight of them in the confusion of the fairgrounds and tries to find them again. The gaze, which can at first be recognized as the driver's, then becomes the gaze of the narrative voice from above, that wanders with difficulty among the crowds, which slow its movement, and then manages to find the woman after having followed her from a distance during a long obstacle course among the stands.

It is important however not to stop at the technical definition of the device, but to make it a part of an analysis that makes clear its expressive potential. The Steadicam has a particular image, created in particular by its technical capabilities, which can lead people to have a limited view of its potential and which inspires stylistic attitudes that basically come down to the search for effects (without appreciation of the device's real worth). It is indeed true that the abuse of the Steadicam in television (talk-shows, variety shows, concerts, etc.) and action and B movies (horror movies, etc.) has determined a stereotypical use of it but, in reality, the expressive and technical potential of this tool allows it to rise above the commonplace (easy solutions to plot problems by providing a dynamic filler or a spectacular effect) in those examples of real ability where plot construction, technique and emotion all blend together and reinforce each other.

The Steadicam and cinematographic space

Talking about using the Steadicam means also talking about cinematographic space. Making use of the analysis done by Gardies in *L'Espace au Cinema*, it is possible to derive a series of procedures for studying a film that allow a greater and more in-depth reading of the meaning and the use of space in movies.

Gardies starts from the assumption that space has never been much considered at the diegetic level[26B] (diegetic-setting space in which the events of the diegetic world are produced), so that an analysis of it, comparable to that which is made of a character (who is also an object of the diegetic world), leads to the identification of a series of characteristics and properties which elevate the meaning of space above its mere encyclopaedic definition.

An analysis of space must emphasize the morphological characteristics of the places that within the film can organize themselves in a meaningful system: this is done by applying to space the same categories used in analysing character.[27] Space, presented as a character with qualities and functions, is thus considered one of the agents of the action.

When space interacts with the character who is the subject of the story, it can determine an exchange with that character and a possible change. The character that within the story is the one who must be competent, that is to say, capable of doing something, is thus flanked by space as a bringer of value. The latter makes it possible for the subject to take a qualitative leap forward or it blocks him, impeding his development. Space is thus considered a 'player' in the story, an element which participates in the overall narrative design and 'operates' so as to create certain dynamics.[28]

Space assumes the characteristics of the character, interacting in the creation of the places for 'doing', being', 'wanting to do', etc. and, according to its attributes and functions, influencing the action. It is interesting to analyse how spaces are shown within the story and how they participate in it, bringing out the characteristics of the narration and the relationships which exist between 'setting' and character. In fact, according to the way they relate to each other, space can be of help to a character, an accomplice, or it can hinder the character and create a series of difficulties which show themselves also in the setting's physical dimension (e.g. *Mamba*).

When analysing space, it is also important to keep in mind the various cinematographic methods of narration and the relationships with the narrative voice that can, in our case, coincide with the use of the Steadicam.

The narrator of the story chooses just how to show us the various settings; it is of fundamental importance, therefore, to see what choices he makes with regard to point of view and the various ways in which events can be shown. Thus, the space that is encountered in movies is described according to its characteristics, but also according to the choices made by the narrator who, in turn, is manoeuvred by the 'grande imagier' – the author. Consequently, it becomes important to see which technical choices are made.

A zoom or wide angle shot determines a flattening or a widening of the field, a Steadicam tracking shot or a static shot results in greater or lesser involvement of the viewer, along with physical entry into the space and psychological entry into the event. Lighting and other factors create the image of space in the story, which is closely connected to character in the construction of 'meaning' and cinematographic content. By diagramming and reconstructing the geography or, better yet, the topography, of the places that comprise the space of the film, it is possible to identify the characters' connection, dependence or independence from the various places and to characterize their greater or lesser complicity in the various roles played by the places.

On the basis of a first census of the technical indications, the properties of the settings and the spoken information, the connection can be made between what is shown, how it is shown and the value that it assumes at the story level. A grid of meanings and places that are closely connected to each other can be made for a deeper analysis of the value of the plot and the creative message. Space therefore becomes a 'dimension', rich in meanings and possibilities that go beyond normal conceptions.

It is important to observe that in the analysis of space and the construction of an eventual topography of the places in the film how and what is shown is of fundamental importance. The viewers' reconstruction of 'space' can be confused or enlightened by what they see, since that is what they must use to tie together and link the various settings and the roles that these might play. The Steadicam is a tool that lets the viewer follow, as on a map, the juxtaposition and the connection between the various settings of the story (e.g., the sequence of Malone's death in *The Untouchables* shows us the entire house). Steadicam shots that explore settings in real time make it possible to reconstruct and recognize the interior geography of the places, which can be useful to the construction of the story.

In *The Shining*, for example, the vastness and, at the same time, the confinement and the limits of the space of the hotel are clearly underlined by the races through the hallways, the scenes in the kitchen and in the room where Jack writes, and by Wendy's various searches and escapes which become a closed cycle. We are shown the same settings over and over again because that is actually the characters' living space. It is possible to make an approximate map of the hotel, both because Jack is shown one by the hotel manager, but also because the various characters return over and over to the same spaces, in scenes shot by the Steadicam that joins the spaces together (Figure 3.1).

As the movie proceeds this movement becomes more hurried at both the physical and psychological level (Jack's unease and insanity) until it culminates in Jack's mad search and Danny's desperate escape in the hedge maze outside the hotel. The Steadicam captures perfectly Danny's panic as he runs through the maze, attempting to escape from Jack who, wounded but relentless, drags himself along wielding his axe, searching for his son, anticipated by the Steadicam that shows us his growing insanity. It then captures equally well Danny's lucidity as he realizes that the only way he can save himself is to interrupt the trail he is leaving in the snow that is giving him away, by walking backwards in his own footprints.

The scenes, which alternate without external reference points between the search and the escape down the paths of the Maze, are in fact perfectly tied to the movements of the characters, who are followed or anticipated according to what is supposed to be shown and, as in other moments in the movie, the camera performs an 'internal' 'ocularization', substituting itself for the character, showing us the movement from the character's point of view. The sensation of unease and strangeness, emphasized also by the physical presence of the maze, is heightened by the Steadicam, which becomes Danny's terrified gaze as he looks for a possible solution or Jack's murderous gaze as he searches incessantly down the turnings of the maze. 'It required enormous force to pull the camera around the turns and a degree of luck to find the right path while essentially looking backward' recalls Garrett Brown.[29] Even in this case, as for other sequences, the space is shown perfectly on the screen, thanks also to

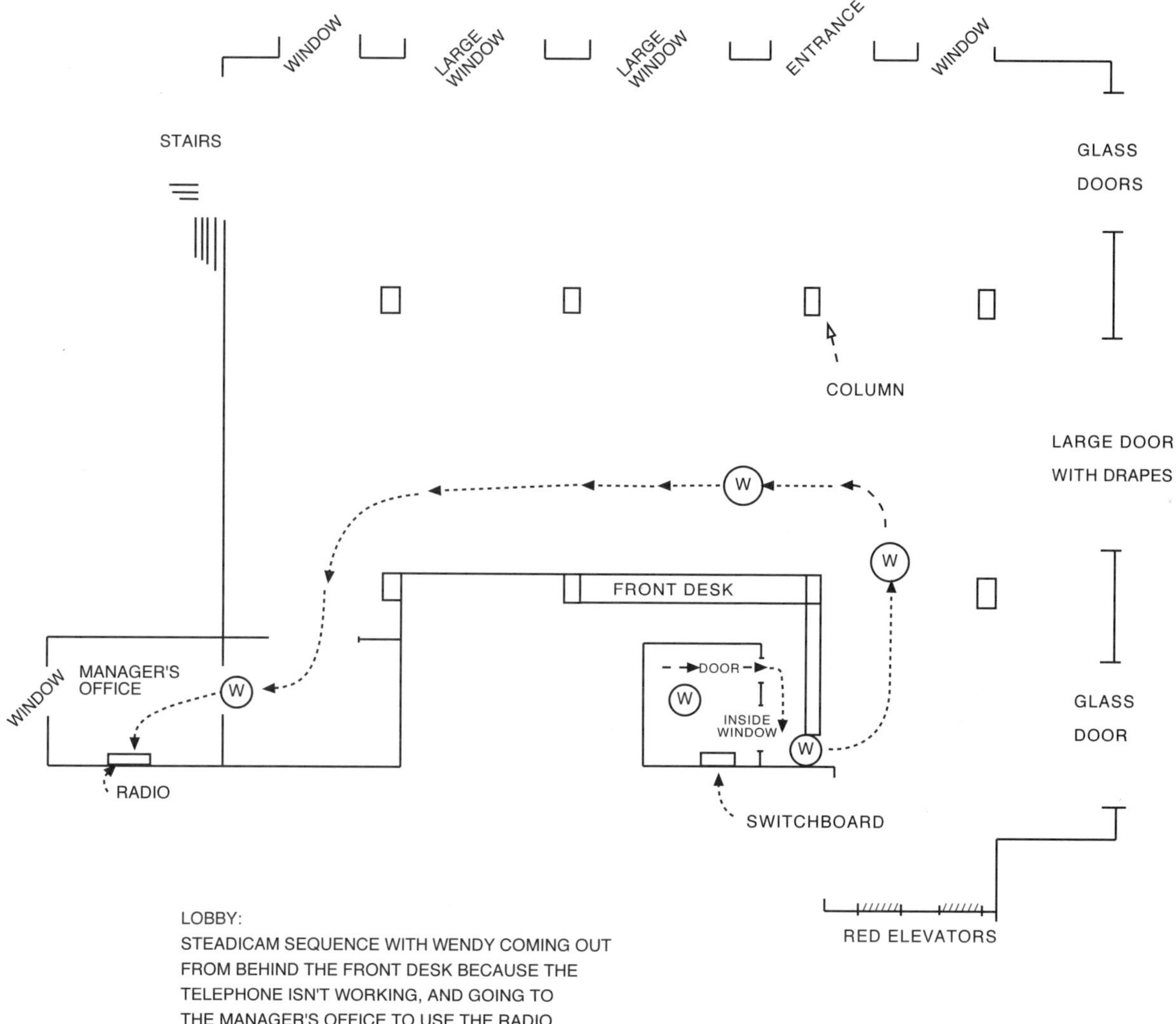

Figure 3.1 Map of *The Shining*: hall of the Overlook Hotel

the use of the Steadicam. The point of view, no longer from high above and dominant, as in the sequence showing Wendy and Danny (seen by Jack) in the maze, lowers itself and enters the dimension of the two characters, underlining the hostile role (for Jack) and the accomplice role (for Danny) played by the maze. 'I think that the most difficult shots on the entire picture for me were the 50 mm close-ups travelling ahead of Jack or Danny at high speed'.[30]

Thus, this tool is used to build up tension, by staying close to the character, with the character, in discovering what is happening. 'The very believable point of view shots as Jack or Danny enter room 237 ... The over-the-shoulder shot of Jack as he climbs the stairs above the lobby to find Halloran'.[31]

In this movie the Steadicam work is discrete and basic at the same time. Discrete, since it is not limited to easily identifiable, long dolly shots (following or anticipating), but is also used to follow small gestures, introduce frames and for short withdrawals that enter the realm of the most unconscious meanings, thanks to its characteristic lightness and fluidity, which reveal, without exaggerating, the presence of a narrative gaze. 'Here were fabulous sets for the moving camera – we could travel unobtrusively from space to space or lurk in the shadows with a menacing presence.'[32] Its use was necessary, since it does things that would be impossible for other devices.

Obviously, the capacity to show on the screen a recognizable space depends on the narrator, whose intentions are given total freedom by the Steadicam that can help to locate the story or follow the psychological paths of the characters and cross the space without the least interest in being 'recognizable'.

In *Mamba*, as in *The Shining*, the entire movie takes place in one space (apart from the prologue which has a particular setting, the desert where the snake trainer lives) – a loft apartment, a single, large environment where the main character lives. Here it is easy to identify the topography and floor plan of the apartment which, although it is a friendly space because the heroine knows it very well, turns against her and becomes a prison when her deluded lover frees the snake in her house, because the door is sealed and locked from the outside. The space thus takes on the double characteristic of being both a particular and friendly place, well-known to the heroine who can move around in it confidently and, at the same time, her enemy and opponent because it is a hiding place for the deadly snake, will not let her escape, and makes it hard for her to hide or to call for help. The space is thus undivided and communicating and it is crossed in every sense of the word by the heroine and the snake. The latter, often in primary 'ocularization', shows us the space from his point of view, spread out, brushing the ground, and these shots are made with the Steadicam.

All the space is then condensed and shown diagrammed on the assassin's computer screen where, just as if it were a videogame, he has put the characters and closed all exits in order to then watch the 'game'. He follows what is going on in the apartment from far away and lets us once again reconstruct the events perfectly.

The heroine, who finds herself involved in a real test of courage in which she must fight for her life, discovers that her loft is the place where she 'can be' and 'can do', precisely because of the will to fight and save herself that she needs to stay alive. She thus manages to dominate the space that had dominated her, upsetting it and taking it apart, and allows us, thanks to the Steadicam shots in real time, to identify with her struggle and to share the difficulties that she encountered in her space.

The Steadicam and real time

We have analysed space in terms of its physical characteristics and the value it has as an agent of the plot. We have looked at it in relation to the various paths taken by the characters and, thanks to the fact that the Steadicam moves through it, discovers it, describes it, it is possible to see how spatial dimension is strictly tied to the effect of real time. The latter, in its turn, influences the perception of space.

Time and its passing are perceived through physical manifestations: seeing a high-speed race or a chase down three fights of stairs shot in real time, without interruptions, makes us 'feel' the physical dimension of time and flight. An example of this occurs in *Bugsy*: 'Warren Beatty runs up some stairs after Annette Bening into the bathroom, slamming one door after another. I finally had the opportunity to get a shot that couldn't be gotten any other way', Jeff Mart (Steadicam operator).[33]

The Steadicam is therefore the only tool which can shoot a scene in real time, continuously, without having to cut to adapt to new situations. As the body of the camera is tightly attached to the operator, the whole structure is 'one being': wherever the operator can go, so can the camera. For this reason, the operator can be in a car, he can get out, climb on a dolly, enter a second-floor window, enter a room. In other words, by taking advantage of the camera's properties of stability, he can go from one situation to another by using a combination shot without the viewer being aware of any change. Potentially, the arrival point is the single take.

> During the entire movie, time coincides with real time and there is absolute unity of place ... long and complex camera movements without ever having to cut to make the two basic elements of dramatic tension, time and space (setting) stand out.[34]

> The dream of being able to tie things together in order to obtain a single movement.[35]

> ... The rope has only one level because the images are only the twists of a single, identical thought.[36]

At the same time, continuous shooting means that there must be a unity of time and action, since the physical perception of time is given by the space that is actually crossed by the camera. In other words, the time of the action is made real by the space that we cross through completely. Thus we see sequences that use the Steadicam, as dollies and cranes were used in the past, to follow characters in long, uninterrupted shots as they go from one place to another, in order to make the physical time needed to go down the stairs, take the elevator, etc. 'interesting' and an integral part of the story.[37] An important example is the long take at the beginning of *Snake Eyes*, which follows the main character as he goes through various rooms until he gets to where the fight is being held.[38]

It should be a rediscovery of the value of reality, gestures, simple actions, so that everything that happens is unique, unrepeatable, important and therefore can be recorded. Actually, it often happens instead that a tool such as the Steadicam is abused, as when a story that lacks large-scale action and/or a strong plot is constructed on tiring reproductions of long walks or chases that border on pure virtuosity[39]. Or there is an attempt to create dynamic depth by making the action more agitated, moving the camera continually, as in *Mary Shelley's Frankenstein*,[40] where the continual use of the Steadicam tires the viewer in a non-constructive way.

The director Brian de Palma uses the Steadicam in all his movies, for both constructing the story and building physically and psychologically the expressive dimension of the characters.

> The idea of the initial sequence shot was to show viewers as much as possible of the world in which they will be immersed ... the first thing to do is to walk through it, trying to show the character not only in his physical space, but also in his way of living.[41]

In De Palma's *The Bonfire of the Vanities* there is a long sequence (running about 5 minutes) of a character arriving in front of a skyscraper and going up to the salon on the top floor, which begins with a view of the car and continues with an internal tracking shot through the garage, hallways, elevator, hallways, finally arriving at the salon. The entire sequence runs in real time, creating a sense of dynamism, but even more of dizziness and apprehension. It becomes the continuum of the search and discovery of the character's truth, an entering and going towards things.

This continuum in time and space is also seen in *The Shining*, with the events taking place in a vast, articulate but single space. The hotel is shown, in fact, through a 'crossing' of it; in this case, not in a single sequence, but in a series of long Steadicam sequences that create a symbolic 'flow', that is to say, the overall continuity of the story (the movie), circumscribing and acquainting us with the setting.

The flow constructed with sequence shots is not the only kind: a movie may also wish to build a symbolic, thematic, expressive flow through the use of editing and the rhythm that it gives the movie. Certain movies which narrate with the Steadicam build a dynamic flow which, despite the cuts done during editing, is imposed through the rhythm of the action.

Carlito's Way, another film by De Palma, builds the final sequence in which Al Pacino escapes and meets his girlfriend at the station with a frenzied rhythm and a crescendo of tension that are obtained in particular by the dynamism of the running: on the street, in the subway, up and down the stairs at the station. The sequence is shot mostly with the Steadicam and, although it is spliced and cut with other shots, it maintains the frenetic rhythm of the escape, swallowing the viewer up into the vortex of the speed and the desire to be saved, skilfully illustrated by Steadicam sequences alternating with other shots that do not slow the rhythm but, on the contrary, blend with the narrative intent to communicate to us the character's frenzy, fear and desire to get to his destination. The rhythm of the race counters the static waiting of the girlfriend as she stands by the train, trusting that he will come but nonetheless afraid.

In *Coup de Torchon* Tavernier uses the Steadicam to create a sense of flow, of continuity in movement, or what Daniel Brian has called 'circuit of wandering'. The on-going search in the unfolding story, the passing of time which, even if it is told in numerous ways, fragmented, anticipated, runs on continuously.

> It is not at all indifferent, in fact, at least in a work that gives importance to style, whether an event is analysed by fragments or shown in its physical wholeness[42]
>
> ... The editing is negative when the spatial unity of the event needs to be respected, when breaking it would transform reality into a simple imaginary representation of it.[43]
>
> The rejection of editing opens itself to the theoretical definition of the concept of setting the scene as the organization of the scenic elements and their relationship with the camera in order to convey their real flow.[44]

Continuous shooting is also linked to the idea of the documentary and its way of filming reality, which is perceived as a whole and must be captured in the same way. Even if didactically it is necessary to break up the action to better show the various phases of a process, the continuous take gets closer to the complexity of the event and is better at capturing it at the moment that it happens, following it uninterruptedly as it unfolds.

Shooting a documentary and shooting for television are the same in that they both involve entering a situation and staying with it without a break, in order not to lose the public's attention for even one second. Not just by chance is the Steadicam used so frequently for television programmes.

Television and cinema *genres* such as *cinema verité*, *free cinema* and *nouvelle vague*,[45] have been influential in demonstrating the importance of the means of shooting in connection with obtaining the effect of reality or of totally exaggerating it. They emphasize this documentary-like continuous view of what is happening and show it in a continuous evolution over time.

Television shots for news programmes, in which it is particularly important to be continuously present during the event, are closely tied to documentary shots, as the aim is to record what is happening as a witness. Similarly, the television show *ER*[46] is based on its capacity to stay with the characters, who are often involved in urgent attempts to save patients, through the constant use of the Steadicam, which 'breathes' with the medical staff and conveys their feelings, a continuous witness.

Another example is the experience of Steadicam operator Jeff Mart. Given Mart's background in news and documentaries, Steadicam was a natural transition for him. He bought a system 'because I wanted a device that would smooth my camera movements as I ran after animals or parades'.[47] The movie industry, as with all mass media, understands, or rather reacts to, this influence, making movies that mirror just that documentary and television-type approach.

In *The Sheltering Sky*, the search for the doctor and the marketplace scene at the end of the movie are all filmed with Steadicam. Pecorini describes the camera moves as 'documentary style'.[48] Another example is *All Quiet on The Western Front*, in which the Steadicam was used for the shots in the trenches, both because there was no other way to do them and for the realistic and almost documentary-like effect it was able to lend to the portrayal of war. The Steadicam embodies the qualities of a perfect witness who has the gift of being able to go anywhere (or almost) and follow events as if it were their shadow.[49]

The Steadicam and remakes

A number of movies have been or will be made more than once in the history of cinema, because each time the story is attractive and new for the person who wants to tell it. Thus, we find that over time we have had one, two, three, four versions of Frankenstein, each of which caught, emphasized or looked for a new aspect of the story and which therefore had a new form each time it was offered to the public.

Often in remakes there is an attempt to go beyond not only the limitations that exist with regard to the expression of the story, but also the technical limitations. Since the technology available to the movie industry is continually evolving, the story can be enriched and retold with greater effect.

With the creation of the Steadicam, camera motion attained an expressive capacity that makes it possible to underline the construction of the movie, to follow the more complex developments in the narrative and to describe the events with greater clarity, heightening the viewer's sense of participation. Thus the werewolf is no longer described exclusively from the outside, as a transformation from man to wolf, but is seen as a being with his own point of view that we can perceive through the visual changes and from a new, low down, viewpoint, in movement, quick, unexpected, thanks to the use of the Steadicam in low mode.

At the same time, in many films less concerned with effect, the Steadicam allows the construction of different dynamics and rhythm. The camera follows a conversation between people on the street, stays closer to the actors, following their paths more efficiently and in a way that increases the viewer's involvement in the story, e.g. *Sabrina*, 1954/1995; *We're no Angels*, 1955/1989; *The Night and the City*, 1950/1992; *Dial M for Murder*, 1954/*A Perfect Murder* (remake), 1998.

Obviously, there is no direct link between the existence or not of a new cinematographic tool and telling a story that has already been told. The story has the inner strength to exist in its own right and technology can be used to express it as well as possible.

John Carpenter, in his remake of *The Thing*, used the new technology available to him to go beyond the limits of the 1950s, when Christian Nyby's[50] black-and-white classic was made. In the original version, there is a lot of atmosphere and expectation, and the audience is left to imagine what is not shown; the cold and snow make it difficult to have a clear view of what is happening. The use of the dolly and the many fades serve to synthesize the idea of movement. In his colour remake, Carpenter makes the story more complex and more visual. The Steadicam, which is also present as an independent narrator, is unleashed to follow the characters in the races down the hallways and is used for point of view shots.

This example shows how using the Steadicam can increase the expressive potential of a story and a movie without, however, legitimizing the idea that a movie made with more means and possibilities is necessarily better.

The beginning and end of a movie

Entering into and leaving a film are particularly beautiful and tragic moments for viewers. Entering the world of make-believe can coincide with a need for entertainment, meditation or reflection on their part. They choose a movie, they dedicate that interval of time to the make-believe and play the game. The movie's beginning is the start of the credits, the first frames that appear out of the dark. For this reason, the graphics at the beginning of the movie, the presentation of the authors' names and the first events are of fundamental importance. All this, accompanied by a soundtrack that is both internal and external to the story, allows us to enjoy the oblivion of the fiction and detach ourselves from the present, to 'get into' the film.

The Steadicam has made it possible for viewers to enter and leave a movie in new ways that we might call 'more physical'. It manages to involve the viewers and take them by the hand so energetically that they almost feel the need to call a stop, even if they are already sitting in the theatre, in order to understand what is happening. This is what happens in *Diner*, *Legal Eagles*, *The Bonfire of the Vanities* and *Snake Eyes*.[51] These movies, all with opening scenes shot in Steadicam, have dynamic beginnings which lead viewers to feel almost as if they were racing along behind the story.

At the end of a movie as well, viewers participate in a particular rite – the inevitable displeasure of leaving the make-believe, the fantasy, the sentiment. Thus, the stories are often made to finish with full shots, which progress slowly and gradually 'to accompany the viewer to the door'. At times, however, the ending can be brusque or paralysing using, for instance, a freeze-frame. At other times the ending is done differently and can take viewers back to the beginning again, closing the story in a circle. For example, in *The Bonfire of the Vanities*, the long tracking shot at the beginning, which was interrupted to allow the story to be told, is concluded at the end of the movie.

However, the end of a movie may not mean cutting viewers off from the make-believe, as in *After Hours*,[52] where the final tracking shot is a movement that continues to lead us into the story, making us think that something else will follow. The movie ends with a Steadicam tracking shot in the empty office, the camera moves among the desks and hallways to the music and then it moves away, inviting viewers to continue to give their imaginations free rein.

Conclusions

> The moving camera is particularly useful in cases in which the scene of the action is not a static environment, in which the actors come and go, but when the actors are, so to say, the constant elements and it is the environment instead that changes. The camera can accompany the hero through all the rooms of a house, down the stairs, along the street; and the human figure can stay the same, while the environment runs like a panorama, continually changing. The movie artist can therefore do what is very hard for the theatrical director, which is to show the world from the point of view of an individual, to take man as the centre of his universe; in other words, make a totally subjective experience visible to everyone.
>
> Actually, it is possible for experiences of an even more subjective nature to be represented in this way. The feeling of 'seeing everything turning around us', dizziness, drunkenness, the sensation of falling and getting back up are easily produced moving the camera in the most suitable way.[53]

With these words Arnheim in 1933 anticipated what the Steadicam fully realized. We have seen how this device can be used to help tell the story and to substitute itself for the gaze and the narrator itself. I have tried to analyse the various functions of the Steadicam, examining how it performs in the different movies in which it has been used, according to the type of movie and the director. As it was impossible to review every film, I have limited my analysis to the earliest films, to the period in which the Steadicam was introduced as an official movie tool, and to some of the films through which it became known. Then, the analysis considers those productions that clearly demonstrate the qualities of the Steadicam. Movie history makes it possible to travel through movie production from 1977 to 1999, and to consider the films made during the last 10 years, during which time there has been an exponential increase in the use of this tool.

The versatile Steadicam, which can go from being a fixed camera to performing any number of camera moves all without needing to interrupt the shot, has undergone a metamorphosis from the time of its debut to the present. If, at the beginning, it was used and experimented with for the effects it could create (stability and fluctuation together, shooting the point of view of someone looking while moving, chases down long and varying routes, etc.), its uses are now more skilled and more standardized. More skilled, since it is not as identifiable as it was. In fact, where it once was noticeable for its diversity and for the peculiarity of its movement compared with other means, we now see movies that use the Steadicam as if it were a dolly or for a stationary shot, since all shots can be made without the viewer being able to recognize the source. At the same time, the Steadicam has been standardized because it has determined what is practically a style, one tied to action movies and 'thrillers' in which it is the absolute protagonist. Tightly linked to the dynamics of editing, it helps to construct movies that seem to be 'all alike'.[54] All action films of the 1990s use the Steadicam, particularly because of the dynamic shots it can make, perfect for capturing the 'action' that is their basic premise. In these movies the rhythm is fast and the events rush along one after another to astonish and enthral the viewer. Basically, the story is constructed by relying on the dynamics of the action.

In my analysis, I have attempted to gather examples of point of view shots done with the Steadicam and to give more thought to the link between the expressive richness of the device and the fact that it represents a stimulus to 'write' stories which can fully exploit such wealth.

> The point of view is substantially a figure which is halfway between meaning and expression, between syntactic position of the camera and special effect within the image, it is a 'compromise formation' in the Freudian sense between the desire to enter the visual horizon of another person, of a character, and the impossibility of leaving oneself to one side.[55]

In the light of this analysis, it is interesting to look at the movie *Strange Days*, directed by K. Bigelow, which unites 'effect' and story construction, exalting the possibility of living 'the point of view of others'. Set in a violent and disillusioned Los Angeles just before the year 2000, a large part of the movie is shot with the Steadicam. The lead character is a man who sells 'dreams' through the squid, an electronic system that is attached to the head and allows the wearer to live the same emotions felt by whoever wore it before and activated it for recording. Practically speaking, it records brain activity and sight, a direct line with what one feels while one acts.

This coincidence is realized, in terms of moviemaking, by the use of point of view (subjective vision), since the wearers of the pre-recorded diskettes (squids) live other people's lives anew, seeing again directly through their brains, what happened to the person who 'recorded' it. The point of view shots are alternated with shots filmed with the Helmetcam, which is worn directly on the operator's head in order to achieve the greatest possible coincidence with the character's point of view. Seeing and feeling blend together; the viewer is swallowed up in long takes of insane flights and violent situations.[56]

A movie such as this is an evident and efficacious example of technical and narrative effects that move along together, and adds another title to the long list of action movies, thrillers and horror movies that are constructed with an incessant dynamism of shots, even if in many of these movies the spectacular dimension becomes more important than the contents: a fast-running story that never lets up and is over in the wink of an eye.

Notes

1 Metz, C. (1980) *Cinema e psicanalisi. Il significante immaginario*. Venezia: Marsilio, p. 53.

2 'The techniques for the hand-held camera are essential to penetrate the reality which one is investigating, adapting the shooting in function of the space. In fact, the director/operator must become a mechanical eye, capable of following the characters involved in the action in what Rouch calls by analogy with the phenomenon of possession cine-transe.' Nepoti, R. (1988) *Storia del documentario*. Bologna: Patròn Editore, p. 98.

3 'Patricia Rollet notes that some of the most important technological innovations of recent years in the field of cinema, such as the Steadicam or microcameras, have the effect of detaching the camera from the human eye, thus completing a longstanding cinematic tie.' Metz, C. (1995). *L'enunciazione impersonale o il luogo del film*. Napoli: Ed. Scientifiche. See the author's interview with Garrett Brown in Chapter 4 (question 5).

4 *La Roue*, 1922, A. Gance: particularly in the sequence called 'Sisif aveugle', in which after an accident (a jet of steam went in his eyes) the driver looks at the familiar objects that he has at hand and no longer recognizes them – the continuation shows them to us: Sisif, who picks up his pipe, feels it and looks at it as he moves it closer to his eyes (descriptive image). Later, this pipe is shown to us (in close up) as he sees it, in other words in a sort of woolly shimmer (analytic image, called subjective). Next come various images of this type showing Sisif looking at an object that we also see in the way that he sees it. Mitry, J. (1965) *Esthétique et psycologie du cinema, II Les Formes*. Paris: Editions Universitaires, p. 61.

5 *Birdy*, directed by Alan Parker, 1984.

6 *Ransom*, directed by Ron Howard, 1996.

7 He divided the subjective viewing process into six elements: point, glance, transition, from point, object and character (awareness of the presence of someone looking); and defined various point of view categories on the basis of the relationship between the subject and the object of the glance. 'The point of view shot is a shot in which the camera assumes the position of a subject in order to show us what the subject sees. The point of view shot is composed of six elements usually distributed in two shots as follows: *Shot A*: point/glance: (1) establishment of a point in space; (2) glance: establishment of an object usually

off-camera, by glance from the point; between *Shots A* and *B*, (3) transition: temporal continuity or simultaneity; *Shot B*: point/object: (4) from the point: the camera locates at the point, or very close to the point in space defined by element one above; (5) object: the object of element two above is revealed; *Shots A* and *B*: (6) character: the space and time of elements one through five are justified by – referred to as – the presence and normal awareness of a subject.' Braningan, E. (1984) *Point of View in the Cinema: A Theory of Narration and Subjectivity in Classical Film*. Berlin, Mouton Publishers, p. 103.

8 *The Untouchables*, Brian De Palma, 1987.

9 *The Maltese Falcon*, John Huston, 1941; *Notorious*, Alfred Hitchcock, 1946; *A Fistful of Dollars*, Sergio Leone, 1964; *Leon*, Luc Besson, 1994; *Snake Eyes*, Brian De Palma, 1998.

10 'We Italians have always used the hand-held camera, even when there was no Steadicam – it's just that we never used it as something to be shown, I mean to say no one was ever aware of it, but in every Italian movie there is a piece which is 'hand-made'. Interview by Serena Ferrara with Giuseppe Rotunno, Centro Sperimentale di Cinematografia, Rome, 7 February 1997.

11 'Most hand-held shots suffer from a distinct jerkiness. Since it is solidly connected to the operator's shoulders or hands, the camera is subject to all of the operator's movement including undesired shocks and bounces that accompany each footstep. When we walk we do not see these shocks in the way the camera see them ... our muscles, joints, tendons and ligaments absorb a large portion of these shocks. What the body does not absorb is corrected by the eyes, muscles and the brain's image processing, turning a bumpy ride into a smooth flight ... the easiest and most reliable way to counter these movement is to prevent them from even reaching the camera and it is through this isolation that the Steadicam works'. Swanson, E. (1994) Steadicam Operators Association www.steadicam-ops.com/Eric Swanson's Steadicam FAQS hosted by Kiwi Film. This document is copyright Eric Swanson 1994.
'The eyes are part of an exquisite human servosystem (the brain) that is constantly adjusting and correcting for body motions so that the scene we see is always steady.' DiGiulio, E., President, Cinema Products Corp. (1976) Steadicam–35 – A revolutionary new concept in camera stabilization. *American Cinematographer*, July, 57 (7), p. 786.

12 *The Duellists*, Ridley Scott,1977, UK; *The Strawberry Statement*, Stuart Hagman, 1970, USA; *Il Conformista*, Bernardo Bertolucci, 1970, Italy; *Saving Private Ryan*, Steven Spielberg, 1998, USA.

13 About Larry McConkey: 'Larry's about the best there is: you can watch *At Play in the Fields of the Lord* and have no idea that it's full of Steadicam shots. He's the kind of Steadicam shooter we all aspire to be' (from the interview of J. Muro, Steadicam operator). Comer, B. (1992) Steadicam hits its stride. *American Cinematographer*, September, 73 (9), 82.

14 Such an effect can surely be found in other types of camera movements involving the use of mechanical devices that are less fluid and therefore more perceptible.

15 'You see, sometimes instead with the Steadicam they do things, they linger, just to show that it couldn't be done with another device; instead that same scene can be done just as effectively, maybe even more effectively, in less time.' Interview by Serena Ferrara with Giuseppe Rotunno, Centro Sperimentale di Cinematografia, Rome, 7 February 1997.

16 In this sense it should be noted that for many years now movie studios have offered tours in order to satisfy the curiosity and interest of the public. In addition, movie tapes, whether for rental or sale, have in recent years begun to include behind-the-scenes footage which shows how certain sequences were made.

17 For example, Lucas 'remodernized' the *Star Wars* Trilogy by using computer graphics which Lucas felt enhanced the story.
18 Rilla, W. from Marner, T. S. J. (1987) *Grammatica della regia.* Milano: Lupetti & Co, p. 24.
19 Truffaut, F. (1985) *Il cinema secondo Hitchcock*. Parma: Pratiche Ed.
20 'There are no neutral images. Any visual, or audio, element of any film ... is the result of many choices which always imply an activity.' Metz, C. (1995) *L'enunciazione impersonale o il luogo del film*. Napoli: Ed Scientifiche. Metz does not considers so-called neutral images a category, but rather a limit in the perception of the enunciating/speaking means; this definition is given to those images that do not have the characteristics of *film d'auteur* images (for example, the camera held intentionally at an angle, the use of colour that changes to underline emotion).
21 Gaudreault, A. and Jost, F. (1990) *Le recit cinematographique*. Paris: Natham Université.
22 'Ocularization: this term has in effect the advantage of evoking the viewfinder and the eye which is looking through it at the field that the camera is going to capture.' Jost, F. (1987) *L'oeil-camera*. Presses Universitaires de Lyon.
23 In Gardies' work, we find the distinction between the three levels on which the viewer's knowledge is constructed: he distinguishes between *location* (where the camera is positioned), *display* (what is seen) and *polarization* (management and diffusion of the narrative knowledge). In Gardies' polarization we find the differences and the correlations between the various sources of knowledge. On the basis of whether the narrator's or the character's knowledge is favoured more or less, we have the polarization – enunciator/speaker, the polarization – viewer and the polarization – character. Gardies, A. (1993) *L'espace au cinema*. Paris: Méridiens Klincksieck.
24 Bernardi, S. (1994) *Introduzione alla retorica del cinema*. Firenze: Ed. Le Lettere, pp. 68–69.
25 Cuccu, L. and Sainati, A. (1987) *Il discorso del film*. Napoli: Edizioni Scientifiche Italiane, p. 33.
26A 'The times the Steadicam is used are therefore perfectly functional to the narrative regime which was established with the illustration – truly Celine-like – of a voyage to the end of the night, a hiccoughing-voyage of which Cordiere, the rebel, is the Messiah. A voyage in which everything is turned upside-down, everything oscillates between logic and madness, in a sort of metaphysical delirium.' Arecco, S. (1992) *B. Tavernier*. Firenze: Castoro Cinema Ed.
26B Diegesis: Everything that belongs to the story, i.e. events and characters of a narrative. See Stam, R., Burgoyne, R. and Flitterman-Lewis, S. (1992) *New Vocabularies in Film Semiotics.* London and New York: Routledge.
27 *Attribution*: elements which characterize a place; *usefulness*: organizes the places into three categories: referential places, 'embrayeurs' places, anaphorical places; *differentiation*: involves the morphological characteristics (horizontal–vertical), the relational characteristics (open–closed), axiological characteristics (public–private), the speaking and cinematographic processes; *modalization*: involves the new information that the subject of the narrative acquires when he enters into a relationship with the space (i.e. the place of doing, of being ...). Gardies, A. (1993) *L'éspace au cinéma*. Paris: Méridiens Klincksieck.
28 Casetti, F. and Chio, F. (1990) *Analisi del film*. Milano: Ed. Strumenti Bompiani. (See discussion: *Attanzialita* pp. 176–8.)
29 Brown, G. (1980) The Steadicam and The Shining. *American Cinematographer*, August, 61 (8), pp. 786–9, 826–7, 850–4.
30 Brown, G. (1980) The Steadicam and The Shining. *American Cinematographer*, August, 61 (8), pp. 786–9, 826–7, 850–4.

31 Brown, G. (1980) The Steadicam and The Shining. *American Cinematographer*, August, 61 (8), pp. 786–9, 826–7, 850–4.
32 Brown, G. (1980) The Steadicam and The Shining. *American Cinematographer*, August, 61 (8), pp. 786–9, 826–7, 850–4.
33 Jeff Mart (Steadicam Operator) in Comer, B. (1993) Steadicam hits its stride (Part 4). *American Cinematographer*, February, 74 (2), p. 78.
34 Chiarini, L. (1965) *Arte e tecnica del film*. Bari: Ed. Laterza. p. 66.
35 Truffaut, F. (1977) *Il cinema secondo Hitchcock*. Parma: Pratiche Ed.
36 Deleuze, G. (1984) L'immagine in movimento. Milano: Ubulibri.
37 In *Raising Cain*, the doctor's long walk with the detectives. As the doctor goes from one place to another she talks continuously and gives us important information about the killer.
38 *Snake Eyes* opens with a technically demanding, seemingly edit-free 20-minute Steadicam sequence, shot by renowned operator Larry McConkey, which follows Santoro (Cage) through the Forum. 'Of course, you only have 500 feet in the magazine', notes Burum, 'so when it got to the end of the roll, we would either have a wall or a person wipe in front of the camera ... we use those moments as our opportunities to cut.' Pizzello, C. (1998) Ringside riddle. *American Cinematographer*, August, 52 (8), pp. 52–9.
39 Some critics have noted these 'filler' functions, such as Roy Menarini, with regard to *Species*, by R. Donaldson, 1995, USA: 'For the rest of the movie, Donaldson is satisfied with a series of circular tracking shots, with a good use of the Steadicam'. *Segno Cinema*, 1996, No. 78. G. Rotunno also criticizes movies which too often invent situations in which to use the Steadicam, not for narrative ends but because it provides a resolution for a weak screenplay. See interview in Chapter 4.
40 K. Branagh, 1994.
41 D'Agnolo Vallan, G. (1998) Morte al Casinò. *Ciak*, 11, November.
42 Barbera, A. and Turigliatto, R. (1978) *Leggere il cinema*. Milano: Mondadori, p. 307.
43 Bazin, A. (1986) *Che cos'é il cinema*? Milano: Garzanti, p. 87.
44 Barbera, A. and Turigliatto, R. (1978) *Leggere il cinema*. Milano: Mondadori, p. 292.
45 They are all movements which belong to a cultural moment involving the search for reality, provocation and the sense of the author. There is an attempt to reduce the amount of organization and expense involved in creating a set to a minimum and to directly follow what is happening.
46 *ER*, television drama series. Comer, B. (1993) Steadicam hits its stride. *American Cinematographer*, Part 4, February.
47 Jeff Mart, Steadicam Operator, in Comer, B. (1993). Steadicam hits its stride (Part 4). *American Cinematographer*, February, 74 (2), p. 78.
48 N. Pecorini, Steadicam Operator, in Comer, B. (1993). Steadicam hits its stride (Part 4). *American Cinematographer*, February, 74 (2), p. 77.
49 In this regard, it is interesting to hear Garrett Brown's opinion: 'Steadicam is almost too facile at this ... these shots desperately need thought – the discipline would be as follows: To imagine that these are dolly shots and that we need to lay all that rail. One would certainly have to consider each aspect of such a shot more carefully, since the labor of laying the rail is so large and essentially unchangeable. Therefore, one would actually design all aspects of the move carefully, rather than just jumping in and following endlessly, or relying on the flexibility of the Steadicam to avoid what should be an act of intense design.' Garrett Brown, personal communication, February 2000.
50 *The Thing from Another World*, Christian Nyby, 1951, USA.
51 In *Diner* the scene begins in the street: the camera follows the character as he goes down it, enters a building, climbs the stairs, goes down a hallway, enters a ballroom. *Legal Eagles* begins with characters on the street, they cross it, go into a building, climb the stairs (almost as if to

music), enter a room where a party is going on. In *Bonfire of the Vanities* Bruce Willis gets out of a taxi and goes to the salon on the 50th floor, all shot without cuts. See also Chapter 2 and this chapter for references to De Palma's work.

52 This film, too, in a certain sense has a circular ending, since it began precisely in that office, thanks to a masterful Steadicam sequence shot running about 7 minutes, that shows the arrival of the various employees, with a sense of dizzy premonition of what will happen, until it finds the main character sitting at his desk.

53 Arnheim, R. (1983) *Film come Arte*. Milano: Feltrinelli, p. 100.

54 V. Storaro: 'Today, simpler lighting equipment, faster lenses and the mobility of the Steadicam have given American movies another aspect, one which is also dangerous at the level of style and language, because I'm a little bit afraid that these films will turn out to all resemble each other.' Consiglio, S. and Ferzetti, F. (1983) *La bottega della luce – I direttori della fotografia*. Milano: Ubulibri, p. 177.

55 Bernardi, S. (1994) *Introduzione alla retorica del cinema*. Firenze Ed., Le Lettere, p. 74.

56 *Strange Days* ably reconstructs the feeling and the effect of subjective vision (point of view), showing the hands and feet of the character to whom the glance is attributed it makes the image truly seem to be his sight. As early as 1947, Robert Montgomery in *The Lady in the Lake* had amply reconstructed the effect, shooting the entire movie as a single point of view, that of the main character, the detective Philip Marlowe. Using devices such as the smoke from a just-lit cigarette, the hands ... all seen directly by him (coinciding with the camera). Montgomery's experiment, different from *Strange Days*, was in part a failure precisely because of the heaviness of the image which, even though it was a point of view, became in the long run almost an 'objective vision', according to J. Mitry. Paradoxically, the effect of subjectivity was lost, because there was no confrontation with other points of view.

Part Three

The Steadicam: Different Opinions

4

Open debate and interviews with movie industry professionals

Open debate

The profile that emerges from the technical description of the Steadicam and an examination of some films on which it was used is of a useful and versatile device. The Steadicam, besides giving the operator freedom of movement, in almost all situations, also frees the actors. In fact, no longer constrained by dolly tracks or other structures, the actors move freely over the whole area of the action.

Bertrand Tavernier chose to use this device precisely for its capacity to follow the actor without limiting his actions: 'I wanted to use it to give a great liberty to the actors, to be able to go everywhere without seeming to do so, to shoot very long takes'.[1]

Giuseppe Rotunno, instead, finds that the same effects can be obtained with a good hand-held camera (and other means) and that, indeed, the abuse of this tool leads to sterility in the construction of stories: 'I think that a lot of what is done with the Steadicam is an escape, especially if the director doesn't know what to do and so, thinking he'll give the scene more weight, he takes the Steadicam and goes'.[2]

Ed DiGiulio sees the Steadicam as an extension of the operator: 'by supporting the total weight of the camera system from the body brace we permit the camera to move with the operator as if it were an extension of its own body (part of its internal servosystem, so to speak) so the operator can easily control and guide the camera in any direction he pleases with a gentle movement of his hand'.[3]

For M. Chion, this extension of the body represents a hybrid between technique and person that it might not be possible to tame: 'Actually, the Steadicam is really a 'cyborg' device, a combination of man and machine, of muscle and mechanics as Boorman said – and the risk is that with such a device you don't feel ... either the one or the other: neither the muscle's tension, nor the machine's precision'.[4]

The argument which developed between Chion and Tavernier in the pages of *Cahiers du Cinema* is interesting for Chion's assertions emphasizing the obvious and at times imprecise use of the Steadicam in *Coup de Torchon*: 'The moves and the shots of Glenn's camera are quite variable, unsteady, at times almost dancing'.[5] Chion makes a comparison between *The Shining* and *Coup de Torchon*, as two of the first movies to use the Steadicam. While the first uses to advantage the spectacular characteristics of the device during the chases down the hallways, done with great precision, the second on the other hand, uses unstable camera moves and follows the characters 'awkwardly'. Actually, for Tavernier this is a desirable effect that helps the construction of the film: 'The Steadicam gave me a style of 'mise en scene' that continually led people into the 'scene' and tracked the characters as they looked at themselves, observed themselves ... Also it gave me great freedom of movement'. The argument continues with an article by Tavernier in which he maintains that he never 'used the Steadicam that much' and a further reply by Chion: 'In a work, it isn't the frequency of a 'method' or a form that counts; it's the way in which it defines the style. For their particularity and their presence at significant moments, *Coup de Torchon* is marked by its Steadicam sequences.[6]

Some 'good sense' regarding the use of this device, and whether it indeed determines how a story will be told, is provided by Garrett Brown: 'Steadicam doesn't ever determine story but offers some storytelling possibilities that permit more flexible and longer takes, if there is reason to continue uncut. Of course it's a tool, frequently badly used like every tool, sometimes used in a manner to charm the gods'.[7]

Interviews

This final portion of the book contains a series of interviews with people who work in the movie industry. They generously expressed their opinions, told their stories, recalled anecdotes and experiences regarding the invention and the use of the Steadicam. These interviews enrich our knowledge of the Steadicam (past and present) by giving us the direct testimony of camera operators, Directors of Photography, and movie directors.

It is interesting to note the different approaches and points of view, the various criticisms and observations which, taken together, communicate a great passion for cinema, movie making and the constant creative invention which very often involves and stimulates technique.

I would like to thank each person interviewed for their kindness in giving of their time: Garrett Brown, Giuseppe Rotunno, John Carpenter, Mario Orfini, Larry McConkey, Nicola Pecorini, Haskell Wexler, Ed DiGiulio, Vittorio Storaro and Caroline Goodall.

Interview with Garrett Brown (by e-mail, January 1997)

What are the principal technical characteristics of the Steadicam?

Invention of Steadicam needs four things: a) expanded masses; b) angular isolation (with gimbal); c) spatial isolation (with spring-loaded arm that mimics a human arm); d) a method of viewfinding that doesn't need the eye on the camera (such as a video monitor).

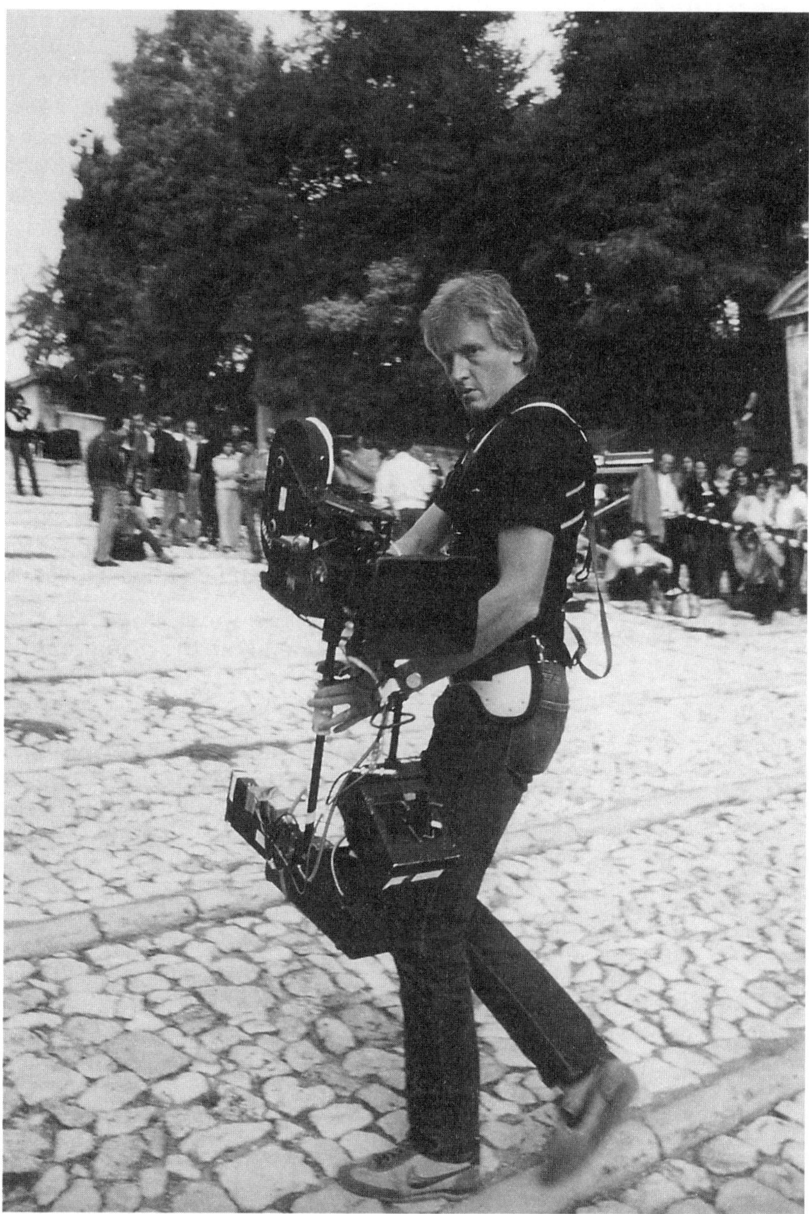

Figure 4.1 Workshop run by Steadicam inventor Garrett Brown during the festival 'Una città per il Cinema'. Photo: Istituto Cinematografico 'La Lanterna Magica', L'Aquila Collection, 1982

Is it difficult to use the Steadicam?
Yes, it takes a workshop, then practice, practice – it's an instrument.

Do you think that the fact that the vision you have in the Steadicam monitor (viewfinder) is so far from the body (as opposed to an ordinary camera where the viewfinder is near your eye) means that you frame the shot in a different way?
I prefer framing with the Steadicam monitor because I am used to it. Perhaps it's a more objective look than a viewfinder, particularly for violent action.

Is there a link between the choice of the shot and the kind of tool utilized? I mean, are the Steadicam's characteristics better suited to certain kinds of shots?
Yes – with overlap, of course, each tool is best for certain shots. Steadicam can stand still and look just like a tripod, but unless you intend to move before or after, what's the point? My favourite kind of Steadicam shot is when it is used just like a dolly (see next answer).

What do you think about the point of view shot, seeing with the character's eyes?
I have studied point of view shots. My favourites are with Steadicam – I don't like hand-held point of views, because I think of the frame as a window and I don't like my window shaking.

Has Steadicam changed the way films are made or is it only a tool?
The process of filming has changed with Steadicam, but only because some new things are possible and some other things are easier. Each successful tool has this effect on the business aspect, as well as on the creative aspect, of filmmaking.

What are the most important and significant movies in which you used the Steadicam?
Out of nearly 200 movies, *The Shining* was the most significant for Steadicam use.

Do you find that today the search for content is lacking because it is easier to fill the eyes of the viewer with special effects (such as unbelievable escapes)?
I have the same requirement of special effects as for stunts or regular shots: absolute believability and appropriateness. Otherwise they are not very interesting.

When you thought up this tool, did you imagine something that could approximate human vision?
Yes ... and I was looking for a fast-running stunt camera. Only later did I realize that it could be great, therefore didn't know what it was good for.

What were the first movies to utilize the Steadicam, up to about 1985?
Bound for Glory, *Marathon Man*, *Rocky* were all shot during 1975. Some others, at least up through the 1980s, are: *Rocky II*, *The Shining*, *True Confessions*, *Greystoke*, *Falling in Love*, *Sweet Liberty*, *Fame*, *Taps*, *Prince of the City*, *Xanadu*, *Baby It's You*, *Indiana Jones and the Temple of Doom*.

Have you used the Steadicam in other fields such as TV, theatre, dance, video?
Yes, except theatre. Others have, but not me personally.

Do you think that this tool is more about the sense of movement and capturing it?
It is about placing the lens where you want it, and moving it to where you want it next, in the manner that you want to move.

When you invent something like the Steadicam or the Skycam are you answering someone's particular requirements?
I invent for myself first – usually because I want one!

Do you think that the use of Steadicam is linked exclusively with a particular genre of movies?
No!

Have there have been situations in which the use of Steadicam was less successful than using dolly and crane together?
Of course. It is just a tool – frequently badly used like every tool. Sometimes used 'in a manner to charm the gods'.

What do you think about camera moves using dolly, crane, zoom – the possibilities and limits?
I love camera movement – some of it historically has been influenced by the limitations of dolly and crane, now we have a better, full spectrum of tools, and now it is less likely that one would be forced into an arbitrary style of movement because, for example, the Steadicam didn't exist.

How much does the Steadicam determine the story and the way it is told?
Steadicam doesn't ever determine the story, but offers some storytelling possibilities that permit more flexible and longer takes, if there is reason to continue uncut. It also permits more sophisticated camera movement in three dimensions – French curves, etc., rather that straight ahead over the dolly rails.

The Steadicam has speeded up a number of situations that would otherwise be impossible or very expensive. Do you think that this speed can cause contents and lighting to receive less attention?
Yes, sometimes. There have been some atrocities because Steadicam is so facile. It's regrettable. One could think of easy analogies: the invention of the tripod meant cameras didn't have to be placed on piled up furniture, and this extra speed may have caused some sloppy work!

What are the difficulties involved in lighting a scene that uses the Steadicam?
Being able to see in all directions during the course of a long shot has required the perfection of some particular lighting techniques: adroit dimmer work, etc., to keep the hot side always as backlight, etc.

Garrett Brown, Steadicam inventor

Garrett Brown began by making TV commercials and opted for movies after he invented the Steadicam camera stabilizer in 1974. During his prolific career he has shot nearly 200 movies with the Steadicam, and invented a series of extraordinary tools for shooting movies, television, sports events and concerts. Garrett currently holds fifty patents worldwide for camera devices, including the Steadicam JR for camcorders; Skycam, which flies on wires over sporting events; Mobycam, the underwater camera; the Go.cam and the Fly.cam, miniature tracking cameras, and the Emmy award-winning Dive.cam.

He has worked steadily to perfect the quality of his inventions and increase their capacity to shoot under the most difficult conditions.

He shared an Oscar (Class I Award) with Cinema Products in April, 1978 for the invention and development of the Steadicam, as well as winning an Emmy in 1989.

Garrett Brown is a member of the American Society of Cinematographers, the Directors Guild, the Screen Actors Guild and the Academy of Motion Picture Arts and Sciences. He also organizes and teaches Steadicam workshops all over the world.

Films

Some of the films on which he worked are: *Bound for Glory*, H. Ashby (1976); *Marathon Man*, J. Schlesinger (1976); *Rocky*, J. Avildsen (1976); *Exorcist II*: *The Heretic*, J. Boorman (1977); *Rocky II*, S. Stallone (1979); *Kramer vs. Kramer*, R. Benton (1979); *The Shining*, S. Kubrick (1980); *Fame*, A. Parker (1980); *The Formula*, J. Avildsen (1980); *True Confessions*, U. Grosbard (1981); *Reds*, W. Beatty (1981); *Taps*, H. Becker (1981); *Wolfen*, M. Wadleigh (1981); *Tootsie*, S. Pollack (1982); *Greystoke – The Legend of Tarzan Lord of the Apes*, H. Hudson (1984); *Indiana Jones and the Temple of Doom*, S. Spielberg (1984); *Legal Eagles*, I. Reitman (1986); *Rocky V*, J. Avildsen (1990); *Philadelphia*, J. Demme (1993); *The Return of the Jedi*, R. Marquand (1993); *Wolf*, M. Nichols (1994); *Casino*, M. Scorsese (1995); *Bullworth*, W. Beatty (1998/99); *Bringing out the Dead*, M. Scorsese (1999).

Interview with Giuseppe Rotunno, Rome, February, 1997

Preface by Giuseppe Rotunno

The Steadicam is a mechanical device like many others: in other words, great movies have been made without the Steadicam. The Steadicam hasn't resolved the problem of movies, because, in a certain sense it has always existed, people had started to think of the Steadicam a long time ago. I mean to say, we Italians have always used the hand-held camera, even when the Steadicam didn't exist yet, it's just that we never made a show of it. I mean no one ever thought about it, but I think every Italian movie has a part that was done with the hand-held camera.

Finally, I think that all technical devices are useful and very important, including the Steadicam, if they help us to tell the story, if they help us to stay within the story. However, I'm completely against the possibility of a movie being conceived for the Steadicam, as if you had to conceive a movie for a camera car or any other device outside the story. The Steadicam, overall, is very important if it is used with awareness of the reason for using it, in other words, if it helps to tell the story.

It is exactly, and only, a device.

How do you choose a camera move?

As is needed. In other words, you must never forget that in a certain sense the camera is the moviegoer, so you can't take it by the throat and take it around just to take it around. I think that a lot of what is done with the Steadicam is an escape, especially if the director doesn't know what to do and so, thinking he'll give the scene more weight, he takes the Steadicam and goes. It's not like that.

An example of Steadicam that instead is very effective is in Kubrick's movie *The Shining*, in which the Steadicam puts the viewer in the position of the characters, suspended in midair; in this case this floating sensation that the Steadicam gives is very effective and perhaps it couldn't be done with any other device. Even if, for example, with Fellini we did it with the arm of a crane with the camera on it, moving slightly, which is always a good way to give the idea of being suspended in midair, that is to say, detaching the actors from the ground and, obviously, putting the viewer in the same conditions. When all these things meet up, story, technique, lighting and, of course, movement, then it becomes something important.

It happened back in *Nouvelle Vague* (New Wave) cinema: the people who had serious cinematographic values remained and the others disappeared – the ones who substituted mechanical means for the story, telling just a very limited technical part, forgetting the story. It's always stories that make history.

Even long shots without cuts have always been done, for that matter – think of Hitchcock's *Rope*.

Does there have to be a different kind of lighting for Steadicam movement?

No, lighting has its own particular significance. Lighting too, in my opinion, is part of the story. It can't be done as a function of the technical device. Above all, it has to be a function of the story. Then it's the technical means that has to adapt to both the lighting and the story. Overall, there aren't any technical or emotional, artistic elements in the making of a movie that aren't part of the story, that aren't tied to the story. You have to keep in mind that the lens is always the viewer, so you can involve it in the movements if necessary, but this can't be done haphazardly, it has to be done at the right time, when it's needed. I cited Kubrick because in that case the thing is explicit, clear.

They say that using the Steadicam saves time; it's not true. Some movies might use shortcuts of this kind, but the Steadicam is not a time-saving device, because to prepare for that shot, Kubrick took a whole day, sometimes even two days, because he took possession of the means he was using, he didn't let it take possession of him. In other words, he dominated it. He used it correctly for his story, and this is true for everything in the movies, but particularly for the Steadicam or the hand-held camera (which is the same thing): you can't abuse it, or try to solve the movie's, or the story's, problems with it. With the hand-held camera, the Steadicam, the crane, a free dolly or an idea for a particular shot, everything has to be always a function of the story. That's my particular point of view and I don't think it's only mine.

Is there a relation between Steadicam use and the kinds of films that abuse it?
I think that when we think of the Steadicam we always think of action films, for example, chasing someone up a flight of stairs, which isn't easy because you need exactly the same amount of time that you need if you're using an offset arm. In other words, even if you put the camera on a dolly, on an arm, you can follow the person as far as you want to.

There are very, very few cases in which the Steadicam is irreplaceable: for example, if on the stairs you have to cross over and enter another stairwell; but precisely because I want to do something that I can't do with another device I have to do what serves the purposes of the story. There are the entrances and the exits which can also let you save time and, among other things, you don't have to go the entire route to tell it cinematographically, you only have to tell a portion of it. In fact, you normally would do just a portion of it to give the movie a better rhythm, to not go on too long.

Now, sometimes instead with the Steadicam they take too long so they can show that it couldn't have been done with another device. But that same scene could be told with the same effectiveness, and maybe even more, in less time.

Does the Steadicam really speed things up?
No, it slows things down. If you follow a moving object, you go more slowly. If you stay still, or it moves in front of you or it goes away or comes closer, the internal dynamics of the scene are more effective. In other words, everything has to be used with awareness and professionalism, because you need to know that if, while you're using that device, you increase or diminish the speed of the story, you are increasing or diminishing the speed of the shot's contents. That's what you need to know how to evaluate and then use the Steadicam too if it's needed, but only if it's needed.

Regarding control of the supporting structure, can the Steadicam be stopped at the desired point?
With great difficulty. One shot that we did in *Wolf*[8] with Garrett took a whole night and then it was cut because it never did come out well. I had already suggested we cut it, because I had designed it with a crane, an arm with the Steadicam on it, which accompanied the characters up to a certain point and then there was a cut, an out of shot. It was a terribly long shot to do and then it was cut after all. Then and there people thought that I didn't want to do it or that I was having trouble with the lighting for it, but the lighting was always the same.

It involved going from the starting point, which was at the top of some stairs, towards a house where there was a party, where the two characters meet, they go down the stairs and towards a certain place. Doing it in pieces, in other words, one part going down using the crane, then cutting away from the scene and then instead of starting from the same place, starting 150 m further along with the house already behind them, would have made it more effective as a story.

Following that movement realistically you have a meaningless view in the background for 150 m. We did it with the Steadicam and they cut that piece, they had to enlarge the scene optically to be able to change it.

You know that to cut directly onto the same scene – they made it worse than what I had suggested.

Are there movies (for example, remakes) that are able to tell the story better because of the technical means that exist today (Steadicam, Skycam, etc.)?
No, I never had a problem with equipment being mechanically inadequate, but then I've made a lot of movies and sometimes the lack of something makes you think better, and more, and find solutions without leaving them to someone else. 'Here, this could go there, I can do it anyway with that'. You have to think what exactly would be most effective and then do it. I never suffered from not having the Steadicam, not even now that it's available, that it's used. I have pictures of Blasetti many years ago with a sort of Steadicam he'd designed – a little helmet with a camera mounted on it, it was the same thing, more or less. Let me say once more, however, that the hand-held camera has always been in use here in Italy and not only here, also abroad, I think.

Can the Steadicam be considered a refinement of a technique that already existed?
Yes, just like film has gotten better, but it's still film. It's more sensitive, it needs less light.

What about the fact that the Steadicam moves sideways, that it can move more smoothly?
It's more limiting than a hand-held camera, if you consider the effect. The smoothness of the movement is another question, but this isn't always useful. The braking is dangerous, in my opinion.

What do you think about Steadicam shots with regard to framing?
By preceding someone who's walking, you don't make things go faster (apart from the fact that you can do it with any device: a dolly, a dolly with a jib arm, a camera car, a car, by hand). If you want to accelerate the movement behind you, you have to take it from a three-quarter view, because then the speed of what you have behind you is greater.

Even dollies, if they're not used carefully, won't increase the speed or rapidity of the movements or, say, the feeling of movement; they can absorb it, deaden it. Following a person means, I repeat, absorbing his movement, because you do the same movements and 30–40 per cent of it is lost, absorbed by your following him. So you have to really understand it.

Also, you see, the positions for preceding someone are always a little bit awkward and then they lengthen the time, as I said, and this is contrary to our modern style because the modern style is to tell a movie more rapidly, in the sense of skipping lots of parts of the story that were once thought necessary. The public today catches on sooner. In other words, if from this hallway you have to go outside and you want to follow someone on the stairs, all you have to see is someone who's running away, you catch him again down below and you've cut out a whole piece giving exactly the same idea, without losing anything of the story but with a speed which is three or four times greater; the editing is faster. In other words, time, the seconds that you take to tell it are more rapid when you cut away than when you follow, because that's real time, the other is cinematographic time.

With regard to screenplay, should it be decided from the beginning if Steadicam is to be used?
Not nowadays, if someone does it it's very rare. You write a screenplay because you think first of all of the story, then if someone wants to do a story for the Steadicam, that's different. But normally someone writes a screenplay, tells about human events, about human moods, and then later studies the means.

Are all camera moves studied later?
Certainly, all of them later. First you have to find where you'll be shooting; after having done the screenplay you look for the locations, to decide where to shoot – there has to be an office, a major street, big stores – in other words, what the story needs and after that, according to where they are, and, again, according to the time that you want to give to that move, that scene, you choose the technical means.

Have you ever used the Steadicam in other fields – TV, dance, etc.?
In TV they don't know how, they move the camera as if they invented it, instead they make you sick at the stomach, it's really annoying.

A story has to have a life of its own and then, afterwards, the technical means should make the passage from the screen to the viewer clearer, taking the words and translating them into images. Let the viewer get inside the story and be captured by it, in other words, become part of it.

Giuseppe Rotunno, Director of Photography

Giuseppe Rotunno first worked as a still photographer at Cinecittà, with Arturo Bragaglia and, later, as a camera assistant before becoming a camera operator on several movies, beginning with Rossellini's *L'uomo della Croce*.

In 1953 he made his debut as Director of Photography on Visconti's *Senso*. He has become an important cinematographer at the international level. As well as for his early work in black-and-white, he is well known for the particularly warm quality of his colour photography.

During the 1970s he often worked with Fellini and, in the 1980s and early 1990s, he worked on many Hollywood productions. He was nominated for an Academy Award for the cinematography of *All That Jazz* (1979). He has been awarded many prizes for his work.

He has been a Professor of Cinematography at the Centro Sperimentale di Cinematografia di Roma since 1988.

Films

His films include *Le notti bianche*, L. Visconti (1957); *La grande guerra*, M. Monicelli (1959); *Rocco ei suoi fratelli*, L. Visconti (1960);

L'ultima spiaggia, S. Kramer (1959); *Il gattopardo*, L. Visconti (1969); *Roma*, F. Fellini (1969); *Amarcord*, F. Fellini (1973); *Casanova*, F. Fellini (1976); *Prova d'orchestra,* F. Fellini (1978); *All That Jazz*, B. Fosse (1979); *Popeye*, R. Altman (1979–1980); *Five Days One Summer*, F. Zinneman (1982); *E la nave va*, F. Fellini (1982–1983); *American Dreamer*, R. Rosenthal (1983); *Rent a Cop*, J. London (1986–1987); *The Adventures of Baron Munchausen*, T. Gilliam (1987–1988); *Mio caro Dottor Grasller*, R. Faenza (1989); *Regarding Henry*, M. Nichols (1990); *Wolf*, M. Nichols (1994); *Sabrina*, S. Pollack (1995); *La sindrome di Stendhal*, D. Argento (1995); *Io mi ricordo, si io mi ricordo*, M. Mastroianni and A. M. Tatò (1996).

Interview with John Carpenter (by fax), December, 1998

I decided to interview John Carpenter under the mistaken impression that he had used the Steadicam in his film *Halloween*. In the late 1970s, in fact, the Panaglide, a Steadicam clone, responded to the same technical and narrative requirements as did thc Steadicam.

I analysed the movie and studied a number of sequences in point of view that demonstrated a Steadicam effect, without knowing that they were actually done with the Panaglide. I think it is important, nonetheless, to include the observations I made upon seeing the movie, since the narrative intention in using the Panaglide is equivalent to that of the Steadicam.

In the interview which follows the discussion of *Halloween*, Carpenter discusses the technical and other reasons which led him to use the Panaglide in response to questions I had formulated about using the Steadicam.

Halloween (John Carpenter, 1978)

The film tells the story of a babysitter who confronts, on the night of Halloween, an escaped maniac from a mental hospital who, when a child, had killed his sister.

I must emphasize that the comments made about *Halloween* concern exclusively the film's 'Steadicam effect' and the use of the Steadicam/Panaglide to recreate subjective vision. This film was one of the first to use this device to represent subjective vision and to show us, without the annoying shaking that would make the camera too evident, what the killer sees as he murders his first victim.

The Panaglide is used from the first sequence to show what the killer sees as he draws close, following every step from the outside (garden) to the inside of the house in a continuous movement. In this way it is used both as the perfect embodiment of the character's vision and as a recording of his movement (through the garden, entering the house, going through the kitchen, up the stairs to the room).

The effect of suspense is accentuated by the sound of his breathing, full of potentially aggressive connotations, as he puts on a mask, takes a knife in the kitchen and moves through the house in search of his victim.

The narrative gaze does not give us an objective distance from things, rather, it involves us in the killer's movements and leads us in a single, long shot to the murder, which is revealed as having been done by a child.

During the film the narrator does not want to give us information about the identity of the killer or, at least, we are not shown his face and thus cannot recognize him. We have thus an 'explicitly denied portrayal' that always shows us only part of him, never his face, or else shows him through what he is seeing as he spies on and follows the other characters. An example of this is the shot in which a boy, leaving school, runs towards us, the camera moves slightly to the left and the boy bumps into someone, looks at him, is scared, the unknown person holds him away from him and then lets him go. We see the head of the man who, after the boy has run away, stays there for a minute, then turns and goes to the left, slightly anticipated by the Panaglide, and finally walks along the school fence following another child, with the camera always at his side but never showing us his face.

We have seen that the story begins with a point of view of one of the main characters, the murderer; everything is seen through his eyes and in first person. For the first five minutes he is at the controls, then, after the murder, a more neutral narration takes over, the vision becomes total and no longer seems to belong to one specific character.

The tension in the movie is created by the question of which character is seeing what is on screen and the narrative voice continues to play this game, simulating and hindering the vision, limiting the audience's knowledge. Thus the narrator, who coincides with the camera, seeks to maintain its role as giver of information and allows itself to linger on and 'reframe' certain situations in order not to give us a total picture of the murderer.

What is your opinion of the usefulness of the Steadicam in filmmaking?

The Steadicam has become a basic photographic tool in the movie industry; beyond useful, the Steadicam has become seminal.

When did you see the Steadicam used for the first time and what about it impressed you?

I became fascinated by the Steadicam after I saw a shot in *The Exorcist II*, of all things. It was a bird's point of view, I believe, swooping down a street somewhere. It was not a hand-held effect – rather, a gliding, sweeping shot. Extremely cool.

When and why did you decide to use it in one of your films?

I first used the Steadicam in a television movie, *Someone's Watching Me*, in 1978. I photographed Lauren Hutton dashing around her apartment, and her moving point of view of same. It was great. Immediately after this, I made *Halloween*.

I used Panaglide in *Halloween*, and have in almost every movie since. Panaglide is a Panavision-built Steadicam designed for use with Panavision anamorphic (widescreen) lenses. The Panavision anamorphic lenses are heavier than spherical lenses (standard 1.85 format), therefore requiring an operator with a great deal of lower-back strength. I strapped on the Panaglide and began walking around with it back in 1978 – for about 15 seconds. I screamed, 'get this damn thing off me!'. It was a very disappointing day – I had dreams of operating the Panaglide myself. No lower-back strength.

Is your filmmaking technique – past and present – influenced by the particular features the Steadicam offers?
The effect of the Panaglide on screen is fascinating. Footage photographed with a Panaglide falls somewhere between the effect of a conventional dolly-operated shot and a documentary-style hand-held shot. The gyroscope in a Panaglide smoothes out the jerks and jitters of hand-held footage [author's note: this is a common misconception; there is no gyroscope in either the Steadicam or the Panaglide], thus it resembles a dolly-shot. But there is a slight sailing or drifting effect. The Panaglide makes the image float [author's note: practised Steadicam operators consider this 'floating' effect the giveaway of an unskilled operator].

Panaglide/Steadicam liberated the dolly move. Now an operator can strap on the camera and follow actors up and down stairs, in and out of buildings, over hills and valleys.

Whenever I direct a movie, I try to know as much as possible about the photographic equipment I'm using. I need to know how long it will take to set up a certain shot and what effect I want that shot to express. One of the issues I've confronted in the past is the moving point of view shot, in which a character is walking or running or basically on the move physically. I want to photograph, then, two different shots, to get the audience to identify with this character.

If you watch Alfred Hitchcock's films, you'll see he used a conventional dolly to photograph actor and moving point of view. I wanted to use the Panaglide instead. The freedom of movement, the gliding effect, the speed and mobility of shooting – it was all a plus.

Do you think the Steadicam has changed the manner of filmmaking?
See above.

To what extent is the Steadicam a tool of the narrator and to what extent can it be a narrator itself?
To discuss the aesthetics of Panaglide as a tool of the narrator or narration, I'd like to stop briefly at a boring history lesson.

There are really only two distinct styles of cinema. One is Russian montage. Think of Eisenstein, the Odessa Steps sequence in *Battleship Potemkin*. A montage is a series of shots cut together very quickly, creating excitement in the audience regardless of image content. A television commercial is exciting to watch because the images flash by so fast. A modern action film such as *Armageddon* is exciting because every scene is a rapid montage. It resembles a person watching a flickering light.

The second basic cinematic style is German Expressionism. It involves long shots, often single takes, usually with camera movement, exploring an environment, revealing characters or action. Think of Orson Welles, the opening tracking shot in *Touch of Evil*, plus the one that occurs later in the picture that takes place in the motel room. The emotional effects of German expression are excitement in the grandeur and sweep of a locale, a melancholy and sometimes anxious feeling regarding characters and locations. The Panaglide can be used to service both forms of cinematic style. It can become narrator or narration.

When making a film, what are the reasons for which you choose the Steadicam for a particular scene (from a technical and narrative point of view)?
See above.

What do you think of the point of view shot? Can you tell me something about using it in Halloween, i.e. the choice to have the Steadicam take the character's point of view? Do you think the Steadicam was essential in realizing your narrative intention?
I love point of view shots and sequences. I made the Panaglide double for both characters' point of view and narration point of view. It was absolutely essential for narrative intention.

What do think about hand-held shots and how they indicate the use of a cinematic tool as well as making the filmmaker's presence felt?
Hand-held shots give the sense of chaotic movement. The audience doesn't really intellectualize it the way you have, sensing the presence of the operator. They accept hand-held as moving chaos.

What do you think of the possibilities the Steadicam offers in terms of continuous or real-time shooting (in the sense of the possibility of following an action without interruptions of space and time)?
See above.

Do you think there is an abuse of the use of the Steadicam?
See above.

Do you always work with the same Steadicam operator(s)?
No.

Speaking as an author and narrator, how do you use the camera – as narrating eye, as third-person narrator, etc.? Is your choice influenced by the means you are using for filming? How?
My choice of using the camera as narrating eye or third-person narrator is influenced by the story, characters and intention of the scene I'm shooting.

Is the Steadicam such a strong means that it ends up imposing a certain style or can it be controlled by the filmmaker?
Any movie technology can be controlled by a director, given that he or she understands its strengths and weaknesses.

Does the fact that the Steadicam is such a versatile instrument affect the way you control the framing and shooting of an image? How much of what occurs in Steadicam shots is planned and how much is determined during shooting by the operator?
I dictate the direction of the Panaglide. During a shot, the operator

watches the framing on a small television monitor attached to the rig itself. I'm right behind him, following along, watching both the shot and the actors in front of the camera.

Do you think the Steadicam will be responsible for creating a film genre (or has it done so already)?
No.

John Carpenter, Director and Composer

John Carpenter began making short films in 1962, winning an academy award for Best Short Subject (Live Action) in 1970 for *The Resurrection of Bronco Billy*. He has worked in the film industry in numerous capacities – as a writer, actor, composer, editor, producer and director. He co-wrote the screenplays and composed the intense musical scores for all his movies. He is particularly interested in horror and thriller genres, blended with the fantastic. He is sometimes credited as Frank Armitage, Rip Haight, Martin Quatermass or John T. Chance.

Films

As a director his films include: *Dark Star* (1973); *Assault on Precinct 13* (1976); *Someone Watching Me!* (TV)(1978); *Halloween* (1978); *Elvis* (TV) (1979); *The Fog* (1980); *Escape from New York* (1981); *The Thing* (1982); *Christine* (1983); *Starman* (1984); *Big Trouble in Little China* (1986); *Prince of Darkness* (1987); *They Live* (1988); *Memoirs of an Invisible Man* (1992); *Body Bags* (TV) (segments *The Gas Station, Hair*) (1993); *Village of the Damned* (1995); *In the Mouth of Madness* (1995); *Escape from L.A.* (1996); *Vampires* (1998).

Interview with Mario Orfini, Rome, July 1998

When did you first use the Steadicam?
I'm not sure, I think it was in *Mamba*.

Does the Steadicam condition your choice of how to shoot a scene?
Yes, the Steadicam can condition your choice of how to shoot a scene and that's why the Steadicam has a lot of mistakes on its conscience – because people treat it as if it were the director, in every sense of the word. It's not the director, because anyway it's just a tool, and the person using it has to know how to direct it.

Eighty per cent of the time, in what I've seen of the Steadicam in Italy – in America much less – it's used wrongly, taking advantage of and abusing its worth; in other words, it's used automatically, without understanding its real value and real effectiveness. The Steadicam, like other cinematographic tools, can modify language and, if it's used haphazardly, it leads to enormous mistakes.

The most important thing is choosing when to use it, on the basis of what you want to express and narrate. Lots of times I've found myself deciding whether to use the Steadicam, the hand-held camera or the dolly, and I've had to think about what was important to narrate, about what I wanted to tell. And when I'd thought about it I'd say, I've chosen the hand-held camera or the dolly or the Steadicam, whichever, but I was always very sure of my choice. I could see in my head what I wanted to do and which was the right tool to use to get the result I wanted. So for me personally it's never been a problem.

Is there a difference between predicting the effect of a dolly shot and the effect of a Steadicam shot?
No, I don't think so, because a dolly might seem to be something simple that you know very well because it's in your genetic code – it was around a hundred years before the Steadicam so it's lodged deep within the layers of the director's memory, the person who knows how to narrate with images and how to translate words into images. The dolly is part of our inherited knowledge, our heritage. The Steadicam comes along as the last tool, so then you have to decide if you'll use the dolly or the Steadicam.

And when do you decide to use the Steadicam?
When it's impossible to use the dolly or the hand-held camera I can depend on the Steadicam, but in this way I'm running the risk of undervaluing it. The Steadicam, besides having a language of its own, has something more, though it can substitute for an aspect of a dolly or a hand-held camera.

When you shot *Mamba* was the Steadicam very important?
No, when I was thinking about *Mamba* I never took into consideration what tools I would use. At the beginning, right before we started to make it, I said I wanted the Steadicam as well, because it could be useful, but I hadn't planned at all where, or how, or when. I thought up all the Steadicams in that movie one morning from 7:00 to 8:00, while I was being driven to Cinecitta. The fact that I had to have a Steadicam available caused a lot of trouble for everyone, but since I was the producer I could decide, and so one was made available.

Were there difficulties with using the Steadicam in that movie?
No, not at all. However, I can tell you that in the last movie I made, *L'Anniversario*, I did have problems with using the Steadicam, not because of the instrument but because of the operator. He was very, very good at his job, but one day when I had to do a difficult Steadicam shot – he had to start in front of the actor and then go around to follow him, with a double circle around a table at which the actor was sitting, then go out the door, with the door acting as a curtain, go away, climb on a dolly that raised him up, and shoot the actor as he appeared in the doorway in a Full Shot (FS) to give the idea of the total breakdown of this character who psychologically had lost his entire vision of life. I needed to show him isolated in this doorway, seen from above. The operator had a 40° fever and he couldn't control the Steadicam – not its weight, which would be a banal consideration of the job that a Steadicam operator does, but he couldn't get the right tension. The operator and the Steadicam are two parts of a whole, and they breathe together. Seeing him in difficulty, I had a feeling of the Steadicam being in difficulty as well, and I did something that I don't think

anyone else would have done. I used the Steadicam sequence in which he had had the most trouble. This situation enabled me to obtain a strange mechanism of liaison: when there was one mistake, it seemed like a mistake; when there were two, three, four, imperceptible mistakes it seemed like the Steadicam was breathing, as if it took a breath and wanted to get closer to the character it was showing us. In the end we got a really beautiful sequence.

Does the fact that the Steadicam makes it possible to shoot a series of free movements mean that you tend to simplify the story?
I don't think it conditions the way you shoot the story. For me personally, no. First I think of how I want to compose the shot. It would be a big mistake if I were to follow the tool and not what I want to tell. You could say that it's more true for television than for movies (except for 'B' movies).

What do you think of point of view shots?
A point of view is almost always shot with a hand-held camera, sometimes with a dolly, and sometimes it is better to use the Steadicam for it. It depends on what you want to say and how you want to say it. The Steadicam is absolutely a tool that you have to know how to use, because if it's used badly it's wrong, like with all tools.

Does the Steadicam impose a certain style?
It can't impose a style, because if it imposes a style it means that the director wasn't able to control it.

Can it lead to the creation of a new genre?
I don't know about that. It can at times be conditioning, and thus I'm contradicting what I said earlier a little bit, when a sequence or a scene is being made. I can say that in the last movie I made I used the Steadicam four or five times and I massacred two of them when I was doing the editing, because I realized that in order to have the softness and flow of the Steadicam I was losing the rhythm. Because with the Steadicam, you also get the intervals when nothing is happening. You can do that in television, but not with movies. For example, there's a scene in which Laura Morante, the main character, goes out, I'm in front of her and I follow her as she closes a series of doors behind her, and I kept jumping from one to the other. You could do an entire movie in Steadicam but it would be an exception. But in my situation I realized in doing the entire sequence with the Steadicam that in the end when we edited it I had to cut a lot to have the rhythm I wanted. That doesn't take away from the fact that the Steadicam parts that we kept in the movie are beautiful, just right.

From an author's point of view, how do the means of shooting influence your choices?
The means must influence your choices, because if you're deciding how you're going to tell something you ask yourself what tool you'll use, and then you choose it on the basis of the various characteristics and on what you're telling.

How do you use the camera – as a narrative eye, as a third-person narrator?
Both things, and not only those, also in a lot of other ways, because there are situations in which you see in first person and then a

second later you feel the need to step aside and look at the situation objectively. For example in my last movie, I had a situation of guests in a house after a dinner party, and the hosts and their friends use a language in which the uselessness of words and gestures is exalted. What they say has no real content. There are two women in this group who have something dramatic in them, and that needs to be seen in a different way. In this case, I thought that to be able to distinguish between these two ways of narrating, I had to do something with the camera, and I shot from up high, flattening the actors, seeing the heads and the noses of the people talking, and other times they were placed a little differently and you could see a little of their faces. But I made it feel like a vertical shot that nullified them, flattening them to the ground.

How do you control the shot with such a versatile tool?
I think that you can calculate everything, and what the operator makes happen is that little extra touch that comes from the camera being sort of a part of the operator's body. That's the sensitivity the operator has. It's like ballet, if you see Carla Fracci or Maya Plissetskaya you realize, you can feel, how they're able to become light, and you can feel when a ballerina is too heavy, too hard, etc. This is what the Steadicam operator gives you, and a good camera operator gives it to you as well, that you don't feel the camera and he and it are one. He feels the image and he makes it his own, moment after moment, capturing it in the lens.

Can using the Steadicam change the narrative message?
No.

Do you think the Steadicam is abused?
Yes, enormously, by everyone who uses it in the wrong way.

What is your relationship with the viewer, with regard to his getting narrative information?
I think that in the end the viewer understands everything, so I put myself in a position to be able to give him what I see, which is very important. I mean to say, I don't become a narrator who is present, a narrator who's also the object of the narrative. In this movie, *L'Anniversario*, I used two cameras a lot, but not one next to the other, like in 'Put a 200 here, and a 100 underneath'. No. 'Put a 200 here and a 40 down there at the far end'. They couldn't figure out where to put the lights and the mikes anymore, but I didn't care and I was right, because like that I always had an 'eye-witness' to the events. In other words, I observed a situation and then to make it more important, to reaffirm the narrative importance of that situation, I asked a witness to watch and to say 'It's okay like this', and the witness was off to one side and it was another camera. For the viewer it was as if the second camera was him looking at the scene from a different viewpoint.

What do you think of shots with the hand-held camera?
The hand-held camera is a tool like the Steadicam, or the dolly. As with all tools, you have to overcome your prejudices or get something straight: behind the gaze of the hand-held camera, behind the gaze of the Steadicam, behind the gaze of any lens, there is always a viewer, the one who's watching. The director is a

mediator, someone who's telling a story. He uses these tools to tell the story. If he's good at his job, he tells it to you well, and if he's not, he tells it to you badly.

The viewer is the one who sees it and he's the one who feels himself embodied by the lens at that moment, so if I use the hand-held camera and the hand-held camera is more present, it's because in that moment the director has chosen to narrate with the hand-held camera. The birth of the Steadicam didn't eliminate the hand-held camera.

In my last movie I used both the hand-held camera and the Steadicam a lot, according to the situation. There were things which were unthinkable for the Steadicam; for example, the husband saying to his wife 'Now I'm going to throw you out of the house' and he takes her and drags her down the stairs to finish packing her stupid suitcase so that she'll leave. At that point, I didn't have any doubts at all about whether to use the Steadicam or the hand-held camera, I used the hand-held camera because the tension of the break-up of their relationship was that of the hand-held camera. If I'd used the Steadicam I would have annulled the roughness of the scene. The action was more physical and if I had softened it, because with the Steadicam I would have softened it, I would have ruined that scene. So they're two different things.

What do you think about continuous shots?
I think very highly of them when they're not abused and when they're not used wrongly. When they're done with the Steadicam, which does the job much better because it can do the 'impossible tracking shot' or the 'impossible dolly' and lets you do things that would be impossible by any other means, almost always the main mistake is wanting to keep the entire shot, to say 'Look what a great 7-minute shot I did!'. Orson Welles would be rolling over in his grave. Instead, you have to use the Steadicam to do tracking shots, dolly shots that would be impossible, but then you have to cut them in editing to eliminate the things that pollute the shot, including the times when nothing is happening.
In the example I gave earlier, the Steadicam helped me create an almost magical sequence. Then, evidently, the Steadicam did its work well, it became a violin that was playing beautifully, despite the fever. You could feel that the bad shape the operator was in matched perfectly the bad shape the character was in, which was what the Steadicam was telling you about, and the whole thing increased the total effect. Although it's true that if a Steadicam shot has a mistake it should be done over, in this case it was the contrary: the tool – the Steadicam, which was breathing with the operator – took on the same feverish and weak conditions the operator was in, recording the feeling, and shooting the character's drama with his same feelings.

Mario Orfini, Producer and Director

Mario Orfini worked for years as a reporter for a variety of European and international publications, writing for Pannunzio's *Monao* and *Espresso*. He also worked as a photographer for the Piccolo Teatro of Giorgio Strehler.

He is a producer with a curriculum rich in discoveries and sophisticated quality films by authors such as E. Greco, R. Faenza, F. Carpi and others. From 1991 to 1992 he was responsible for production at Titanus Distribuzione.

Recently he has been financial co-producer for the film *New Rose Hotel*, directed by A. Ferrara.

He is the president of Millennium Productions.

Films

He directed *Explosion* (1971); *Noccioline a colazione* (1978); *Mamba* (1988); *Jackpot* (1992); *L'anniversario* (1999).

Interview with Larry McConkey, Perugia, October, 1998

I would like to know what you think about the point of view shot.

It's the most difficult thing I have to do, but it can be the most rewarding. One nice thing about the Steadicam is that it can mimic the motion of human eyesight better than any other currently available technique. As you walk, your head is naturally bobbing up and down with every step, along with some side to side motion, and accelerations to the front and back that are less significant visually, but next time you think of it, notice while walking that you tend to focus on something in the distance and keep that steady, while the rest of the world, normally the foreground, moves up and down relative to it, and of course, a little side to side as well. This is a remarkable form of image stabilization that is just natural to us, and the Steadicam, because it is inertially stable, tends to do the same thing. In fact, a good operator will not only make the background steady but the foreground as well. This is a kind of hyper-natural form of image stabilization. So first of all that's why the Steadicam is so nice for trying to represent point of view shots – because it's seems pretty natural.

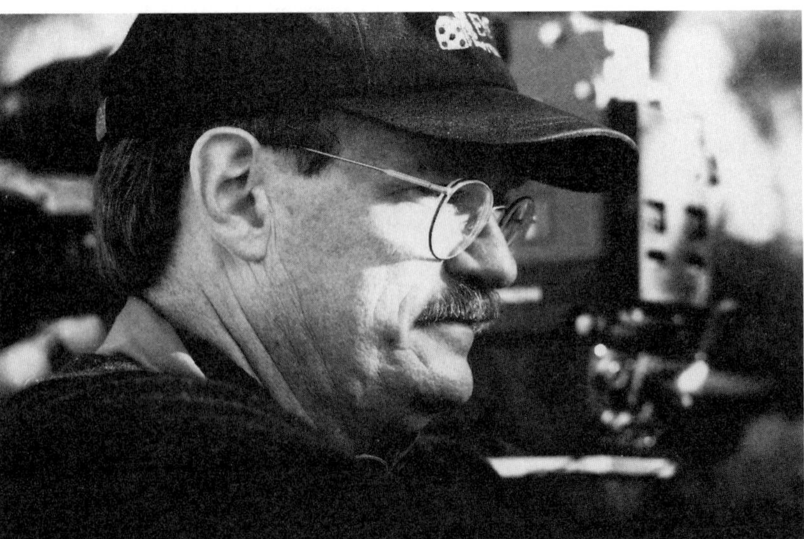

Figure 4.2 Larry McConkey at the International Steadicam Workshop, Perugia, Italy, 1998. Photo: Serena Ferrara

The more difficult part of representing an actual point of view is deciding what to show in the very narrow field of view that almost all lenses provide, particularly the normal-focal-length lenses that present a perspective that closely matches our own eyesight. As you walk, you tend to glance quickly around at a number of things all around and your mind constructs an apparently seamless presentation of the visual reality. In fact, most of your visual sense is nothing but an imaginative reconstruction from memory that your mind fits to the available clues that your eyes and other senses provide. So, to represent this complicated process with a Steadicam point of view, I use a technique of presenting one clearly defined visual idea after another, allowing the audience to construct their own sense of the overall visual reality from this series of ideas. I go through the space defined by a shot and imagine being the character, what he or she is concerned about, what he or she is feeling. I am in essence playing the role myself, using camera technique rather than acting technique, so I try very hard to get the actor to play the scene first, and ask questions about what I should be thinking, feeling and doing. The trick is to turn those ideas into specific shot making techniques.

Yes, but don't you think that when you watch a movie, often the very smoothness of a Steadicam shot brings your attention to that fact that it was shot with a Steadicam?
Well, there are two answers:

First, before Steadicam, it used to be the convention that if you want to tell the audience 'You are watching a subjective shot', you do it hand-held, and the inertial unsteadiness, the shaking of the shot is what alerted the audience that this was supposed to be a point of view. I think it's an overused and less convincing technique, but it is easy and it lends itself nicely to suggesting a spontaneous reaction to the scene, which is possible, but more difficult with a Steadicam. These days the audience is being trained to recognize another convention for point of view when they see a very smooth, very wide-angle shot that moves somewhat aimlessly through a set. I don't like either convention very much.

Secondly, bad technique and execution will call attention to the process rather than the action, no matter how it is done. But if what you do is present the audience with a series of ideas, clearly executed, they don't notice the crane, dolly, tripod, Steadicam or hand-held nature of the shot, they just see the ideas, and then it's a good shot. I feel the Steadicam, handled well, is one of the most expressive and powerful tools you can use for this, but it is a two-sided sword and, handled badly, it can be one of the most offensive, crude and obvious tools we can use. That is always the challenge for me ... walking that tightrope between sublime and subversive. I am always at the edge of completely subverting my intentions through the smallest failure of technique, physical condition, mental preparation and concentration, emotion or sometimes most significantly, political skills. That challenge is a large part of the attraction of the job for me.

I think it's much harder to do a subjective shot well than anything else. Because what I want to do within a point of view is to express a series of purposeful, simple ideas; for instance, as part of a shot, I may want to portray a character who's absolutely determined and absolutely clear about what he wants to do, and nothing is going to stop him – he wants to go through that door ahead of him, and confront something on the other side. He doesn't care about anything else in the world, he just wants to go through that door and there may be no extraneous movements in the frame – nothing to grab the audience's eye other than the set. To do this I need to place that door very deliberately and precisely in some part of the frame and it becomes my target: ideally, it never wavers from that part of the frame, it just gets bigger. Any little bumps distract from the idea of going to the door and they are very noticeable because anything but a steadily growing image of the door is new information, a new idea, and the audience will be startled by it, and they will notice the movement of the camera instead of the simple but powerful idea that the character is moving resolutely to the door. The more perfect your technique, the less you feel the Steadicam and the more you see the idea.

How do you organize and execute a long, unbroken shot?
One reason editing is nice is that it allows you do a section of the scene from a fixed position, or as a dolly or crane move, until it stops working for some reason. A new angle is established and the scene continues, perhaps with some unnecessary action cut out as well. If I am asked to do an unbroken Steadicam shot in the same situation, I have to figure out another solution. I may want to get to that same second angle, but without making the audience feel like they are just waiting for me to get there, or feeling that the camera is rushing to a new position for no apparent reason. As a general rule, I want the camera movements to seem expected, desired, even inevitable by the audience. I don't want arbitrary movements, unnecessary movements of either the actors or myself that don't contribute directly to the story. Often that means that I must manipulate the physical space. I might move parts of the set or people to create a different space where the actors can move logically and allow me to respond with the camera without calling attention to myself, as I would by moving in a direction or speed that might seem undesirable to the audience, and also to end up where I want to go.

This often introduces some new ideas into the scene, but to be helpful they have to be consistent with the story, they can't seem arbitrary. So I must respect the needs of the actor, and the ideas of the director, and get help from anybody who can supply it. For instance, in *Goodfellas*[9] I needed to tamper with the shot, I needed something for Ray Liotta, the main character to do, because otherwise he would just be walking through the club and the audience would just be waiting to get inside. I thought if we asked him to deal with other people along the way at strategic places where I needed help to keep the shot going – maybe he tips them or maybe he just talks to them – suddenly those events become the story, how he talks to these people, what he says to them. These technical challenges lead to solutions that enhance the drama. It's magic when it works like that, but that's what makes the difference between a long shot and a great shot.

Is it always necessary to shoot with the Steadicam or is it maybe possible to use other means?

I think that the best way to do anything is the simplest way, I mean the simplest looking way, not necessarily the simplest to execute. The simplest, whatever it is.

The Steadicam is capable of very complex things and sometimes there is nothing that can handle a complex shot as well. But if you are a good operator, it's also capable of beautifully simple things. There is nothing more pure than the camera simply panning at a perfectly constant rate in a wide space or tracking sideways with perfect direction and smoothness – just those simple ideas, just pure movement through space. Now the Steadicam can do these things, but there are other instruments that also do them and often do them easier or better. But I don't like to impose limits on myself without first attempting what initially seems too difficult, or at least unnecessarily difficult with a Steadicam, and I have done many shots that at first I didn't think were appropriate for Steadicam. Sometimes you can get exactly the same shot two different ways – which is the more appropriate often depends upon the priorities of the moment. Sometimes it's better to use a Steadicam because it's faster, sometimes it's better to use a Steadicam because the operator can make a more beautiful response to a little sudden change in the scene, sometimes it's better to use a dolly because the Steadicam operator is tired.

When asked to do a shot that I knew would be fairly simple shot with a dolly, I have at times responded by asking 'Why don't you use a dolly?' I might not get much more explanation than 'I want *you* to do it' or 'Let's just see how it goes ...'. After operating Steadicam for about twenty years now, I've learned it can be worthwhile trying to stretch my abilities in attempting these shots. Earlier in my career I would have thought some things should only be attempted with a dolly – simple, beautiful moves without deviation, just perfect tracking, booming or panning moves. But I have learned that if everything is going well I can make those same moves – if I'm in very, very good form and if there's no wind, and if I'm rested, and if the equipment is in perfect shape. I can make those moves, plus I can make adjustments during those moves just as a good operator and dolly grip might, but I can make the adjustments with one mind, whereas the dolly operator and grip are often making very subtle corrections for each other and what you see is a series of very small corrections. I can do the same thing but without the corrections, so those same little adjustments look more organic and human and they can sometimes even convey emotion. It is in the little subtleties that I find the most satisfaction and I might look for the opportunities to respond emotionally, almost intuitively to an actor. One example might be: I watch the actor's eyes and some small change in them makes me want to look more closely to see what he is thinking. In my mind I think 'what's happening?' and the response I make with the camera is almost nothing. And on the screen you see a little schh... sound that Larry made to synthesize the action of panning. It is a small but sudden movement, and it's a deliberate but almost instinctive reaction by me. I'm responding as if we were linked together, like a breath, so my camera becomes like another person and the audience becomes connected through that person to the other actors. The audience becomes more empathetic, more involved. The actor cannot help but respond to my camera as well, and we become even more closely linked together, and hopefully, the audience feels like *it* is participating in the scene.

Larry McConkey, Steadicam operator and Director of Photography

Larry McConkey works as a Steadicam operator – specializing in 'long takes', e.g. *Goodfellas*, *The Bonfire of the Vanities*, *Raising Cain*, *Snake Eyes*, *Carlito's Way* and others – and also as Director of Photography for documentaries, music videos, commercials and one forthcoming film, *White of the Eyes*.

He teaches as a Steadicam Master in workshops all over the world.

Films

His films include: *Birdy*, A. Parker (1984); *After Hours*, M. Scorsese (1985); *Legal Eagles*, I. Reitman (1986); *Mosquito Coast*, P. Weir (1986); *The Untouchables*, B. De Palma (1987); *Witches of Eastwick*, G. Miller (1987); *Casualties of War*, B. DePalma (1989), *GoodFellas*, M. Scorsese (1990), *The Bonfire of the Vanities*, B. De Palma (1990); *Miller's Crossing*, J. Coen (1990); *The Silence of The Lambs*, J. Demme (1991); *At Play in the Fields of the Lord*, H. Babenco (1991); *Raising Cain*, B. De Palma (1992); *Carlito's Way*, B. De Palma (1993); *The Age of Innocence*, M. Scorsese (1993); *Mission Impossible*, B. De Palma (1996); *Ransom*, Ron Howard (1996); *Snake Eyes*, B. De Palma (1998); *Celebrity*, W. Allen (1998); *Summer of Sam*, S. Lee (1999); *Bringing Out the Dead*, M. Scorsese (1999); *Three Kings*, D. O'Russel (1999); *Mission to Mars*, B. De Palma (2000); and many others.

Interview with Nicola Pecorini, Volterra, November 1998

What do you think about the Steadicam?
My opinion of the Steadicam has a lot to do with how I discovered it with respect to what I was doing before, which is that I had worked in 16 mm for Switzerland's Italian television for almost three years. I was part of a 'film team', which means that I had a 16 mm camera, then there was a sound man, a journalist and/or a director. We'd go around doing a little bit of everything, a soccer game or a documentary on spiders or an interview about elections in Germany, so I was used to always being frustrated with regard to camera movements, in the sense that I never got what I wanted, unless I could have done them by hand, on roller-skates. It was all a thing of trying hard but not getting very good results.

Then, while I was on vacation in America in 1981 I discovered the Steadicam. I did a course with Garrett and it was a revelation for me, because for the first time even by myself I could move the camera, I mean I could do 'camera movements'.

The Steadicam is an incredible device that lets you move the camera where and how you want, and it has another enormous advantage, which is that the same person moves the camera and

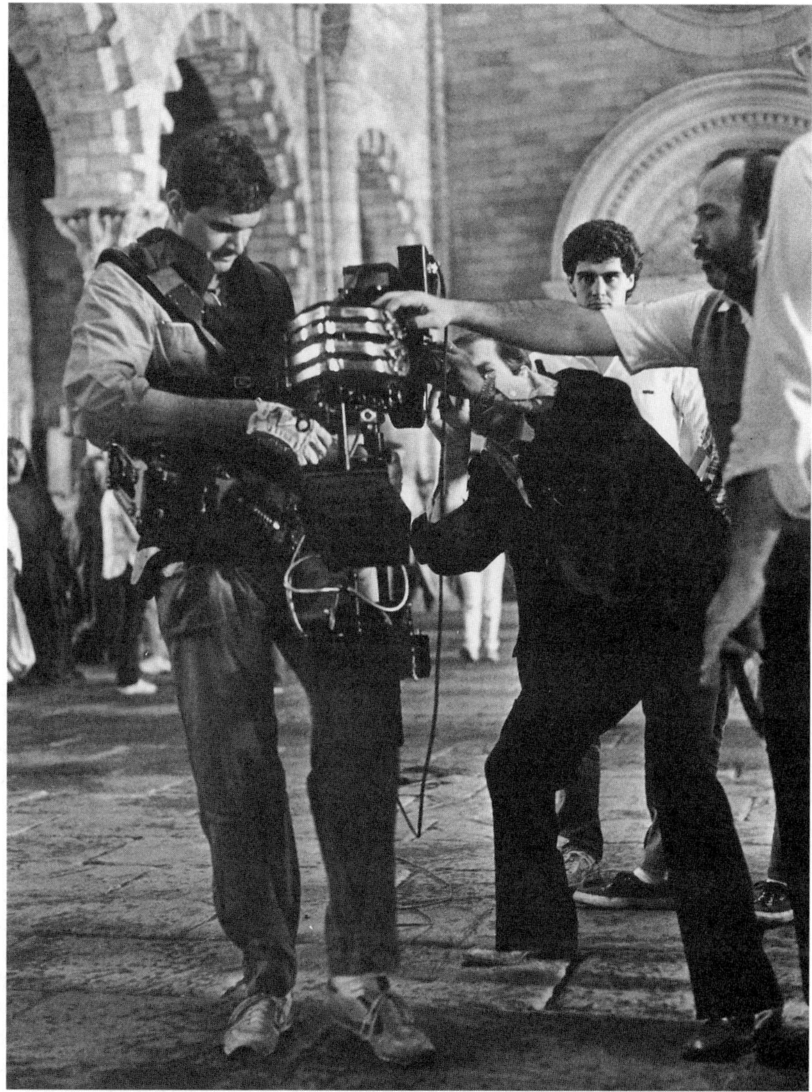

Figure 4.3 Nicola Pecorini and Vittorio Storaro on the set of *Ladyhawke*, Cinecittà, Italy, 1983. The operator is working with a Steadicam Model II, modified. Photo courtesy Nicola Pecorini collection

does the shot. I didn't realize that right away, partly because what you need for doing documentary television is so different than what I later discovered you need when you're making movies.

But above all, working more and more on movies, and more and more at a high level, I realized that one of the incredible advantages that the Steadicam offered was the fact of deciding when to start the movement, when to finish it, where to finish it, where to begin it, to adjust things if the shot's not working, to adjust to the unexpected that can happen in normal life. In my opinion, this is the most incredible thing about the Steadicam. Actually, if you look at the last 50 years, it may be the greatest innovation ever introduced in how movies are made, especially in how movies on location are made.

In 1922 there were dollies which were absolutely comparable with the dollies we have today, in other words, the 'technicality' of making movies was already extremely advanced. It was halted when the sound cameras came out, because instead of moving a thing 60-cm long, you now had to move something that weighed 2 tons and measured 2.5 m by 3.15 m, which was impossible, so technically there was a return to 40 years before. Cinema was blocked, and the Steadicam made great mobility possible again, especially if you think that the Steadicam came out in 1976, so all those things that are available today, minidolly, minigib, all those things didn't exist. You either got on a normal dolly, on a crane, or basically you didn't move the camera.

I should also say that the introduction of the Steadicam was a good thing not only with regard to the possibilities for using it – in other words, the kind of shot that it lets you do – but also technologically. For example, all these things like radiofocus or remote focus, remote control, video transmission, all this technology that was developed above all to be used with the Steadicam, is now being used in lots of other ways. Now, for example, it happens really often that the assistant doesn't get up on the dolly arm anymore to do the remote focus, which also makes things a lot simpler and quicker, and the grips don't have to work so hard. In other words, life is simpler and more complete. If there weren't the Steadicam, everyone would still be there with those wires, and all that stuff.

So for me that's what the Steadicam is, and for me the Steadicam adventure, which is over now, was a great thing, because due to various circumstances I was there at the beginning, so you feel this thing of being a 'pioneer', which is really great.

Then, well, personally I've gotten a little tired of it, partly because I always had a sort of disenchanted view of the Steadicam. I mean, it was a tool like any other. Gradually, as I found other tools for moving the camera I realized that it's like how I was at the beginning, jumping around and bothering everyone I was working with saying 'Let's do it in Steadicam, let's do it in Steadicam!', and then you could do it with the normal dolly, there wasn't a real reason for it. There's this way of thinking that the Steadicam is everything, that you can't do anything without the Steadicam, and in the end you tend to take everything to extremes and lose sight of what the film's needs are as a film in general, and to consider your contribution to the movie more important than it is.

In fact, this thing happens a lot. For example, when I went to America, I had a different approach to the Steadicam, which was 'We need to do this, okay, 10 minutes, ready', which is very rare as I found out later, because the others tend to say 'Oh, we have to construct it, it'll take two days', a rehearsal here, a rehearsal there, etc., etc. It gets too exaggerated for the customer because he says 'Okay, if the Steadicam makes things more complicated instead of simplifying them, I might as well just use traditional tools'.

I remember that at the beginning of my Steadicam adventure (I'm talking about the early 1980s when there were really only a few of us using it and I was one of the few who could make a movie from A to Z), there was a certain – not envy, but my American colleagues would call me every once in a while and say 'You know, I'd like to make a movie from A to Z, how do you do it?'. First of all, you don't drive a hard bargain, because one of the reasons that they would drive a hard bargain is very simply because if you do that you can ask to be paid more, which means that if you ask for US$2000 a day to do the Steadicam work, obviously they won't have you doing the whole movie because it's not worth it. It becomes something which has to be planned months in advance and if something unexpected happens and they have to change the shooting script one day, which happens all the time when you're making a movie, you're not available and they have to call someone else, and in the end it's frustrating because you can't even say 'I did that movie' because it's not true. You contributed slightly to the movie, but there are movies that – at the beginning they didn't even put your name on, but when they started to put the name of the Steadicam operator, there would be seven names,[10] and you'd say 'Who did that? Who did that shot? Me, no, him, I don't know!'.

I mean, it becomes a purely mercenary relationship that, in my opinion, is counterproductive for the artisan who's doing it, for the mercenary who's doing it. I don't know how you want to define it, but I've always disagreed a lot with this kind of system, with the result that I made a lot less money than they did. But I have to say that I haven't regretted it, because I think it's let me do a lot more interesting things than they have, and it's let me stay with a lot of movies from the beginning to the end, which I wouldn't have been able to do otherwise. Larry, for example, made the choice of doing only, exclusively, Steadicam, he doesn't even do B camera when he's on the set, whereas I find that I like to begin a movie, work on it, and finish it, so in the end I've found myself doing everything, A camera and, when it was needed, the Steadicam.

Do you think there's an abuse of the Steadicam, owing to its capacity for movement, and because it can make shooting times quicker?

Yes, often. It's a little bit in movies like it is everywhere but, for example, when the zoom came out it was absolutely abused, when the Tecnocrane came out, it was abused. I mean, there was a bit of masturbatory use of the tool with the Steadicam too and obviously we Steadicam operators were partly responsible for that, because at the beginning you're so enthusiastic, you think you can do incredible things and in the end you do things which don't have that much sense. I think that in the end, as I said before, it's still just a shot, by which I mean that it has to have a logic, a purpose, be useful to the story. If it has that, okay, it can be Steadicam, you can throw it off the balcony, you can do what you want, you can leave it fixed where it is. If it's only an exercise in style then in my opinion it doesn't have much sense. It's true, Kubrick used it for an exercise in style in *The Shining*, it was exactly at the level of an exercise in style, but he's Kubrick, and at any rate in the end he makes masterpieces, even if flawed. But yes, I've done a lot of stupid things, really lots of them, and just as many times I've refused to do them. There is an abuse of the tool that however at the beginning was pretty justified, because Garrett's invention was so clever, for example, the fact that you can boom up and down and you can change the height. Now with the new model it stays where you put it, first you had to hold it; it has a 90° radius. That's an incredible freedom that the Steadicam has compared with any other tool, because the speed with which you can do it is incredible.

Back at the beginning when all its possibilities were being discovered, obviously there was an awful lot of experimentation. Then, in my opinion, that went on a little too long, because in the end those are the possible variations, you can't do God knows what. It took a few years; I'd say that the Steadicam experimentation went on until 1983–1984, after which they kept on doing more or less everything but they didn't invent anything new. Until 1985 they were doing good experiments both with its use and its applications. For example, in 1987 you could rent Steadicams in Italy. Before that, it was a disaster if you broke a Steadicam, you had to beat your head against the wall. Still, I think that the period from 1981 to 1984 was the best period, and the most fun, because we were discovering a new world of our own, and we did a lot of silly things that I don't regret.

Do you think the Steadicam is capable of influencing the style of a movie, compared with a normal camera?
No, I don't think so, it's like saying, do the C major chord cadences oblige you to do a certain thing? No, with the C major chords you can do whatever you want. I mean to say, for me the Steadicam is like a saxophone instead of a violin, in the end you can play the same thing. They have a different sound, but in the end the music can be the same.

But does the Steadicam force you to use it in a certain way?
No, there are clichéd ways of using the Steadicam, it's true, but not for me. For me that's impossible, because I can use the Steadicam in fifty different ways. I mean, now, as Director of Photography, I always want it on the truck and lots of times I use it just because it makes things easier. For example, I have to be free to move with the dolly but the pavement isn't one of the best. I mount the Steadicam arm on the dolly and I can go without any problems. I can shoot everything I want, even if there's a dislevel, I skip it, if there's a wire I skip it, nothing's a problem. That's not a Steadicam use, do you see what I mean? But I also know that if I mount the Steadicam on the dolly, if it doesn't go to the mark, or if the operator doesn't push the dolly to the mark, hop! I've gone to the mark, hop! I've bent down a little bit more or a little bit less. It gives me that option, too. Still, I find that for example, since I don't like to operate the camera if I'm doing the photography because they are two different jobs that pile up, and if I'm not the one doing it, or someone that I trust absolutely, I'd rather not do it. I find that the Steadicam, despite everything, still has that big handicap, which at times is an advantage, which is that you have to have a handle on it. It's useless to ask for a guitar solo if you don't have a guitar player.

And what about television use/abuse of the Steadicam?
Well, I have to say that I enjoyed doing things for television, since I happened to be there at the right time, and I got a lot of satisfaction from the viewpoint of curiosity about applications. In

Italy I worked on a New Year's show on Channel 5,[11] in 1982, with Raimondo Vianello and Sandra Mondaini. Davide Rampello was the Director and there, too, we did some very interesting things in Steadicam, especially because they were new things, strange things. However, because they worked there, they became clichés, like 'we can go around the singer with the microphone'. It's okay if you do it once, but when you've done it four times, it's already boring. The intelligence of the user, in my opinion, isn't the cliché. I mean, someone who lives off clichés will find clichés in any thing he does; it's not the Steadicam, it's not the tool.

So it doesn't condition you in the sense of choosing the shot, but what's important is how you use it?
Exactly. Every once in a while it can be the only choice. For example, it's happened to me to run over suspension bridges made of ropes,[12] and that was the only way to get the shot.

What was the first time you used the Steadicam in an important way?
The first time I used it was in *Ladyhawke*[13] with Vittorio Storaro, in the fall of 1983. If I'm not wrong, Garrett got me that job, actually, because Vittorio had called Garrett with whom he had made *One from the Heart* the year before, which was all in Steadicam. Garrett couldn't do it, and he gave Vittorio my name.

It's a movie in which you don't notice the Steadicam.
No, I don't want the Steadicam to be noticed.

What do you think about how the Steadicam is used in America, Italy, or Europe in general?
No, it depends on the person, I don't think you can generalize, and anyway usually it's a question of budget, in my opinion.

Is its use more widespread in America?
No, not necessarily more widespread. I wouldn't know what percentage of productions or how many productions use it, but I think it's about the same. The fact is that in America, as I was saying, partly because of the politics of these 'semi-fanatics', the Steadicam costs a lot, so it gets used on a day-to-day basis. In Europe, where even if you use the Steadicam you get paid peanuts, as far as I can see there's a more generalized use of the B camera/Steadicam than in America. Even if it's true that in America it's easy to find a B camera operator who also does Steadicam, or an A camera operator who does Steadicam.

Is there a difference, I mean at the visual level, in how you can control the camera and the shot because you're looking at a monitor?
I've realized that having got so used to the Steadicam, I find it easier to work with other devices as well, like hot heads, in which you have to look at a monitor instead of through a camera eyepiece.

You can control everything.
It's easier, you do fewer stupid things, you make fewer mistakes.

It's a different way of looking.
Absolutely. For me the really big handicap with the Steadicam,

which is still there, and I got a little bit upset with Garrett because he listens to those 'fanatics' who are sort of like those bicycle riders who have a bicycle that weighs 1.237 kg, but then they wear a watch that weighs 340 g. If you take all the weight away, then why do you wear a Rolex? I mean, it's not logical. And lots and lots of these Americans are like this, I mean, the thing made of titanium, or of magnesium – and I kept saying, 'Garrett, when you make the new model, the master, I want a PC-type screen, as big as this, that's the only thing I'm asking you for, I want to see the detail', because I can't keep having to guess what's there, who was there, in view, not in view. You can't tell, because it's too small.

But if it's too big it's awkward?
But just something as big as this! A mattebox or a sunshade is like this! I mean, if it's down there, parallel with the sunshade, if the sunshade can go, so can it. Then if one day you need to have it really narrow, you put on the little monitor, but generally speaking I want the big monitor. That's always been a big handicap with the Steadicam, because you can't see the details and you don't know how many times you have to be someplace and then the door opens – what do I know about what happened, and who can tell? It was in frame but I really can't see whether it opened or not.

And tiring situations, in the sense of resistance?
Not a problem.

Shooting when it's hot or cold?
The cold is dangerous, mostly because you get sick – even if it's cold you sweat when you've got the camera on, then you take it off and the sweat becomes icy.

If you have to do a sequence over and over, do you have the same control that you have with other cameras?
It depends on the shot.

On how tiring it is?
Well, if it's physically hard and takes a long time, then yes, of course, you undoubtedly become less clear-minded.

In this sense, how does the Steadicam compare with other cameras?
You know, in my experience, which has basically been above all with good actors, the first takes are good. The problem is that a great many Steadicam operators flub the first takes, then they start to get tired and they can't get them right anymore. At any rate, believe me, it's hard work! Once, when I was filming the 1987 World Championships of Athletics, I made the official movie for CONI.[14] After shooting they tested us with the Steadicam on to see our anaerobic response, things like recovery times after physical effort. They told me that it's like being a 100 m sprinter, in the sense that you can do it over and over but in the space of a day it becomes a big effort.

How do you prefer to use the Steadicam, do you like using it for a long take uncut, or do you prefer short pan shots?
It depends. It's nice to do long takes every so often, but as I said before they have to have a reason for being there. If they don't, I

couldn't care less about them. I remember once some French people asked me to do a long take that made no sense at all, and in the end it couldn't be done. Why should you do it if there's no sense to it?

Do you prefer to work over and over with the same director or director of photography?
No. I mean, there are people you like to work with more and that you get along with, but something for which I've always been grateful to the Steadicam is that having found myself in a situation in which for a certain number of years I was either the only Steadicam operator, or the only one who could be trusted, or one of the few who could be trusted in Italy and in Europe in general, I ended up working with tons of people – something that would have been impossible otherwise in the 'normal' professional scene in Italy, because in Italy there's a very 'mafia'-type system for awarding jobs. There's an unspoken rule which exists in photography and also for grips, electricians, make-up artists, everyone who works in movies, that if you're not someone's relative you don't work in movies. No one in my family worked in movies, so the only way I had to get work was the Steadicam. Not only that, but especially in the area of photography, the blackmailing power that sometimes even the directors of photography have is so big that if you don't join their retinue ('court') from the lowest possible rung of the ladder and move up rung by rung, then usually you don't move up those rungs at all. Luckily I avoided all those rungs because I was always in touch with everyone and worked with everyone. Practically the only one I've never worked with is Luciano Tovoli, but I've worked with everyone else. That way you learn, you learn a lot more, even from the ones who don't know what they're doing – actually, maybe you learn more from the ones who don't know what they're doing than from the ones who do. So the question isn't if there are, or have been, people – directors and directors of photography – that I got along with better than others and that it was a pleasure to work with again. There are others with whom I kept working and I didn't really know why I kept working with those assholes, but you know, that's work, too – after all, you don't have to marry them.

The Steadicam is so versatile, you can do so many things with it, that the person asking you to do something must trust you a lot and understand what you're doing.
Yes, but I think it's a lot at the level of helping, making a film better or worse. The kind of involvement, understanding, communication that you can establish with a director of photography as a Steadicam operator can be just as important as the kind of understanding, involvement or whatever that the grip has with him, or that an actor has with him. I mean, when that alchemy snaps into place it's very important, but it's not specifically something having to do with being a Steadicam operator. It's very important in every field and with all professional people: if it doesn't happen, it doesn't happen, and it's a problem. I've always been firmly convinced of something, and I've never changed my mind about it: you can have the greatest screenplay in the world, the greatest cast and troupe in the world, on paper, but if there isn't harmony on the

set you'll get a shitty movie. If, on the other hand, you have a screenplay that's not all that great, but there's harmony, it could even become a good movie, because something happens that in the end you can feel, you can see. There's something extra, there's the fun, the research, the curiosity, something that develops mentally. Yes, that's what it is, I think.

However, first you asked me about fatigue. I always thought of the Steadicam as mental exercise more than physical exercise, so like with all mental exercise, yes, it's tiring, but when you solve your mental crossword puzzle, your ideas, your mental journey, at the end you don't even feel the fatigue anymore, because you got where you wanted to go. Yes, physically there were times when you worked really hard, like going up and down stairs. I remember once I did a film for television with Salvatore Nocita and Annie Girardot, and there was a scene in which she got up and went running after her son. There were something like four flights of stairs to do on foot. We did about fourteen takes, more or less, that's like fifty-two stories, running. That evening I remember my legs hurt, but the next day it was just like having been skiing and the snow was icy and your legs hurt.

Now that you're a director of photography, do you find that there are particular technical difficulties in doing the lighting for a Steadicam sequence?
Well, the Steadicam is more problematical, and Peppino if he was honest will have told you about that very well. That's the reason he doesn't like the Steadicam. It's more problematical where you move around more, because then you see more, and you never know where to hide the lights. Basically, though, the problems are the same. In this sense as well it's not different from other devices.

It can be controlled?
Yes, as I said. If you do a long tracking with a normal dolly you're sure to have the same problems.
The thing is that one of the advantages of the Steadicam is that you can move in curved lines, which you can't do with other devices. It becomes one of the disadvantages, as well, since you use more of the set so you have to prepare more of the set. For me it's easy, because I grew up with the Steadicam, and having already had to deal with so many of those problems I know what they are and what I have to do.

It's not that I choose not to use the Steadicam because it makes problems for me, if it's useful I use it, and if not I don't.

What do you think about the fact that there are people who become Steadicam operators without having had any training as camera operators?
Too many.

In other words, the fact that they don't have the sense of the shot that you get from having been a camera operator?
Yes, and then in my opinion the real disadvantage, more than that, because after all you can have that sense naturally and you'll be okay, is that it comes from an idea of the job of Steadicam operator that I think is wrong, where they take it as a shortcut, where they're lacking the basic information that is fundamental for becoming an

operator. Also, they have this idea, I call it the 'gymnastics vision of the Steadicam'. Meaning, being able to jump from a wall 1.2 m high instead of 1.05 m, which yes, can be useful, but it doesn't change absolutely anything, because you can make the wall whatever height it needs to be so you can jump down from it. That's not the point. I mean, the grips are there on purpose for that. It's really a bad thing.

But it's something that's becoming more widespread?
Yes, too much.

What about coming from television, where there's another kind of experience?
Yes, but that's still okay. When I ran the Steadicam courses here in Italy, sometimes we'd take these people without experience to fill the courses and pay our expenses, but not very often, because usually we had too many applicants for the places we had, and we tried to avoid them all together. On the admittance form we asked how many years of experience people had, and we gave precedence to people with more years of experience, of course, because I've always seen it as a specialization, not as something unto itself, so I need you to be a camera operator, and if you're not a camera operator I don't want you.

Is there a time you used the Steadicam that you particularly remember?
Bertolucci has used it a lot. He was very opposed to it at the beginning, but then he had to use it in *The Last Emperor*. The first time he used it was in that movie. The entire sequence of the boy at the coronation was done with the Steadicam for two basic reasons. One was that the Chinese don't take anything 'into that room' so we couldn't take any other equipment in, and the other is that you never knew what the little boy was going to do. In the scene when he's looking for the cricket, he was five years old, and for him it was really just a game to look for the cricket, and every time it came out differently. You couldn't lay down tracks, it would have taken too long, so that's why the Steadicam was used.

What's changed now that you're director of photography?
Well, I liked being a cameraman a lot, because every time I worked I learned something. Then you get to a certain level where you don't do anything that exciting anymore, you don't learn all that much anymore. You find yourself solving other people's problems. Excuse me, but at that point I'll be better off making my own problems.

Nicola Pecorini, Director of Photography and Steadicam operator

From 1978 to 1980 Nicola Pecorini worked for Swiss Television. He became a Steadicam operator in 1980. With Garrett Brown, he founded the SOA in 1988 and organized and taught at Steadicam Workshops in Italy and the USA.

He worked as camera operator and Steadicam operator on many important Italian and American movies, such as Bernardo Bertolucci's *The Last Emperor* and Oliver Stone's *The Doors*. In recent years he has been Director of Photography on a number of films, including *Fear and Loathing in Las Vegas* and *Rhinoceros Hunting in Budapest.*

Films

Pecorini's films include: *Fear and Loathing in Las Vegas*, T. Gilliam (1998); *The Brave*, J. Depp (1997); *Rhinoceros Hunting in Budapest*, M. Haussmann (1996); *American President*, R. Reiner (1995); *Little Buddha*, B. Bertolucci (1993); *Cliffhanger*, R. Harlin (1992); *Bitter Moon*, R. Polanski (1992); *The Sheltering Sky*, B. Bertolucci (1990), *The Doors*, O. Stone (1990); *The Last Emperor*, B. Bertolucci, (1987); *Rent a Cop*, J. London (1987); *Isthar*, E. May (1986); *Ladyhawke*, R. Donner (1984); *Aerosmith 'A hole in my soul'* (videoclip) A. Morahin (1987); *Springsteen 'Born in the USA Tour'* (live music) A. Rosato (1985); *Simon and Garfunkel Reunion Tour* (live music) R. Cohen (1983). Also, more than sixty other feature films plus TV movies, TV shows, live music, music videos, commercials, industrials, reportages, documentaries, news.

Interview with Haskell Wexler (by telephone), March 1999

What do you think about the visual potential of the Steadicam?

The visual potential of the Steadicam is almost continuously to be

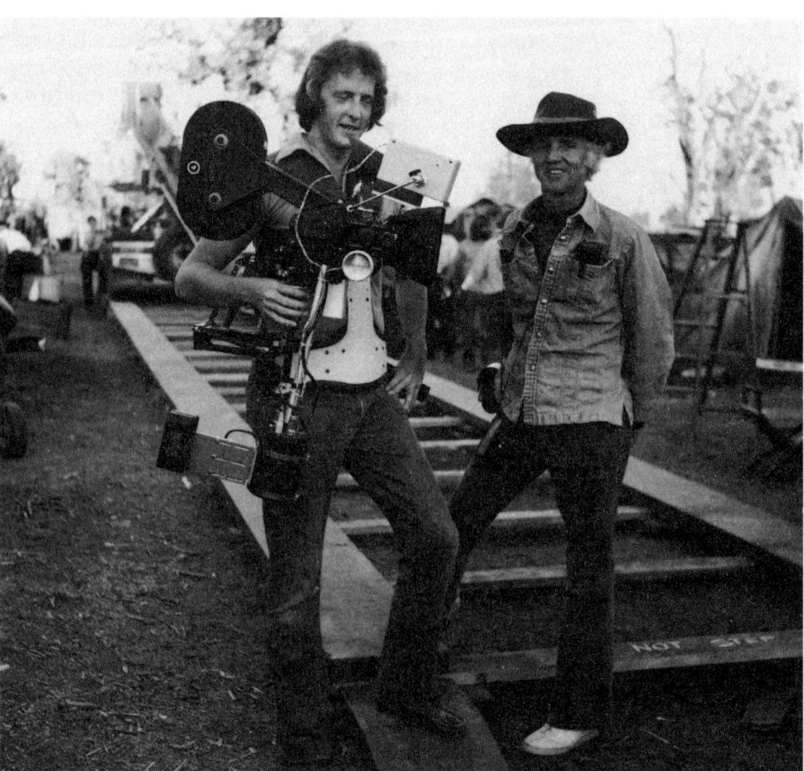

Figure 4.4 Garrett Brown with DP Haskell Wexler (first to use Steadicam) on the set of *Bound for Glory* in 1975. Garrett holds Cinema Products' first 'sled' prototype. Photo courtesy Garrett Brown collection

discovered because potential means, at least in English, possibilities and the possibilities are only restrained by the ability of the Steadicam operator.

In your opinion, what is the Steadicam best used for?
The Steadicam is a tool to move the camera, we have many tools to move the camera, many complex and useful tools to move the camera, now even more than when the Steadicam was invented, though the Steadicam is best used in situations where other ways to move the camera are not practical or possible.

When did you first see the Steadicam used?
I am a friend of Garrett Brown; when he was inventing the Steadicam I saw him. There was a 'Keds' tennis shoes commercial where the shot involved moving fast over the ground following rock-and-roll kids in tennis shoes running at an airport. Garrett used his first Steadicam in that commercial.

What type of situation in a movie would make you choose the Steadicam?
When do you decide to use it during a film?
For example, if you have a camera-car shot and the road is very rough, it's possible to mount a Steadicam on the camera-car and you erase or minimize the roughness of the road. Now of course there are other tools that also do that. There are gyroscopic helicopter mounts which also fit on the camera-car that can do it, but the Steadicam is easier and simpler and faster for that situation. And now Steadicam is also used very often in what we call a combination shot, that's a shot where the camera begins on some other camera-moving device which extends the up and down range of the camera, because the Steadicam has a limited range from low to high and high to low. By combining it with a crane or some other device, you are able to get spectacular shots.

What kind of a relationship do you have with the Steadicam operator?
Basically your relationship to the Steadicam operator should be the same as you have with the operator when a camera is on a dolly. Usually I lay out the shot with a special finder, I put the lens up near the Steadicam, and the finder has a colour radio transmitter that, in a rehearsal, shows on a video monitor what I would like the camera to do. Usually we take that rehearsal Steadicam shot without using the Steadicam because the operator has a long complicated job, there's a physical drain on him. Then the operator watches the monitor and sees what happened, makes some alterations, sometimes for practical reasons, verifies it in rehearsal with the assistant controlling the focus by radio and then they go ahead.

Have you tried using the Steadicam yourself?
Yes, I tried many times.

You've put it on?
Yes, I've got to mention that when I spoke of the Steadicam previously in this series of questions, many of the times the Steadicam is not on the body. Of course in the combination shots the Steadicam would be on the body. But dollies and cranes extend

the range of the Steadicam and it's possible to hard mount the Steadicam, as in the example I gave earlier of the Steadicam on a camera-car on a rough road – the Steadicam would not be on the body mount, it would be hard mounted on a camera-car.

How do you plan the lighting for Steadicam shots?
It's the same. Very often Steadicam shots are regular shooting so you plan the shot as you would normally plan it. The Steadicam is another way to move the camera.

Does the fact that you can move around with the Steadicam and focus in a lot of directions make it different from using a crane or other things?
No, you have to understand that when you lay out the shot with the Steadicam you can actually use the Steadicam itself and you can stand right there with the Steadicam operator during the rehearsal, look through the monitor, record it, so there aren't any questions about it. The only thing that I usually do in the lighting for Steadicam shots is to be doubly careful that no light hits the lens, because it's not possible for the grips to easily see the Steadicam throughout the shot. The contemporary dollies and cranes can move and do move in any direction, there's the Technocrane for example, there's a telescoping crane and the overhead crane when the track is overhead, and they do pretty much what a Steadicam will do, only it too often takes more trouble to do it. I make pictures and things like that where the camera is very big and heavy, and also, most camera operators, including myself, prefer to do shots where you can literally look through the camera because we can easily see and quickly focus on things. The Steadicam was made possible by separating the eye from the camera, when the eye has to be on the camera but the nature of a person walking or moving, the body movement, gets transmitted to the camera. What really primed the camera for these crane shots I'm talking about is the Steadicam, the ability you have to transmit the camera image remotely, and that's a key philosophy that came along with the video assist.

How do you feel about shooting with a hand-held camera?
Well, being hand-held is another way to move the camera so, when it's appropriate, it's good. Often in a documentary-type situation where there's more chaos than is normal on a feature film, hand-holding can give a different image, a different feeling, than the Steadicam. The Steadicam's virtue can also be detrimental: if someone wants to transmit a certain idea of emergency or unsmoothness, roughness.

What do you think about the use of the Steadicam in documentaries?
In some documentaries, yes. For example, in video and so forth, absolutely. When you shoot rock events where the operator has to be perhaps on the stage or move around the band and not get the audience in the frame, and for an intimate picture. Also for certain documentaries that are in plain video, when you want minimum equipment, the Steadicam can be useful.

What do you think about point of view shots and the fact that now they are often shot with the Steadicam?
Well, point of view means the camera has to represent the point of view. That means if you have a person who is sitting in a wheelchair and going down a hallway and you want that person's point of view, the movement of the camera, the height of the camera would be usually the eye-height of the person. If they are going through a crowd of people and are looking for another person, then the point of view would be more like the head, and the eyes will move left, right, up, down and so forth, whatever the meaning of the scene is. So it becomes a question not so much of what device you use as what mood you want to give as a point of view of the character in the film.

Is it possible to foresee the effect that the use of the Steadicam will have on a particular shot or is it too 'free' for you to imagine the result beforehand?
Well there's a video transmitter on the Steadicam, so any judgement you want to make you can make by looking at video in rehearsal, of course, and you try to foresee the effects of this shot, like any shot. Again, I go back to my original statement, it is a special tool to move the camera, and everything else is not done by a magic wand.

Yes, but when you make a hand-held camera shot you usually do it by yourself because it's especially difficult to explain to somebody else what you want with the hand-held camera, and I think maybe it's the same with the Steadicam?
It is quite the same, also, even if somebody can do what you want it's not so easy to foresee what you want on the screen. I'll give you an example. We have a scene of a woman who comes in a door and she walks by a man and she sits down in a chair for a moment, then she gets up from the chair and walks down a little hallway and enters the bathroom. Okay. I am the director of photography. I have the video finder, I have also the Steadicam, but I have the video finder in which I have the various lenses that are going to be used for filming. I stand outside the door and she comes toward me. I back up, I pan, tilt, then I keep on as she goes from the chair, walks down the hall and goes in the bathroom. Okay, what I just did is a colour video picture. I stand with the operator and we talk and he says 'Look, maybe I should start outside the first door and not bring her in'. Then I say 'Well, that would cut with the previous thing' or maybe I'll say 'It's a good idea'. So then we would do the shoot, we'd do what we saw on the monitor. In other words, if you are making a documentary or you are making something where you are not in control of what is in front of the camera, then of course you are obliged to rely on the general intelligence, the filmmaking intelligence of the operator.

How do you feel about technological research in filmmaking and the innovations it has made available? Do you think that technologically advanced products tend to increase or decrease creativity in filmmaking?
I'll say categorically that technology neither increases nor decreases creativity in filmmaking. Creativity does not spring from technology,

technology can free a certain creativity, but it's not *ipso facto* something to do seriously with creativity.

Do you think that the use of the Steadicam has meant the creation of a recognizable style, with negative effects?
No, I think in general if you recognize a shot as a Steadicam shot it's not a good shot. In other words, to answer your question, I do not if it's used properly. Now if it's floppy, of course, it would have a negative effect so that again, it's what image you want to project on the screen.

Have you found that sometimes the Steadicam is used for convenience and not for artistic reasons or because it's needed to achieve the desired effects?
I think you mean that sometimes people get sloppy and they say okay, let's just chase somebody, chase them all around, go here, go there, just get it done. Convenience usually means for budget reasons or for time reasons and not for the best reasons for the film. I assume that's what would be meant by convenience. Well, when you make a film, any kind of film, everything is supposed to be done to direct the person's eye, their interest, to the proper aspect of the drama. That's the duty of the director of photography: it's to make the eyes go where I want them to go. And so when you're making a movie it's not like you're following a football game and say 'Just go bring the camera on and be creative'; or like giving a person a palette and brushes and saying 'You're a painter'. That's not art, and that's not good movie making. So in answer to the question, I'll just say yes.

Could you can tell me something about the film *Bound for Glory* as the first use of the Steadicam?
At that time, I'd done the commercial with Garrett and in *Bound for Glory* I wanted the shot that shows the whole camp and then to go down in the camp and see the people, see their faces, hear them talking; and when we saw it (at that time we did not have video transmission so nobody except Garrett saw the film until it was on the screen) it was so exciting, the fact that a camera could move like that. Everybody in the screening room watching the dailies just gasped and they gasped for a few years afterwards. Now it's almost like a cliché, a cliché camera movement, because it's very common. It's a special tool with many, many possibilities but it is not a sacred tool – it's a marvellous artistic device to have in your equipment, but it's a tool.

When you do a very long shot, that runs maybe 5 minutes, where the Steadicam goes down corridors and stairs and through an open door and so on, are there particular difficulties or is it about the same as using a crane or something else?
No. The particular shot you're talking about would be just like one that actually Garrett and I did in Las Vegas, up and down, different floors, stairways. Basically what you have to do is go with the Steadicam operator and the actors and play it out, and then you have to have some respect for the Steadicam operator's body so that you don't have him wear the suit and the camera for take after take. Also it's important for him to see any obstacles that might trip

him up. He assumes that usually they are there and faces to the side so he sees to focus, but he has to know where his feet are going all the time. So really in a shot like that, it mostly takes the skill and practice of the operator. The device itself, if properly balanced, will work fine. In general, what you should know is that most directors of photography will prefer to do shots where you can look through the camera.

Yes, and not with the distance.
Yes. We like to look through the camera, but when we have a shot where you need to use the video then the Steadicam is one of the most useful tools to move the camera. It's as simple as that.

Haskell Wexler, Director of Photography, Director, Producer.

After many years making educational and industrial films, Haskell Wexler moved into feature films in 1959, when he was the cameraman for the famous semi-documentary film *The Savage Eye*. He became increasingly appreciated for his camerawork, winning an Academy Award for the black-and-white cinematography of *Who's Afraid of Virginia Woolf?* in 1966.

In 1965, he co-produced and photographed *The Loved One*. In the same year he produced, directed, wrote and photographed *The Bus*, a documentary about a group of civil rights protesters travelling from San Francisco to Washington. In 1969 he made *Medium Cool*, which was set at the 1968 Democratic convention and dealt with the problem of violence in modern-day America. This movie, which received much critical acclaim, was directed, written, photographed and co-produced by Wexler.

Later, he collaborated in directing several political documentaries, while continuing to work on major feature productions as a cinematographer. In more recent years he has worked on many period and social consciousness films, including *Matewan* (1987).

He won an Oscar for the cinematography of *Bound for Glory*. Two of his many documentaries won Best Documentary Oscars, *The Living City* (1953) and *Interviews with my Last Veterans* (1970).

Films

Among his films (as cinematographer and director) are: *The Savage Eye*, B. Maddow, (1959); *Who's Afraid of Virginia Woolf?*, M. Nichols (1966); *The Thomas Crown Affair*, N. Jewison (1968); *Medium Cool*, H. Wexler (1969); *One Flew Over the Cuckoo's Nest*, M. Forman (1975); *Bound for Glory*, H. Ashby (1976); *The Man Who Loved the Woman*, B. Edwards (1983); *Latino*, H. Wexler (1985); *Matewan*, J. Sayles (1987); *Colors*, D. Hopper (1988); *Three Fugitives*, F. Veber (1989); *Blaze*, R. Shelton (1989); *The Babe,* A. Hiller (1992); *The Rich Man's Wife*, A. Holden Jones (1996); *Bus Rider's Union*, H. Wexler (1999); *Limbo*, J. Sayles (1999); and many others.

His non-fiction films include *An Interview with President Allende* (1971); *The CIA Case Officer* (1978); *Target Nicaragua: Inside a Secret War* (1983).

Interview with Ed DiGiulio, Los Angeles, March 1999

I started Cinema Products in 1968, 30 years ago or so. I sold the company 10 years ago to a group of high-level industry-type people, but I continue in my role as the creative engineering force to develop new products and bring us into other areas.

Garrett came to me in 1974. He had originally gone to Panavision, because it was a very well-established company at that time and my company had only been in existence for 4 or 5 years. But the founder and President of Panavision, Bob Gottschalk, was a very paranoid individual, and he suffered from what we call the NIH factor. NIH stands for 'not invented here'. Bob Gottschalk was a firm believer that if something was not invented inside Panavision it was not good. And Garrett Brown, before he revealed his idea to anybody, understandably had them sign a non-disclosure agreement form, but Gottschalk didn't want to do it.

At the same time, Garrett was slowly running out of money because he had invested a lot in developing his prototype, and someone suggested that he gave me a call, which he did. He asked me if I would be interested and I said 'Yeah'. He asked if I would sign a confidential disclosure agreement. I said 'I have no problem with that' because we are not thinking of doing anything in this area. So he came out, and he showed me the film first – I didn't have to sign a non-disclosure to see the film – and when I saw what I saw on the film I said 'Great! let me sign!'.

Then he opened up his sack and he had this pile of junk: I mean it was what you would expect from an inventor – to put things

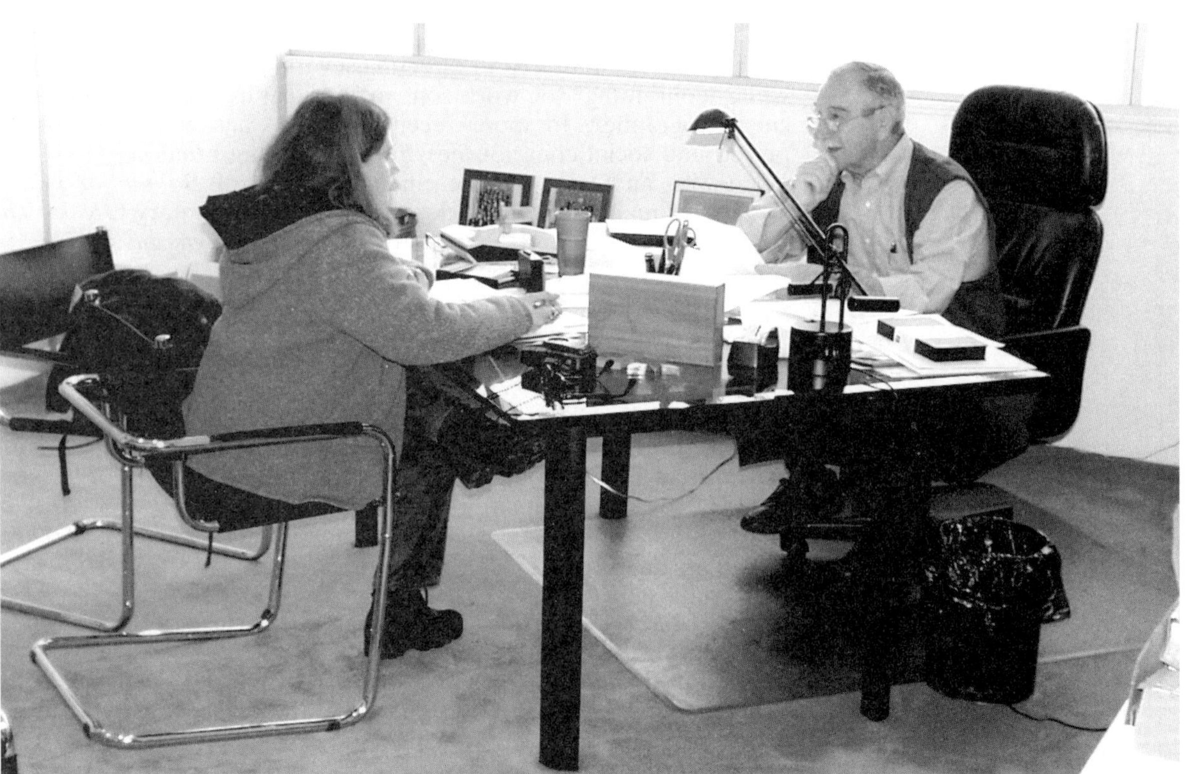

Figure 4.5 Ed DiGiulio with the author during the interview at Cinema Products, Los Angeles, March 1999. Photo author's own, taken by Francesco Ferrara

together as expeditiously as possible. So at that point we made an agreement. That was in 1974 and from that point it took a year and a half and about three-quarters of a million dollars. It took a lot of work – we had to develop the video, the monitor and the arm. My brother designed the final arm and shares credit as co-inventor with Garrett.

When we signed the agreement, we said that we would mutually agree on the name for the product. Garrett's idea was the Brown stabilizer and I came up with the name Steadicam. Well, Garrett said to me 'Ed that is a stupid, hokey name'. I said to Garrett 'You know, you are absolutely right, Garrett, it is a corny, hokey name, but the beautiful thing about it is that it says what it is, totally unambiguously. So he is a great person and he agreed, you know, extra commissions (laughter), some special contracts or something, but he finally agreed and now as he looks back he says I did right, because it's a good name. That's one of the amusing early things that we did.

What is your opinion of the Steadicam?
Well, I have observed that it has provided the industry with a totally new means of artistic or creative expression. It was totally impossible to do before Steadicam and, in fact just the other night at the Academy Awards, there were two Steadicam operators with their cameras and in the old days you wouldn't have had that. I know because I've been going to these things long enough – 10 years ago you would have had the big studio camera on a Vinton dolly with two guys pushing cable. They were moving around the stage, here you have two guys going up and down the stairs, going around and behind the stage, and the director was cutting and switching cameras. You never saw the Steadicam, but these two operators replaced all of the dolly movement, and even a lot of times they would just be standing with their static Steadicams acting like tripods, and good ones.

So that's what I think it is then for the industry, and I just described to you how I first got involved, and it was lucky for me that Mr Gottschalk at Panavision was paranoid.

Can you tell us about working with Garrett Brown on improvements to the Steadicam over the years?
Well, I've worked closely with Garrett over the years and he continues to be what he always was from the beginning, a very creative and talented individual. We also benefited from the fact that Garrett went on to become the premier operator of the Steadicam, and really the best way to improve a product like that is to work with it yourself and then you know what shot is coming out. Garrett, for example, came back in the early 1980s and we produced the Model III. The Steadicam Model III was based totally on Garrett's ideas.

What were the major changes in the evolution of the Steadicam?
We started out with the mistaken notion that the camera should be an integral part of the Steadicam. The first units that we made had a camera built in, so it was a dedicated system. We realized very quickly, within the year, that what we really needed was a model that would handle any camera, so that's why we came out with the

first unit, the Universal Model One, which was just a platform. The sled was a platform on which you put any camera and, in the Model One, the monitor was part of the base. Then we realized that was not a good idea because it wasn't always conveniently visible, so we came out with the model Universal Two, where the monitor was able to move up and articulate on the centre post. And then, the next major change, as I mentioned before, was the Mark Three, which enjoyed 10 or 12 years of good life as a product, and that took us to the 1980s. Of course the major change now is the Master series, which came out in the early 1990s, and we've had great success with that. Hopefully we're going to improve upon that with some new ideas that Garrett has contributed.

How do you feel about shooting with the hand-held camera?
Serena, you have to do one thing for me, look at that aluminium roof and turn your head like that, does it move?

No, it stays still.
It stays still – your brain and your eyes adjust, right? So right after World War II, the French came out with 'Cinema Verité', where they use the hand-held camera, and everything they shot looks like that movie with Ray Milland – *Lost Weekend*, the 'drunk' film. Everybody looks like they're drunk, and what happens is that when you and I go to the movies we don't want to know that we are looking at a movie. We want to be drawn in, into the proscenium, into that frame and be part of the movie. If the filmmaker does anything that destroys this illusion, I mean, at the outset to destroy the illusion, then I say 'I'm watching a film'. So that French 'new wave' film, as it was called, came and went very quickly, because I think people finally realized that from a perceptual standpoint it was the wrong thing to do. Shooting pure hand-held for cinematographic purposes is absolutely wrong and stupid and should never be done, and you still see it in movies on occasion and it's wrong. It's absolutely wrong. If you're doing a newsreel from Bosnia, and I'm watching television, I know I'm watching television, I'm watching war footage. No problem. But for a movie, no, because you are destroying the illusion.

Do you think that the use of the Steadicam has tended to determine a particular style of film making?
Well, yes, of course. As I said, it has given an all-new language to filmmaking and there are any number of films in which you can see that.

How do you feel about using (and possibly abusing) the Steadicam for making long shots?
Oh yes, long shooting, that became a context with Larry McConkey. It's the same thing we had when the zoom lenses first came out and they were used and abused, I think the zoom much more so than the Steadicam. Then, little by little, they realized that you shouldn't abuse it, like when we see a garden rose zooming in and out. So yes, I think doing something extra long just for the sake of doing it is foolish and not necessary.

What do you think about the Panaglide?
I don't know what Garrett told you, but it was a funny story about Bob Gottschalk. As I said, he was a paranoid President. When I

started, our companies were, in fact, within two blocks of each other, so Gottschalk of course was very annoyed any time we were developing something that would compete with him, because Panavision then, like now, didn't sell anything – everything they design and manufacture is for rent only. And our company was just the opposite. We don't rent anything, everything we make we sell, and who do we sell it to? We sell it competitively to the other rental companies, and that was really annoying for him. So there was this rivalry always.

When we came out with the Steadicam, he went to the trouble of getting our patent. In Japan they published the patent before the real shoot, so he was able to see exactly what we were creating. Then he went and made the Panaglide to compete with us, but he used a different material and design for the arm; instead of using springs he used these gas cylinders and the problem with the gas cylinder is that it had friction. If an operator with the Panaglide jumps up and down you can see the camera doing this. Also, they didn't have our special monitor. They used just a black-and-white monitor and so that wasn't good either. What happened was that as soon as our patent was issued in 1976, we brought suit against Panavision and the lawyers for Panavision told Mr Gottschalk it was better to sell it. So we talked about it and negotiated the settlement. Then they paid us royalties – we collected, oh, I don't know, a couple of hundred thousand dollars from Panavision. Then Mr Gottschalk died and the man that came in to take his place was the chief technologist at the Warner Corporation (at that time Warner Brothers). He ran the company for the next couple of years and he invited Garrett to come in and he wound up getting arms and vests from us. So the Panaglide came to disappear.

Was it difficult to create interest in the Steadicam and encourage operators and filmmakers to use this new tool?

Absolutely. In the beginning it was extremely hard to get people to appreciate this tool and of course it was thanks to Garrett and films like *Rocky* that people really started becoming interested, but the problem was training operators. You had to have a trained person and, back in the beginning, it was not that easy to convince somebody that this would be a good thing to do, so it was long and difficult. We didn't think of doing the workshops right away but when we realized that this was the key, the way to get trained operators, that's when we started the workshops and that was the final step in getting it over the top.

How do you feel about people starting out directly as Steadicam operators without having any experience as camera operators?

That's an interesting question, because I think in the beginning we were primarily dealing with people who had not had prior operating experience and, as a consequence, some of them were not successful. Now we are getting more and more camera operators coming to learn about the Steadicam and that's a much better situation, because they already know about composition and framing. It's always preferable to have the background.

In your opinion, does the fact that the operator sees the shot in a monitor instead of through a viewfinder make a difference?
If you weren't getting a good quality image, if the videotape wasn't really sharp and clear, it would be a problem. That's why we made it a point with our special monitor to have it be a high resolution monitor – it's like 670 lines resolution – and I think for composing under certain situations that the operator will be able do that better looking at the monitor than with his eye on the viewfinder.

Yes, but also when you have the camera near your eye you see with one eye and look around with the other and instead, here there's a certain distance – so the way you move and look around is different, and perhaps how you think about framing is different.
Yes, but I think that's a more convenient way to go. Back in the beginning, when we spent these three-quarters of a million dollars, we went through every kind of thing. We had fibre optics, that was Garrett's idea, then we tried to put a little video on a helmet, then we all agreed on putting it down there where the guy can see with both eyes free. That's why we kept it down, because that way he is looking at the monitor and looking at the floor, so he can protect himself from tripping and falling.

Have you ever thought about changing something in the Steadicam?
We always think about changes and we are constantly coming up with new ideas.

How do you feel about technological research in filmmaking and the innovations it brings? For example, the fact that the use of computers in post-production makes it less of a challenge to shoot a scene perfectly and relieves the operator of some of his responsibilities in this sense?
Well, I don't think the computers relieve them.

I mean if you do something not very good, you can improve it, but it's artificial.
Yes, you can correct the takes, no questions about it. I think that's put the wrong emphasis on what technology brings to filmmaking: the real emphasis should on be the kinds of films that you can make now that were totally impossible before – *Titanic*, for example. When I first heard that he was going to do *Titanic* it sounded like a stupid idea – a remake. We had seen the film of the *Titanic* and I never dreamed of the incredible artistry that he would bring to it by virtue of the fact that he could use all these computer-generated images and I think that's where the impact of the technology is really felt. The fact that they can use it in a film for illustration is a good thing. Not film restoration, but the classic use as I just said. Something to correct errors is trivial. But in terms of the kind of films you can make, *Jurassic Park* would not have been possible, not with the impact that it had.
In the final analysis, one of the things I always like to say is that filmmaking is an art form and technology is its palette and so the thing that makes filmmaking an exciting art is the technology that supported it. That's why I make the point about the Academy of

Arts and Sciences pushing that every time. I am charmed by the film technology of the Scientific and Technical Awards categories. I'm inside the Academy, and I'll always keep pushing for greater recognition for our effects.

Edmund DiGiulio, engineer, camera inventor, developer of many cinematographic tools, Vice-Chairman and President of Cinema Products Corporation

Cinema Products was founded by Ed DiGiulio in 1968 and has received several Academy Awards for scientific/technical achievements in professional motion picture camera design and engineering; in particular, the first Class Award (1978) went to the inventor Garrett Brown and the Cinema Products engineering staff who developed the Steadicam.

Ed DiGiulio is also a fellow of the Society of Motion Pictures and Television Engineers, a fellow of the British Sound and Television Society and an associate member of the American Society of Cinematographers. He is a member of the Academy of the Motion Pictures Arts and Sciences and currently serves as a Chairman of its Scientific and Technical Award Committee.

Interview with Vittorio Storaro, Rome, July 1999

How do you feel about the Steadicam?
The Steadicam is undoubtedly something that had to happen, someone had to invent it because in so much cinema, particularly in the 1960s ('Free cinema' as it was called in England, 'Nouvelle Vague' as it was called in France, etc.) there was this need for freedom of movement.

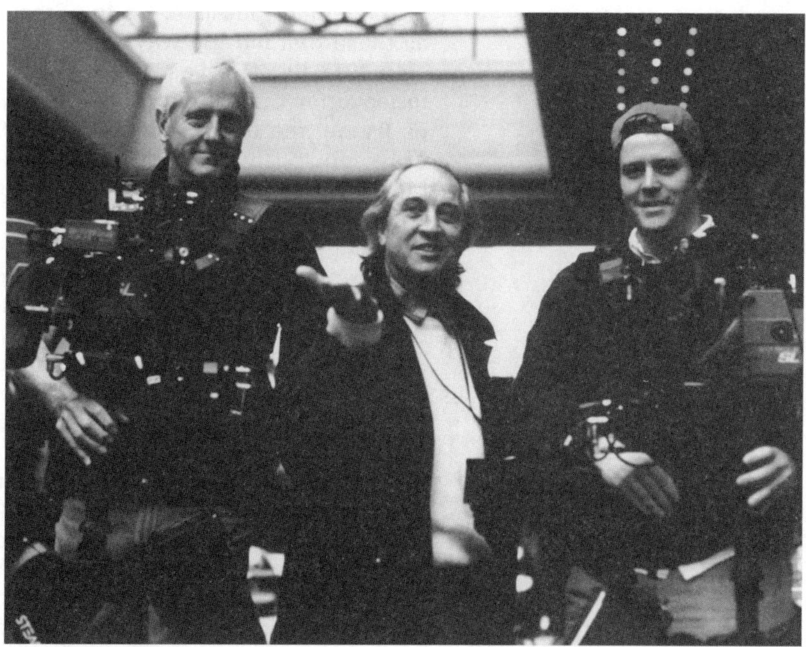

Figure 4.6 Vittorio Storaro, who strikingly photographed Warren Beatty's *Bulworth*, is seen here with his two Steadicam operators: Garrett Brown and son Jonathan Brown, on the set at the Beverley Wilshire Hotel, 1998. Photo courtesy Garrett Brown collection

The camera has taken a certain route; at the beginning it was fixed on a tripod then, during the silent movie era, directors wanted to be able to move it, to give it the narrator's point of view: it was put on wheels, on trains, on cars, on carts, on wheelchairs, wherever, so long as it could be moved.

Curiously enough, some technological innovations sort of blocked a certain possibility of expression. Sound, which was one of the first great innovations in 1927, stopped camera movement: during shooting the cameras were enclosed inside little 'telephone booths', 'little aquariums' because of the noise they made. Then gradually, technology evolved again, blimps were put on the motors and the film magazines, and the camera could be moved again.

When colour came along it brought another problem, for lighting, which black-and-white cinema had developed a lot as a means of expression, because at that point they were afraid of shadows. Then gradually, during the 1970s, with my generation, light and shadow were allowed to meet up again, giving us that continual dialogue which had previously existed in black-and-white cinema.

The arrival of new wave cinema brought back this sense of freedom; the camera, that is to say, the author's, the director's, the writer's, or the movie maker's eye, had to be able to move freely everywhere, no matter what. Unfortunately, the arrival of this kind of freedom once again caused problems with lighting, as with the camera moving so freely it became important not to see any studio lights.

During the 1960s, Raoul Coutard and Jean Luc Godard with *A Bout de Souffle* (it's one of the classic movies) in France, and Gianni Di Venanzo in Italy, with all the movies he made with Antonioni, Rosi, Fellini, Maselli, revolutionized the lighting system, letting us use light freely again. The use of natural light plus a certain kind of mixture of natural and artificial light, the use of artificial lights that were already available, made this great freedom of movement possible. So the Steadicam had two forerunners such as these that led the way a bit, during the 1960s and up to 1974.

In 1975 I was in Los Angeles with Francis Coppola getting ready to leave for the shooting of *Apocalypse Now*, and Ed DiGiulio had us try out the first Steadicam. Both Francis and I tried it and neither of us, obviously fairly well-acquainted with the hand-held camera but not at all with the Steadicam, thought that it was something we could use. In fact, we didn't use it. I had anyhow tended to operate the hand-held camera myself, like the famous scene in *Il Conformista* (*The Conformist*) running along behind Dominique Sanda as she fled through the woods – since then I had always done the hand-held camera shots, up to *Apocalypse Now*, by myself. The introduction of the Steadicam stopped me from continuing what I might call this expression of myself, but it happened at the right time, when I had become so involved in lighting that anyway I no longer felt that I wanted to participate in moving the camera, including the hand-held camera, and that therefore it was right to delegate it to someone else.

Of course, if the Steadicam had been invented when we made *Il Conformista* we would have used it, even if the hand-held camera gives that sort of human trepidation that in some cases makes it more dramatic, but those are very rare. Generally speaking, we always wished for a stabilized hand-held camera. So Garrett Brown came along at that moment at the right time for us, but probably late for movies as a whole because if it had been invented years before it would certainly have been used.

Giving the narrator's point of view the possibility of going anywhere certainly opened a very important door for cinematographic expression. At the same time, like all innovations, it had certain consequences. The first is that with the camera now moving and going everywhere you can't let the studio lights be seen: the danger, again, is that it can make lighting be considered just a generic thing which allows the camera to move freely, and this has been a trap for many moviemakers.

Luckily for me I, however, needed to do a different kind of thing: to move the light and not just the camera, especially working with Bertolucci. He personally decides, and feels passionately, the camera movement and I feel and decide the lighting movements. Therefore, I've always felt the need to have something that will let me control all the lighting from one point – the lighting control console.

In 1981, while working on *One From the Heart*, I first had the chance, after having seen it on a trip to Las Vegas with Francis Coppola, to use the lighting control console, which had been introduced in television a year before. It makes it possible to control all the lights in the studio from one point. Zoetrope Studios bought us this console for *One From the Heart* and, in fact, the idea with *One From the Heart* was to give the camera an enormous freedom of movement. Three camera operators worked on *One From the Heart* : Enrico Umetelli, Tom Ackerman and Garrett Brown. In *One From the Heart*, as I have a very particular style, in agreement with Coppola and with his approval, I gave the Steadicam a passionate character. Every time there was a rush of feelings between the main characters, determining an emotional state, the Steadicam got in there with them, so it was always seen as almost an emotional freedom, not restricted to certain strict set-ups, as a dolly might have been. It was used as part of a vision of cinematographic style and not just for the freedom of not having to lay tracks.

I had met Garrett Brown during *Reds*, he had basically done a sequence, a shot – the arrival at Bakunin, and I was certainly struck not only by the possibilities of the device, but also by the great virtuosity with which Garrett used it. When I was planning *One from the Heart* I thought he was the right person to call.

Garrett is very complicated, with all his interests, being everything from inventor to operator, and it's very hard to find him available. However, he accepted, signed the contract, but he said right away that on some dates he wouldn't be able to be there. Each of those times he brought a substitute, whom I saw rehearse the shot, and I was never able to shoot a single frame, because no substitute, at least at that time, matched Garrett not only for technological virtuosity, but also for the sensitivity with which he used the Steadicam. So, since the film had mostly only one set, in one place, in one studio, with Coppola who was fairly agreeable towards certain things, we put off some sequences waiting for Garrett. I think that Garrett left a very clear mark on *One from the Heart* with his camera work, in my opinion as important as that he did on *The Shining*, even if that is better known, or what he did at the beginning with *Rocky*. After Garrett, lots of students, lots of people have become more or less capable of manoeuvring the Steadicam; Garrett, however, designed it, has lived with it and he uses it almost as if it were an extension of his own body.

What I've seen with some people I've met, sometimes only briefly, on certain films, for a few days, a few sequences, is that the various workshops that prepare new Steadicam operators, rightly enough can't go beyond a certain depth. They prepare you by teaching you about the technological structure, the way to use your body, all that's very good, but what is lacking in my opinion in that kind of workshop is the imaginative side. I mean, I've never met a Steadicam operator who has a sense of aesthetics, a sense of composition – obviously, you can't learn that in the ten or fifteen days that the class lasts, but at least the 'seeds' of an idea could be planted. Usually what they get is the idea of potential, that is to say, they think they're supermen, that they can do anything, which is understandable since they start from the idea of being willing to do anything, ready for anything, to say 'no problem, I'll do it', which is a good mindset to push you to do unthinkable things, sometimes very dangerous things. But it's not only jumping from one place to another, running at a certain speed, arriving more or less in time, getting down from a helicopter, climbing stairs, jumping on a bridge and running 100 m with that kind of weight and that amount of equipment, which is what it means to be a camera operator, physical things which, don't get me wrong, are necessary for someone who has to carry a serious weight in that particular situation. There's also a whole other concept, which is the story, the idea, the figurative concept, the composition. Unfortunately, partly because of the technological problem, in the sense of how much you can see in the little monitor, and partly for the running, sweating and walking backward, the operator is barely able to centre the character or keep him within that space, and he certainly can't compose an image.

Of course, there are some sequences and shots in which basically what's important is that the character more or less happens to be in the frame a certain percentage of the time. In other films, look at *One From the Heart* or *The Shining*, composition is of fundamental importance. And you can see that in those cases, these kids, who sometimes are very mature and serious people, aren't educated, I mean, they haven't learned how to do framing and I've often insisted to Garrett that he should enlarge the monitor and make it visible. I understand the problem with colour, despite the fact that composition is often also chromatic, but at least in balancing the images, the fact of being able to see them well and not only in how much you see, but in understanding what you see, these kids should at least have an inkling of the meaning of the film. Unfortunately, one reason is that often, in movie productions, they are hired for only one sequence, or for one special shot, for two, three days: one, they don't know anything about the movie; two, they don't know anything about the story; and three, they don't have anything to refer to regarding the cinematographic sense of the movie, because this kind of information isn't usually given to them. When it happens with me I try, even if only quickly, to give them a minimum of background, so that they can understand what kind of dimension, style, sensation and feeling they have to try to pick up on. It's true that this is a handicap, but it's also true that there isn't an education in this direction. Things are getting better, a little at a time. The Steadicam has been a little bit 'overused'. Any technological innovation like the zoom, like colour, etc., is exaggerated at the beginning, used even where it's not needed, where there's no purpose to it.

I hope all that is in the past and that today the Steadicam can be used more intelligently, because it's a very great device to write with, but I think it should be used in a more appropriate way, within a particular writing style, consequently with particular rules of grammar, with a particular syntax, with a particular language, otherwise it's very dangerous. Dangerous because there's this continual travelling, going around, that can even become distracting for the viewer. The concentration of an emotion, a feeling, is lost, and strength is lost at the very moment when it is absolutely indispensable for giving that kind of feeling. If the Steadicam isn't used knowledgeably, not only is the figurative aesthetic sense dulled, but so is the sense of lighting aesthetics. Today many people who are used to the new films, the new lenses and the Steadicam for shooting, use only, exclusively, 'available light'. That natural light or that artificial light remains on and therefore you can shoot everywhere and you lose the sense of the studio, the research, the will to understand what lighting will give the right atmosphere for that movie, which is fundamental.

What I mean is that the Steadicam – Garrett knows these things very well so he won't be upset – is a great device, which gives great freedom, but if it's being used by someone who doesn't have a healthy and correct idea of what it is, it can be very dangerous.

Does the fact that you look at a monitor instead of through a viewfinder, therefore with both eyes and from a certain distance, make a difference with regard to how the shot is conceived?

Yes, this is an interesting question because it brings us to current times. The use of electronic images is becoming continually more widespread in movies. In 1980 I was asked for the first time, by Warren Beatty on *Reds*, to have a small video camera along with the movie camera since, being both actor and director, he couldn't see himself as a director would when he was in front of the camera. I didn't believe in that kind of thing because at that time I still followed the teachings I had been given, I thought of the emotion of seeing the daily rushes for the first time on the big movie screen, the mystery of discovering certain things, the psychological weight that a camera operator has, etc. etc., all those ridiculous things, because I was ignorant, I wasn't acquainted with the device. Seven years later, I had confirmation of this, when Bernardo Bertolucci called me for *The Last Emperor*. I said to him, 'Let's take this new thing' and he said to me again, as I'd already heard him say, 'No, I'll never look at it anyhow, I'm not interested, because I love the emotions of the projection', etc. When the first shot of *The Last Emperor* was done, I said 'Bernardo, you can see it if you want to', and he said 'How's that?' and I said, 'If you come over here' and I let him watch it and he was shocked and from that moment on a new world opened up to him.

I mean, there's no doubt that the introduction of the electronic image in movie making, that is to say, the possibility of seeing a shot in a monitor and then also during play-back and therefore of seeing it again has relieved the camera operator of a big responsibility, all that information that he had to get during a shot and respond to. Sure, it's taken away from his importance, that's true, but it's also taken away responsibility that shouldn't have been weighing on him.

Today the director, the cinematographer, the assistant director, can see on the monitor the timing, the rhythm, the things that are more or less valid in a shot, and they see it on a monitor with two eyes; before, they saw those things after the director. And certainly to know how to transmit the necessary emotion technically, to propose it through a lens, a camera movement, or a dolly, I would look through the loupe, of course there was a certain feeling, because you isolate yourself from everyone else, when you look in a monitor there's all kinds of distractions around that can take away your concentration on that particular composition, it's true, but it makes so much more communication possible, if you use certain tricks, a few black screens around the monitor, a minimum of privacy when you look at it, you can get back that concentration on seeing a composition. And at the same time that the camera operator is feeling that emotion; simultaneously those of us watching the monitor, the director and myself, basically, or other collaborators, we are living it as well, and therefore we can understand and make certain decisions while we are watching and understand what we're thinking at the same time that we see our idea being carried out. I think this is important.

The Steadicam operator, to get back to your question, has to concentrate so much on that little green screen, which is a bit too small and in my opinion a bit too green, and not get distracted by all the things happening around him, that is complicated. The screen should be made bigger, certainly, and it should be more visible in the sense of illumination, this is a question of technology; however, things are gradually getting better, and he can isolate himself and pay more attention to composition.

Nowadays, since the 1980s, camera operators have lost this big responsibility and also this great importance that they had on the set, today they're sort of 'implementers', even too much, in my opinion, because today the person who takes responsibility is the one watching the monitor. You don't say to the operator anymore 'How was it?' and according to if he says 'good' or 'not good' you'd do it again or not, but you watch it and you decide. Also, however, the operator will surely become more of a teleoperator, in other words a television camera operator, and he'll see with two eyes, and consequently a certain kind of methodology will change. Certainly, we'll have to adapt to this new way of seeing not only that image, but that image as a part of the external world, and it will be up to the operators a little bit to be capable of doing that well.

How much can the effect of a Steadicam shot be controlled and predicted compared with a hand-held camera, and is it important to be the one actually using it to be sure of the effect?
No, because at any rate it's extremely rare to find a director or a cinematographer who use the hand-held camera themselves, they've always delegated the job to an operator, so it's the same.

And can you control the effect?
No, you don't control it, you have to delegate it to a person who surely knows how to do it better than you do. Today the fact that you can see it on the monitor lets you understand what he's doing – first you saw it a day or a week afterwards, when it was projected, and today you see it simultaneously, so you can direct him, scene by scene, shot by shot.

Does the fact that with the Steadicam you can do endlessly long sequences, going up stairs, through doors, combination shots, in other words, do a lot of things in just one sequence, make it harder to do the lighting, or is the same as with any sequence?
No, it's certainly harder, I mean it's clear that a single, fixed frame can be given better lighting, in other words, more accurate lighting, and when the camera moves the lights have to be kept out of this movement, so they have to be further away and therefore less precise. In this sense, any camera movement makes lighting less precise. That doesn't mean it will be better or worse, it will be different, but the important thing is that it's right for the scene. That emotion that movement gives can make up for the emotion which has been lost, and that's all right. There are two fundamentally important things: the light has to be made as free as the camera, if you don't do this you go backwards, you return to that 'non-light' of the period when colour was first introduced, when everyone was afraid of shadows. You end up putting a lot of light everywhere, like they do now in television, unfortunately, so that the camera can go everywhere, which is the danger with a lot of movies.
It's important to study a lighting system which has the same freedom as the system of moving the camera, which lets the lighting vary as the camera moves, maintaining a figurative concept through the lighting according to where the camera is going. The lighting console lets me use lighting in a certain way, at that moment, from that angle; in other words, I'm not forced to use lighting in a certain way because otherwise you'll see the lights when the camera goes in a certain direction. When the camera moves I can turn those off and turn on others, so I can combine lighting movement and camera movement.
If, as the cinematographer, I don't have the possibility of moving the light in the same way that the camera moves, practically speaking I take away what the lights can express in favour of what the camera can express. Therefore, in my opinion, the Steadicam makes it absolutely necessary to be able to move the lighting. If you don't have this possibility, the Steadicam does damage.

So did the innovations in lighting come afterwards or at the same time?
They came more or less at the same time, for two different reasons. I didn't come up with this idea for that reason, I needed it for an expressive thing within the scene, because I wanted the lighting to change during the same shot. When the Steadicam was introduced, it became even more useful because I could move it according to the camera movement. One didn't lead me to the other.

How do you decide to use the Steadicam in a movie – from a narrative and technical point of view, when do you decide that a certain movement should be done with the Steadicam?
I used the example earlier of *One from the Heart*, where it was tied to the characters' feelings. With *Bullworth*, directed by Warren Beatty, which dealt with a senator's election campaign, we had to illustrate the various movements and situations that that created. In America, during the election campaigning, there's a TV station which follows everything a candidate does, all day long. I decided to use the Steadicam to show this descriptive aspect of 'Senator Bullworth's day', being particularly careful to introduce it in the scene just when the main character has a sort of personal revelation and decides to overturn the usual rules for how a candidate should act and start always telling the truth.

All the first part, before this character's 'awakening', we did 'fixed', with the normal, fixed camera, never moving it. We feel this static atmosphere, and then when he decides to tell the truth and discovers how strongly he feels about it, and nothing else matters because anyway he's committing suicide so there's no problem in telling the exact truth so he says whatever comes into his mind, from that moment on he takes off on an emotional voyage of discovering the truth, and he offers this truth to the electorate. From the moment that this happens it's all shown through the Steadicam, and we did the whole movie with Garrett, because I thought of Garrett Brown, he hadn't done this thing for a long time but he told me he'd be interested in something at this level, with me and Warren. He said he'd come, and that he'd like to bring Jonathan Brown with him, because there always had to be two Steadicams.

Eighty per cent of the movie was shot with the Steadicam, giving this emotional component of freedom, transgression, not following the rules, not staying within the tracks. We had that kind of freedom of movement and at the same time through the TV monitor I could see what Garrett was doing and with the console I would change the lights according to where he was going. The lighting varied according to the movement of the camera or to express something on its own. The camera dictated and instead of being a slave to that, the light was a willing participant in this freedom of movement.

We were constrained by time, in the sense that Warren Beatty knows how to say 'action' but he doesn't know how to say 'stop' and he likes to redo the shots again and again. The Steadicam has a limit, which is the limit of the small magazine. For us it was a little bit of a problem because with every shot we had to change the magazine.

That was one problem and another was the psychological drama which today all of us filmmakers go through when we compose an image, because we can't compose complete and final images anymore since their life on a movie screen will unfortunately be extremely short and they'll be 'decomposed' for television. They're going to be cut, since television space has different proportions, horizontal and vertical, than movies have. For this reason I came up with the idea, with my son Fabrizio, of a system called 'Univisium', a name derived from combining the words unite and vision, a system that can be used in the future to unite cinematographic and television images, putting the two compositions – that of modern television and the 65 mm of future cinematography – together in a balanced way. It will unite the 1 to 2.21 of the 65 mm, the big screen, and the 1 to 1.79 of high definition in a new proposal, 1 to 2, a perfect, basic proportion, the one of the Parthenon, the golden proportion[15] and there will be a much larger area than that of the normal panoramic, much more clearly defined and better quality, also because anamorphic lenses won't be used. It will be freer, less awkward, without distortions. It will be a big stimulus, not only at the technological level of improvements in quality, but also at the creative level. With the 'Univisium' system every camera magazine travels at three perforations per frame, not four anymore, making it 25 per cent faster, so each magazine lasts 15 minutes instead of 11 minutes as they do now. This system is a big advantage for the Steadicam, because it will have 25 per cent more time available to it. Likewise, everything costs 25 per cent less, because it uses 25 per cent less negatives, transportation, development, printing and so on. So I think that with the 'Univisium' system the Steadicam will take a great leap forward.

The Steadicam has been around for 20 years now. Is there something that has changed from the first time you saw it being used or used it, has there been an evolution, for instance with regard to style, has it imposed a certain style?

Basically, in my opinion, even if it's natural to think of a producer, an assistant director, or a director who, on locations where it would be complicated to do a tracking shot, finds it convenient to use the Steadicam, I think that basically it should be seen by the directors or cinematographers who set the style of the shot as a language, in other words, as a way of writing a certain sequence with the camera, the choice of saying use a camera car, a dolly, a zoom, or a Steadicam. I think that it offers a lot of possibilities, like any other device, and that it should be used according to what you want to tell.

Being so emotionally tied to the Steadicam, also because he's capable of using it in a certain way, Garrett really thinks that the Steadicam can replace every other piece of cinematographic technical equipment, and that he can go anywhere moving the same way. I don't agree with him and I've always told him so. I mean, a tracking movement, whether forward, sideways or backwards, is a very particular movement, which is different from the movement of a Steadicam, which is different from the movement of a dolly, which is different from the movement of a crane, which is different from the movement of a hand-held camera. In other words, the Steadicamera has a Steadicam movement, there's this floating feeling that is almost aquatic, let's say, that has an emotion of its own, that has a beauty of its own, a style of its own and it should be used when that kind of movement is needed and I think it shouldn't be a substitute for the movement of something else, even if it's been done a lot because a dolly couldn't be used, so they picked up the Steadicam and took two steps backward. But it's different, it's something else.

What do you think about point of view shots?
For example, with *L'uccello dalle piume di cristallo,* directed by Dario Argento, just before I worked on *Il Conformista.* At that time I loved the hand-held camera, we're talking about 1969, and I did all the point of views of the murderer with the hand-held camera, and certainly with that film, at that time – it was in techniscope, so it was panoramic format – there was this sense of discovery, of moving ahead, etc., it had a certain emotional, anxious feeling. It's true that the Steadicam is a little bit dangerous in this sense, where you feel it move, it seems like a point of view, a subjective shot, which is different from a *tracking* shot. That's why I insist that there are two different movements, and you have to establish at the beginning the style, how it will be used, not to confuse the viewer, because there's the danger of creating confusion.

Today it's easy to know how to do a dolly shot or how to use the hand-held camera, that's a point of view and this is the director's objective shot. The Steadicam can be dangerous in this sense but, let me repeat, when it's not used properly. In other words, it's great if it's used as a point of view. In that case, it has to be given specific characteristics, of a point of view, so that it makes its presence clear to the viewer and doesn't confuse him. Then, I think, its style is being respected.

Has the Steadicam changed moviemaking? Has it imposed a certain style?
No, style means how it's used. It has imposed an availability, it certainly has changed how a lot of people see and think, opening the door to important new possibilities. Then, there are people like Kubrick, Bertolucci, Coppola, etc., who have used it in a very direct, creative way, so to speak, and others who have used it as a form of freedom. So a lot depends on who's using it.

Can you give a negative example and a positive one?
The danger is that this great possibility of movement that the Steadicam offers can make the lighting somewhat static, because it has to be done so that the camera can go anywhere, and if there aren't alternative solutions for lighting it becomes an 'all over light', therefore, a non-light. Not to give examples which could be unpleasant. This is the danger, the negative factor. As a positive factor, it undoubtedly increases freedom of expression.

Vittorio Storaro, Cinematographer

Vittorio Storaro has been a cinematographer since the 1960s. His work with Coppola, Beatty and especially Bertolucci is particularly acclaimed. He is the creator of the 'Univisium' system for obtaining the same image from two different mediums (a new aspect ratio 1:2, a balance between 65 mm and high definition).

He won Academy Awards in cinematography for *Apocalypse Now*, *Reds* and *The Last Emperor*, and received a nomination for *Dick Tracy*.

He is currently teaching cinematography at the 'Accademia dell'Immagine', L'Aquila, Italy.

Films

Among his films are: *L'Uccello dalle Piume di Cristallo*, D. Argento (1969); *Il Conformista*, B. Bertolucci (1970); *Last Tango in Paris*, B. Bertolucci (1972); *Novecento* (Act I/Act II), B. Bertolucci (1976); *Apocalypse Now*, F.F. Coppola (1979); *La Luna*, B. Bertolucci (1979); *Reds*, W. Beatty (1981); *One from the Heart*, F.F. Coppola (1982); *Ladyhawke*, R. Donner (1985); *Ishtar*, E. May (1987); *The Last Emperor*, B. Bertolucci (1987); *Tucker: The Man and His Dream*, F.F. Coppola (1988); *Dick Tracy*, W. Beatty; *The Sheltering Sky*, B. Bertolucci (1990); *Little Buddha*, B. Bertolucci (1993); *Flamenco*, C. Suara (1995); *Tango*, C. Saura (1997); *Bullworth*, W. Beatty (1998); *Goya in Bordeaux*, C. Sura (1999); *Mirka*, R. Benhadj (1999); *Picking up the Pieces*, A. Arau (2000); *Dune*, J. Harrison (2000).

Interview with Caroline Goodall, Volterra, September 1999

What do you think about the Steadicam and actors?

The problem for the actor is that when the Steadicam operator arrives on the scene, the Steadicam becomes the star and no one else is important. This is very hard on actors, especially important actors, stars, who have their ways of doing things, who know what they are doing. They would need to work with the director on the scene – suddenly the Steadicam becomes the star and they're told what to do and they don't like it, and you need an operator who is very sensitive, who is a tool of the director of photography and also on the side of the actor, and not against the director.

Another problem is there are so few maestros of the Steadicam, and because many operators think of it as a short cut to earn more money and become a DP: therefore they do a quick course in the Steadicam, arrive on the set without any real experience and they are frightened, the Steadicam often doesn't work properly and, in order to offset that fear, they become difficult, presumptuous and self-important and actors generally find themselves lost in the scene as a result, because it's all about where you are moving for the camera.

The problem is that it can actually become a handicap for the actor, because 'Stop!', after three passes something happens to the Steadicam, he has seen a boom in the shot, he has seen a light because he has gone the wrong way, the actor has to stop. Also what happens is the director realizes he can do a very long scene now, because he's got the Steadicam, so therefore they're asking actors to do five- or six-page scenes when normally, if they were using a dolly, they would be actually doing the scene a different way. So therefore they're expecting a lot from an actor.

It's very interesting because no one asks the actors how they feel, everybody thinks, what a wonderful tool for directors, also a wonderful tool for actors, for example it works in *ER*. What are the reasons *ER* works? Because it's a television series, because they use a Steadicam all the time, but they are so rehearsed: the Steadicam operator sees what they are doing, and follows the actors. That particular director used to say 'Follow the actors' and not the other way. He definitely needed the two to understand each other, to jell together.

Because the Steadicam was invented by Garrett Brown to help the actor, originally it was for the director to allow the camera to follow what the actor is doing, without the actor having to hit a mark, walk in that door, walk out of that door. It's also obviously to give you a special shot, but also it is a wonderful tool for the director.

Caroline Goodall

Caroline Goodall was born and educated in England, graduating with honours in English Literature and Drama from the University of Bristol.

At 18 years of age she starred in her first TV series, *The Moon Stallion*. For the next three years she combined her degree course with professional acting work on stage and film.

Her stage work in the UK is extensive. She has worked in the West End at the Royal Shakespeare Company, Royal National Theatre, The Royal Court and has been directed by Alan Ayckbourn, John Caird and Mike Bradwell, among others.

She toured Australia acting in *Richard III* for the RSC and initiated a fruitful career in Australia, during which she starred in four mini-series and two films.

In 1990 she was asked by Steven Spielberg to play Moira Banning in *Hook*. She worked again for Spielberg as Emilie Schindler in *Schindler's List* and also with Renny Harlin (*Cliffhanger*), Barry Levinson (*Disclosure*) and Ridley Scott (*White Squall*).

Recent features in Europe include *Harrisons Flowers*, directed by Elie Chouraquiu, *The Secret Laughter of Women* and *Les Epedees des Diamants* (*Diamond Sword*) with Jason Flemyng. She has also starred in numerous European TV films and mini-series, including the recent *Trust, Sex and Death* and *The Sculptress*.

Caroline is married to cinematographer Nicola Pecorini. They divide their time between homes in Tuscany and Los Angeles.

Notes

1 Chion, M. (1981) Le system Steadicam. *Cahiers du Cinema* (Technique), no. 330, pp. VII–VIII.
2 Rotunno, G. (1997) Interview with the author, February.
3 DiGiulio, E. (1976) Steadicam – 35: A revolutionary new concept in camera stabilization. *American Cinematographer*, July, 57 (7), p.786.
4 Chion, M. (1981) Le system Steadicam. *Cahiers du Cinema* (Technique), no. 330.

5 *ibid.*
6 Chion, M. (1982) Response. *Cahiers du Cinema* (Technique), February, no. 332, p.XII.
7 Brown, G. Interview with the author, January 1997.
8 *Wolf*, Mike Nichols, USA, 1994.
9 See Chapter 2, 'Shooting with the Steadicam: Preparing and programming the shot'.
10 For example, *Dead Bang*, J. Frankenheimer, 1989, filmed with five Steadicam operators.
11 Italian TV channel.
12 For example, *Cliffhanger*, R. Harlin, 1993.
13 The first Italian film was *Phenomena*, D. Argento, 1984.
14 CONI: Comitato Olimpico Nazionale Italiano.
15 For more information see Storaro's web site www.Univisium.com. See also Bankston, D. and Holben J. (2000) Inventive New Options for Film. *American Cinematographer*, February, 81 (2), pp. 96–107.

Appendix

Introduction to the analysis of a film

Watching a movie

In analysing a movie to determine the presence of the Steadicam and its role, we have to concentrate our vision on the means of shooting. The movie must be seen more than once – the first time to understand the story, not under research conditions but as an 'average viewer', to be able to be taken in by the fiction and get the movie's more immediate message. Then should come a more analytical viewing, to extrapolate the basic structure of the movie through its deconstruction – to imagine the screenplay while seeing the movie, noting the sequences, the most important scenes, the significant pieces of dialogue and everything which can be understood with a slower, more careful viewing. Deconstruction of the movie makes it possible to reconstruct it with the logic of the director, identifying the logical and artistic connections that determined how it was made.

I developed a 'presumed' screenplay of *The Shining* in order to study how the Steadicam was used in that movie. With the movie broken down into sequences, we can see how often the Steadicam is used and how it is used, as it follows, anticipates, discovers the various characters moving through the different parts of the hotel, and helps the viewer to reconstruct the space in which the action takes place.

The hotel has a particular structure, which is shown to us in a somewhat similar way as we are shown the hedge labyrinth outside it, as its outer limits are unclear. The rooms form a closed ring along the corridors; the salons, the kitchen, the stairs, run confusingly into one another at the beginning, but thanks to the presence of the Steadicam, the viewer is able to piece together the various spaces and locate them.

The camera has chosen to bear witness to the story from a point close to the characters; at the same time it lends itself to taking on their views of the action, in order to penetrate more deeply into the story's physical and psychological spaces.

The movie, which develops in the increasing insanity of the main character, uses the Steadicam to move in the actual spatial dimension of the hotel and in the time that is passing – Danny playing in the snow with his mother, racing down the corridors on his tricycle, Jack working in his office – and in the imaginary but very realistic dimension of Jack's past and his fantasies (mixed with the present).

The Steadicam follows both the physical and mental routes taken by the main character, introducing them right at the moment he starts down them (the subjective camera) while also showing the imaginary dimension, often a confusing component since it can enter perfectly into what he is imagining (which seems real and then frightens us because it changes into a nightmare, taking away any certainty we had).

Maps of *The Shining*

What follows is the first part of the screenplay of *The Shining* to give an example of a working method that has allowed me to reconstruct some of the principal spaces in which the story takes place and that helped me to better understand the interaction between space, story and characters.

The first part of the movie is where, in particular, the spaces are described by the various routes taken by the characters followed by the Steadicam and, thanks to its capacity for keeping the character at the centre of attention during every movement, we go down the hallway of the hotel with the Steadicam, making the complete circuit together with Danny.

Legend [1]

Definitions of the terms used in the following screenplay.

- **ELS**. Extreme long shot; shows the landscape or a specific setting from a considerable distance. Sometimes is used as an 'establishing shot' to set the location or background for the following scenes.
- **LS**. Long shot; shows characters somewhat distant (especially in the context of their physical environment). Sometimes used as an 'establishing shot'.
- **MLS**. Medium long shot; presents character closer to the camera from knees up, but still as part of the setting. Also called 'American shot'.
- **MS**. Medium shot; shows a character or characters from the waist up; sometimes called 'mid-shot'.
- **MCU**. Medium close up; shows a character from the mid-point of the chest to the top of the head.
- **CU**. Close up; presents the full head and shoulders of a character or some important part of a subject in a close detail.
- **ECU**. Extreme close up; brings to immediate view a small object or some portion of a face or object.
- ***D***. Danny.
- ***J***. Jack.
- ***W***. Wendy.

Screenplay deduced/derived from The Shining *(Stanley Kubrick, 1980)*

00'.00"	Exterior day, ELS aerial (helicopter shot) of a car, in the mountains. Series of ELS/LS, that follow the car. *It is as if the camera were a dominant eye which geographically locates the arrival point of the car as somewhere very far away*	music
01'.05"	The camera leaves the car, then goes back to it. We begin to see snow in the landscape	
02'.24"	Aerial ELS of the Overlook Hotel *idea of the surroundings of the hotel – idea of the vastness of the hotel, there are a few cars in the car park and the mountaintops are now covered with snow* *The camera moves around it (left–right)*	disturbing music
	Title on black background: THE INTERVIEW	
02'.42"	Jack goes into the hotel, crosses the hall and enters the lobby, he talks to the employee who shows him where the office is. He goes to the office. *The entire sequence is shot with the Steadicam without interruptions; we can already see the structure of the first room of the hotel*	'Hi. I have got an appointment with Mr Ulland, My name is Jack Torrance'.
03'.46"	Fade. Exterior daytime LS of a series of buildings. The camera moves towards the buildings.	
03'.53"	Inside the kitchen, MS Danny and Wendy sitting at the table.	
04'.19"	CU ***D*** (A)	***D***: 'Mum?' ***W***: 'yah!' ***D***: 'We really will go in the Overlook hotel for the winter?'
04'.23"	CU ***W*** (B)	***W***: 'Sure, it will be lots of fun'
04'.26"	(A)	
04'.29"	(B)	
04'.32"	(A)	
04'.34"	(B)	
04'.37"	(A)	
04'.39"	LS of the manager's office	
04'.48"	CU of the manager (A)	The manager tells Jack what his job will entail.
05'.05"	CU of ***J*** (B)	***J***: 'Oh it sounds fine to me'
05'.12"	(A)	
05'.21"	(B)	***J***: ' five months of peace is just what I want'
05'.33"	(A) ... the dialogue continues, alternating A and B, with the insertion of C (CU of the assistant manager), until:	

		The manager explains about the 'tragedy' that happened during the winter of 1970, when a caretaker suffered so much from the isolation when the hotel was closed that he killed his family ... with an axe.
08.'17"	Cross dissolve MLS. Interior of bathroom. ***D*** (in profile) in front of the mirror. Slight tracking shot forwards with Steadicam.	***D***: 'Tony do you think Daddy'll get the job?' 'he already did, he's gonna phone Wendy up in a few minutes to tell her'
08'.34"	MS. Interior of kitchen, ***W*** is washing dishes, phone is ringing	ringing phone
08'.47"	Interior of hotel, ***J*** is talking on the telephone in the lobby (in the background we can see the large entrance hall with columns)	
08'.56"	MS. ***W*** in the TV room	
09'.03"	MLS. ***D*** in front of the mirror, camera moves forwards until we have a close-up of ***D***'s reflection in the mirror	strange music
09'.26"	LS. Elevators red with blood (taken in slow-motion)	
09'.39"	Twins	
09'.40"	LS. Elevators and blood	
09'.42"	CU. ***D*** is crying	
09'.43"	LS. Elevators and blood	
09'.49"	Fade in black done with blood that covers the lens	
09'.52"	'CLOSING DAY' Aerial LS pan shot that searches out the Torrances' car	
10'.10"	Interior of car	
11'.30"	Cross dissolve: aerial ELS. The camera follows the car through the mountains and fog	
11'.44"	Cross dissolve: exterior day ELS. Hotel, garden and mountains behind	
11'.48"	Cross dissolve: interior hotel, manager and assistant manager cross the lobby, crab – tracking shot with Steadicam towards the entrance, where ***J*** is waiting. *This tracking shot allows us to learn even more about how the entrance hall is made*	The manager: 'I suggest you have a quick look at your apartment ...'
12'.35"	Cross dissolve LS. Hallway near room, with the two elevator doors, the group (***J***, ***W***, manager, assistant manager) come out, the Steadicam tracks sideways, right–left, following (*we thus have our first view of the Colorado room*)	The manager: 'This is the Colorado lounge'

12′.52″	From CU to MS. ***D*** throws darts, he picks them from the target, he turns, the camera zooms into an ECU of***D***	
13′.15″	LS. The twins in the room	
13′.21″	CU***D***	
13′.25″	LS. The twins look at each other and leave	
13′.37″	CU***D***	
13′.43″	LS. ***J***, ***W*** and manager in the hallway, anticipated by the Steadicam, they go through the door of their apartment	
13′.55″	LS. The group goes in, the camera is in front of the entrance, the Steadicam anticipates and follows ***J*** and ***W*** as they look in at ***D***'s room and then go to see the rest of the rooms (bedroom, kitchen and bathroom) *The Steadicam's movement, following and anticipating the characters, allows us to get to know the rooms with them, with the effect of involving us more and providing us with more knowledge of the space*	The manager: 'here are your quarters: living room, bedroom, bathroom and a small bedroom for your son'
14′.13″	Exterior, day. The group walks around the hotel	
14′.17″	Exterior, day. They continue to walk around the hotel to go to the garage to see the snowcat	
14′.40″	MLS. ***W***, ***D*** and the head cook go into the kitchen, anticipated by the Steadicam as they wind their way through the equipment (*here, also, the uninterrupted Steadicam tracking shot allows us to see the arrangement of the spaces*) (see Figure A1)	***W***: 'such an enormous maze'
15′.17″	Interior LS. Walk-in refrigerator, the camera is on the opposite side as the group walks in	
15′.45″	LS of the group as they leave the refrigerator, Steadicam anticipating, we see the kitchen and then follow them to the pantry	
16′.20″	Interior LS of the pantry, sideways tracking shot that follows the cook as he shows the stored food	
16′.40″	MS to CU of ***D***	
16′.46″	MS (low angle shot) from ***D***'s point of view	
16′.56″	CU ***D***	
17′.00″	MS ***W*** and the cook	
17′.13″	Cross dissolve: kitchen – LS hallway and furnaces: the manager, ***J*** and ***W*** walk down the hallway anticipated by the Steadicam	
18′.09″	Cross dissolve on the cook's face	
18′.19″–22′.10″	Dialogue between the cook and ***D***, the shots alternate between shot/reverse of the two characters in CU, they alternate three times with a shot in MS with the two characters sitting at the table (*behind* **D** *we can see the kitchen knives hung up*)	The cook explains to ***D*** about 'the shining' and ***D*** speaks about Tony
22′.21″	'A MONTH LATER'	
22′.24″	Exterior, day. LS hotel, a chimney with smoke coming out	
22′.31″	Interior hotel, MLS hallway, point of view at the level of Danny's tricycle. The Steadicam follows Danny on his tricycle from the kitchen hallway as he turns left, enters the Colorado room, crosses a series of carpets, next to the billiard room, crossing	

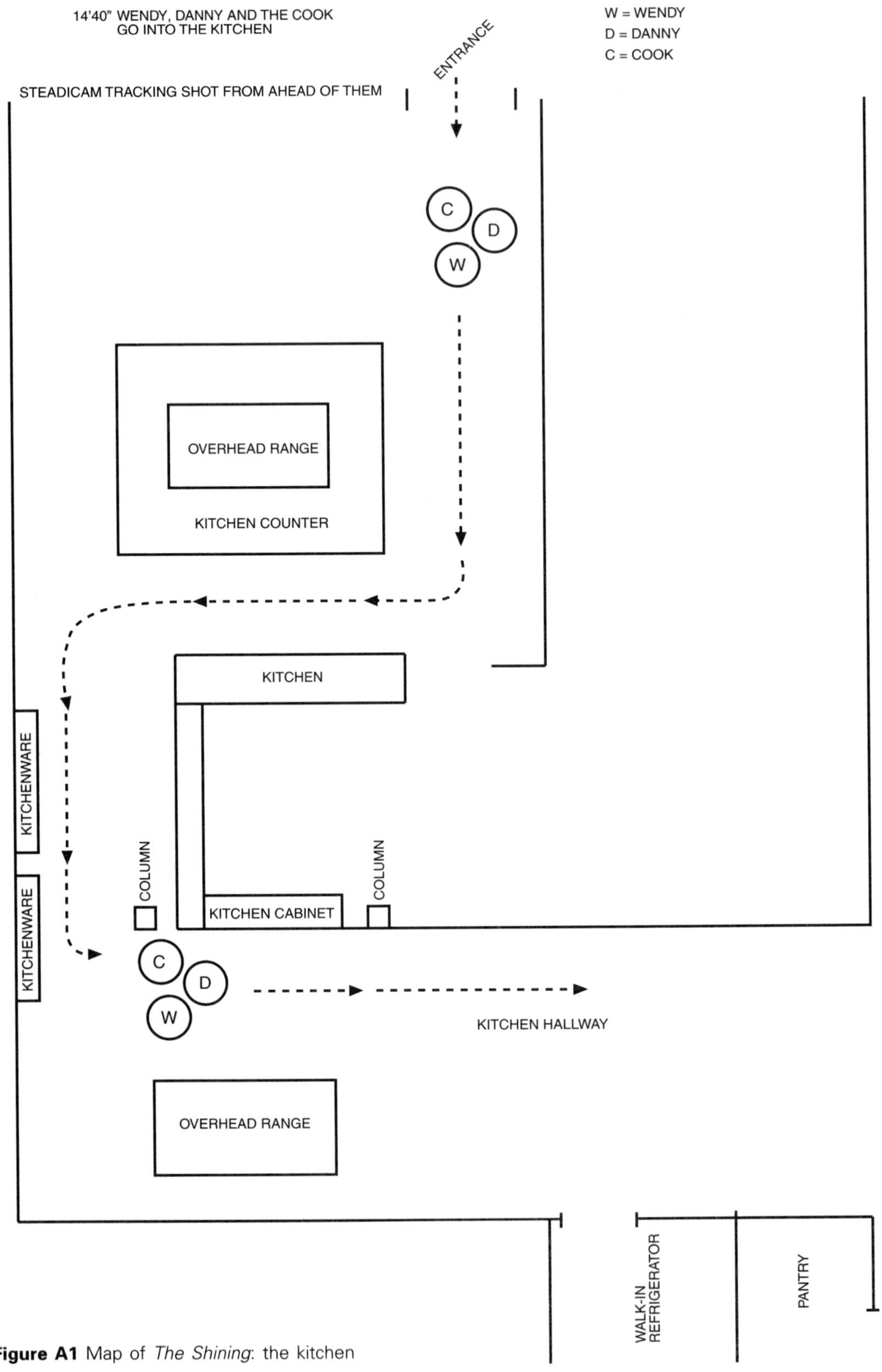

Figure A1 Map of *The Shining*: the kitchen

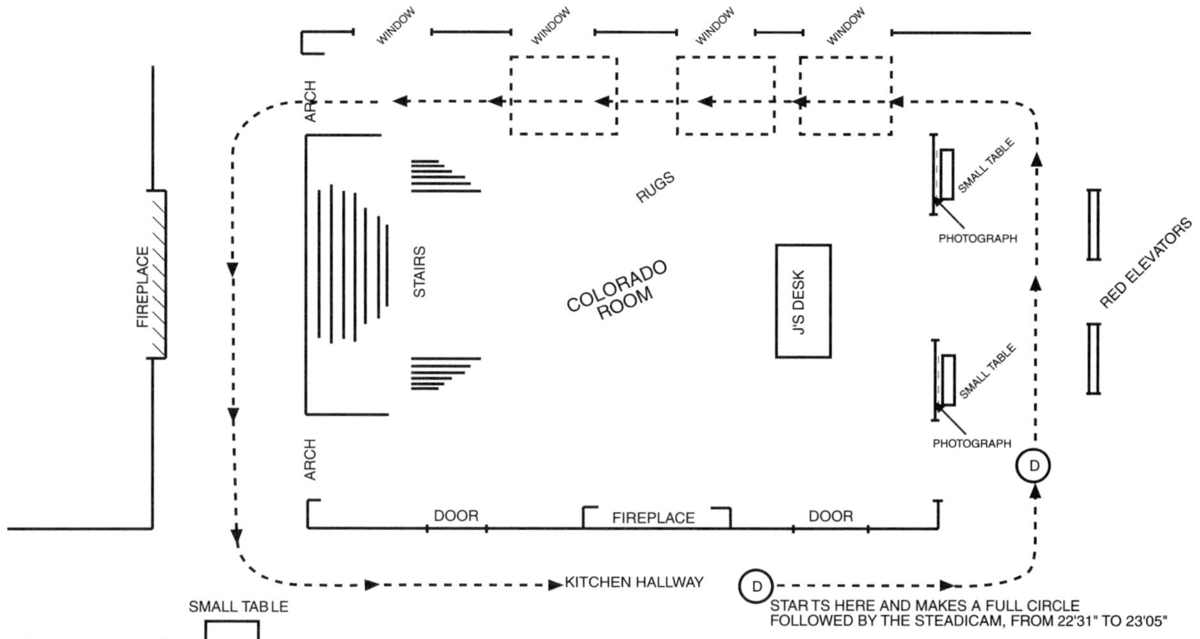

Figure A2 Map of *The Shining*: the Colorado Room

	the room to find the stairway on the left, goes past the stairs, goes under an archway and continues to the left down the hallway next to the room, until he goes part way back down the kitchen hallway (see Figure A2) (***D** makes a complete circuit followed by the Steadicam, this lets us see the space better and at the same time drags us suddenly into the reality of the story and the character*)	Sound of the tricycle's wheels on the wooden floor alternating with the sound they make on the carpets in the Colorado room
23′.05″	MLS hotel hallway, ***W*** comes into view with a teacart, she goes towards the camera and towards the door of their apartment, followed by the Steadicam (*the spaces start to be fairly recognizable and we can understand their position*)	
23′.16″	CU of ***J*** sleeping, zoom backwards and we see he is reflected in the mirror, ***W*** brings his breakfast, all the action is seen in the mirror	
24′.26″	ECU, typewriter, the camera widens the field until we see ***J*** in the room who is bouncing a ball off the wall	
24.′42″	Exterior, day. LS ***W*** and ***D***, followed in parallel by the Steadicam, they run towards the hedge maze. Instead of following them the whole way, the camera stops on the sign that shows the design of the maze	disturbing music
25′.00″	LS, tracking by Steadicam preceding ***W*** and ***D***, *the sequence is shot in wide-angle to increase the oppressive effect of the hedges*	
25′.16″	LS from behind, Steadicam following	
25′.50″	Cross dissolve, MLS. ***J*** walks through the room and goes up to the model of the maze, we see that it is the entrance hall of the hotel, with the front desk	
26′.06″	Reverse-angle shot MS, ***J*** in front of the model	
26′.16″	CU ***J***	

26'.21"	Centre of the model seen from above, zoom in	disturbing
26'.47"	***W*** and ***D***, in LS tracking shot, Steadicam preceding	music
27'.02"	TUESDAY	
27'.05"	Exterior, evening. LS hotel	
27'.05"	Interior, evening. LS hallway and rooms, seen from behind ***D*** with the Steadicam at tricycle level; ***D*** makes a fast circuit (*the tricycle's route, followed by the Steadicam allows us to gain even more understanding of the arrangement of the rooms in the hotel*)	sound of tricycle wheels on the floor
27'.44"	MS (low angle), ***D*** in profile looking at Room 237 (A)	
27'.49"	CU, ***D*** with frightened look	disturbing music
27'.56"	LS, ***D*** on tricycle, in the middle of the hallway, the camera is behind him, he stays facing the door, gets up and tries to open it. The camera is in MS on ***D*** and follows him	
28'.35"	MLS, twins (B)	disturbing music
28'.37"	(A) ***D*** scared, goes back to his tricycle and drives away	
28'.55"	LS, Colorado Room, seen from the hallway, Jack typing seen from behind	noise of typewriter// disturbing
29'.08"	CU ***J***"	music
29'.19"	LS, Colorado Room (*which confirms Figure A2*), ***J*** from behind who types, ***W*** enters from the far side of the room	
29'.45"	MS of ***J***, ***W*** in profile at the left edge, behind ***J*** we see the elevators (A)	
29'.49"	CU, ***W*** (B)	
29'.55"– 31'.07"	Series of (A) (B), dialogue between ***W*** and ***J*** with two ECU on ***J***	
31'.22"	MS, ***J*** stays at the desk while ***W*** goes away	
31'.27"	Exterior, day. LS, ***W*** and ***D*** followed by the Steadicam, they run over the snow, in the background we see the hotel and the snowcat	
31'.39"	Zoom in from MS to CU of ***J***	sinister instrumental music
32'.06"	SATURDAY	
32'.09"	Exterior, day. ELS, hotel, much snow	
32'.14"	LS, Colorado room, fire burning in the fireplace, the point of view is from the wall of the grand staircase	we hear the noise of a typewriter noise of steps
32'.16"	MS, ***W*** in the radio transmitting room	
32'.47"	***W*** leaves the room, behind the front desk, Steadicam precedes her, we see the elevators, the lobby, the hallway, she passes next to the camera and goes to the manager's office, goes in and tries the radio (*this Steadicam sequence allows us to better reconstruct the space and confirms the arrangement of the layout of the lobby*) The camera tightens on ***W*** in MS (A) (see Figure A3)	

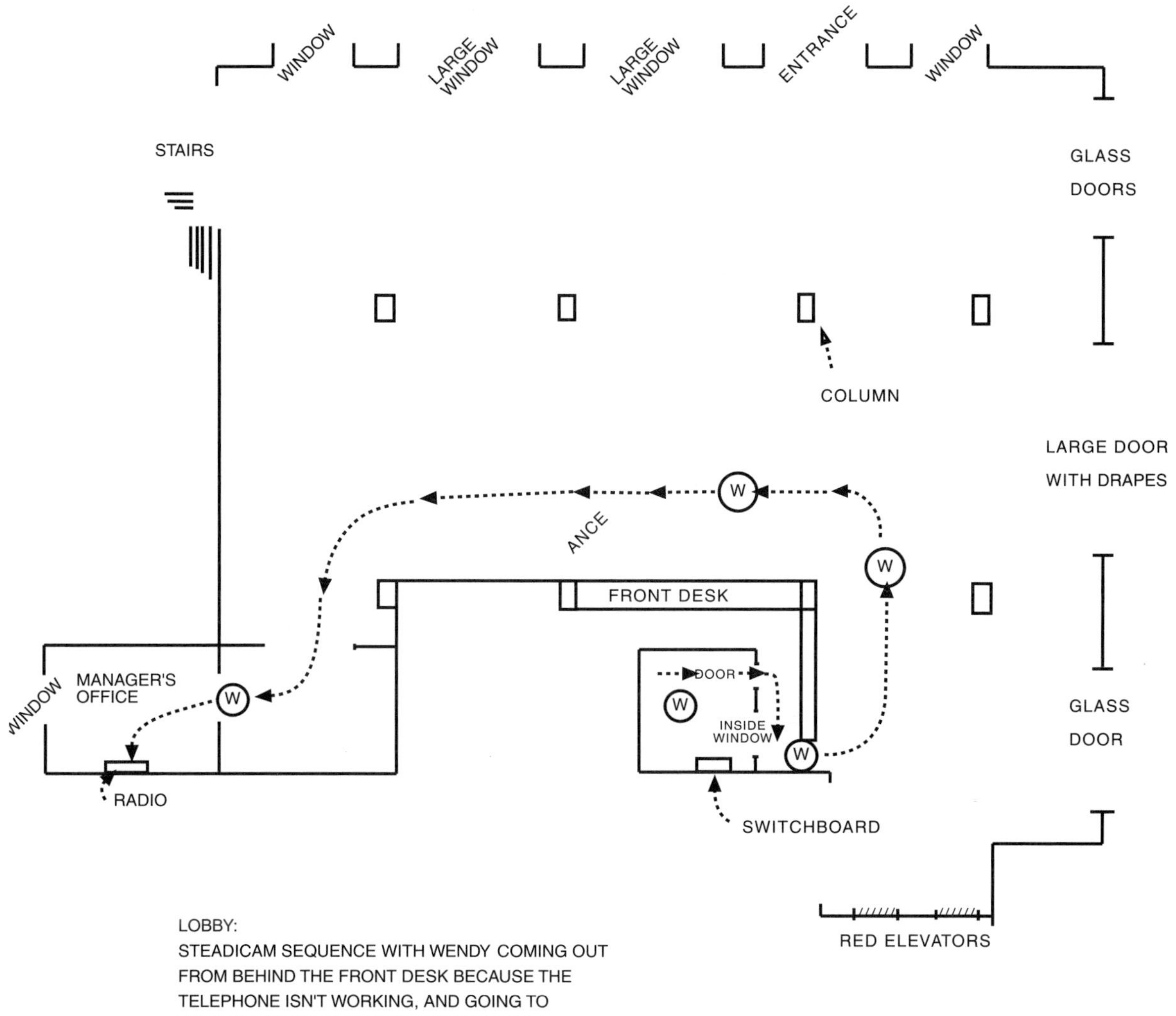

Figure A3 Map of *The Shining*: the hall of the Overlook Hotel

33′.20″ MLS, Ranger Station with which ***W*** is in radio communication (B)

33′.27″–34′.12″
Series of (A)–(B), alternating, dialogue between ***W*** and the Ranger over the radio

34′.27″ LS, kitchen hallway, ***D*** fairly far back riding his tricycle. The Steadicam follows keeping its distance, he leaves the scene by turning left, the Steadicam lingers on the empty hallway; we see that the hallway at the far end is a different colour because the rooms start there
(*the Steadicam takes the role of narrator and acts independently of the characters*) — sinister music

It is important to remember that this kind of work is only of reference to better individualize the 'role of Steadicam' and for this reason the dialogues are alluded to evidence the context of the scene.

Note

1 Koningsberg, I. (1998) *The Complete Film Dictionary*, second edition. Penguin Reference.

Filmography

Cabiria	Giovanni Pastrone	Italy	1914
La Roue	Abel Gance	France	1922
Der Letzte Mann	Friedrich W. Murnau	Germany	1924
Bronenosec Potemkin	Sergey M. Eisenstein	USSR	1926
The Jazz Singer	Alan Crosland	USA	1927
The Maltese Falcon	John Huston	USA	1941
Notorious	Alfred Hitchcock	USA	1946
The Lady in the Lake	Robert Montgomery	USA	1947
Rope	Alfred Hitchcock	USA	1948
The Night and the City	Jules Dassin	USA/UK	1950
The Thing from Another World	Christian Nyby	USA	1951
Dial M for Murder	Alfred Hitchcock	USA	1954
Sabrina	Billy Wilder	USA	1954
We're No Angels	Michael Curtiz	USA	1955
Touch of Evil	Orson Welles	USA	1958
A Bout de Souffle	Jean Luc Godard	France	1960
A Fistful of Dollars	Sergio Leone	Italy, Spain, Germany	1964
2001 A Space Odyssey	Stanley Kubrick	UK	1968
Il Conformista	Bernardo Bertolucci	Italy	1970
L'uccello dalle piume di cristallo	Dario Argento	Italy/Germany	1970
The Strawberry Statement	Stuart Hagmon	USA	1970
Bound for Glory	Hal Ashby	USA	1976
Rocky	John G. Avildsen	USA	1976
Marathon Man	John Schlesinger	USA	1976
Star Wars	George Lucas	USA	1977
Exorcist II: The Heretic	John Boorman	USA	1977
The Duellists	Ridley Scott	UK	1977
Coma	Michael Crichton	USA	1978
All Quiet on the Western Front	Delbert Mann	USA	1979
Kramer vs Kramer	Robert Benton	USA	1979
Rocky II	Silvester Stallone	USA	1979
Fame	Alan Parker	USA	1980
La Mort en Direct	Bertrand Tavernier	France/Germany	1980
The Shining	Stanley Kubrick	USA	1980
Coup de Torchon	Bertrand Tavernier	France	1981
Taps	Harold Becker	USA	1981
An American Werewolf in London	John Landis	USA	1981

Wolfen	Michael Wadleigh	USA	1981
Raiders of the Lost Ark	Steven Spielberg	USA	1981
Reds	Warren Beatty	USA	1981
Diner	Barry Levinson	USA	1982
The Thing (remake)	John Carpenter	USA	1982
The Twilight Zone – The Movie	John Landis, Steven Spielberg, Joe Dante, George Miller	USA	1983
Terror at 20 000 Feet	George Miller	USA	
Risky Business	Paul Brickman	USA	1983
Birdy	Alan Parker	USA	1984
Phenomena	Dario Argento	Italy	1984
Runaway	Michael Crichton	USA	1984
Indiana Jones and the Temple of Doom	Steven Spielberg	USA	1984
Ladyhawke	Richard Donner	USA	1985
The Emerald Forest	John Boorman	USA	1985
After Hours	Martin Scorsese	USA	1985
Legal Eagles	Ivan Reitman	USA	1986
Aliens	James Cameron	USA	1986
Hannah and Her Sisters	Woody Allen	USA	1986
The Last Emperor	Bernardo Bertolucci	UK/Italy/China	1987
The Untouchables	Brian De Palma	USA	1987
Ishtar	Elaine Maine	USA	1987
Evil Dead II	Sam Raimi	USA	1987
Le città d'acqua	Carolyn Carlson	Italy	1988
Mamba	Mario Orfini	Italy	1988
Casualities of War	Brian De Palma	USA	1989
Dead Bang	John Frankenheimer	USA	1989
We're No Angels (remake)	Neil Jordan	USA	1989
The Sheltering Sky	Bernardo Bertolucci	Italy/USA	1990
The Bonfire of the Vanities	Brian De Palma	USA	1990
Rocky V	John G. Avildsen	USA	1990
Goodfellas	Martin Scorsese	USA	1990
Bugsy	Barry Levinson	USA	1991
The Silence of the Lambs	Jonathan Demme	USA	1991
Terminator II: Judgment Day	James Cameron	USA	1991
Fried Green Tomatoes at the Whistle Stop Café	John Avenet	USA	1991
Point Break	Kathryn Bigelow	USA	1991
Raising Cain	Brian De Palma	USA	1992
Bram Stoker's Dracula	Francis Ford Coppola	USA	1992
One from the Heart	Francis Ford Coppola	USA	1992
Bitter Moon	Roman Polanski	France/UK	1992
The Fugitive	Andrew Davis	USA	1993
Carlito's Way	Brian De Palma	USA	1993
Philadelphia	Jonathan Demme	USA	1993
The Age of Innocence	Martin Scorsese	USA	1993
Cliffhanger	Renny Harlin	USA	1993
The Return of the Jedi	Richard Marquand	USA	1993
Jurassic Park	Steven Spielberg	USA	1993
The Crow	Alex Proyas	USA	1994
Mary Shelley's Frankenstein	Kenneth Branagh	USA	1994
Wolf	Mike Nichols	USA	1994
Nick of Time	John Badham	USA	1995
Strange Days	Kathryn Bigelow	USA	1995
Casino	Martin Scorsese	USA	1995
Species	Roger Donaldson	USA	1995

Sabrina (remake)	Sydney Pollack	USA	1995
Mission Impossible	Brian De Palma	USA	1996
The Rock	Michael Bay	USA	1996
Ransom	Ron Howard	USA	1996
Scream	Wes Craven	USA	1996
Anaconda	Luis Llosa	USA	1997
Armageddon	Michael Bay	USA	1997
Break Down	Jonathan Mostow	USA	1997
Con Air	Simon West	USA	1997
A Perfect Murder (remake)	Andrew Davis	USA	1998
Saving Private Ryan	Steven Spielberg	USA	1998
Snake Eyes	Brian De Palma	USA	1998
In Dreams	Neil Jordan	USA	1998
Fear and Loathing in Las Vegas	Terry Gilliam	USA	1998
Bullworth	Warren Beatty	USA	1998
Matrix	Andy and Larry Wachowski	USA	1999
Bringing Out the Dead	Martin Scorsese	USA	1999
Eyes Wide Shut	Stanley Kubrick	USA	1999

Bibliography

Almendros, N. (1984) *A Man with the Camera*. New York: Farrar, Straus, Giroux.

Andrew, D. (1984) *Concepts in Film Theory*. New York: Oxford University Press.

Arecco, S. (1992) *Bertrand Tavernier*. Firenze: Il Castoro Cinema Ed.

Arnheim, R. (1983) *Film Come Arte*. Milano: Fertrinelli, p. 100.

Assayas, O., Le Peron, S. and Toubiana, S. (1982) Entretien avec John Carpenter. *Cahiers du Cinéma*, 339, 15–24.

Aumont, J. (1989) *L'oeil interminable – Cinema et peinture*. Berkeley: University of California Press.

Baldick, C. (1990) *The Concise Oxford Dictionary of Literary Terms*. Oxford: Oxford University Press.

Ballerini, D. (1999) *Steadicam. Una rivoluzione nel modo di fare cinema*. Alessandria: Falsopiano Ed.

Bankston, D. and Holben J. (2000) Inventive New Options for Film. *American Cinematographer*, February, 81 (2), pp. 96–107.

Barbera, A. and Turigliatto, R. (1978) *Leggere il cinema*. Milano: Mondadori.

Baroni, R. M. et al (1989) *Emozioni in celluloide*. Milano: Raffaello Cortina Ed.

Bazin, A. (1986) *Che cos'e il cinema*? Milano: Garzanti.

Benigni, M. and Paracchini, F. (1994) *American Movies '90*. Milano: Ubulibri.

Bernardi, S. (1980) *Stanley Kubrick – e il cinema come arte del visibile*. Parma: Pratiche Ed.

Bernardi, S. (1994) *Introduzione alla retorica del cinema*. Firenze: Ed. Le Lettere.

Bernardo, M. (1983) *La macchina del cinematografo*. Torino: Gruppo Ed. Forma.

Bernardo, M. (1995) *L'immagine filmata*. Rome: La Nuova Italia Scientifica.

Bernardo, M. and Blumthaler, G. (1990) *I trucchi e gli effetti speciali fotografici*. Roma: La Nuova Italia Scientifica.

Bignardi, I. (1996) *Il declino dell'impero americano*. Universale Economica Feltrinelli/Onde.

Boorman, J. (1985) *The Emerald Forest Diary*. New York: Farrar, Straus, Giroux.

Bordwell, D. (1986) *Narration in the Fiction Film*. London: Methuen & Co. Ltd.

Bordwell, D. and Thompson, K. (1994) *Film History: An Introduction*. New York: McGraw-Hill.

Bourget, J. L. (1983) *Le cinéma américain 1895–1980*. Paris: Presses Universitaires de France.

Braningan, E. (1984) *Point of View in the Cinema*. Berlin: Mounton Publishers.

Bringuier, J. M. (1989) Laying 'The Steadicam Effect' to rest. *Steadicam Letter*, 2 (2), pp.1–9.

Bringuier, J. M. (1996) The 'Moveman'™, Future Jewel – case for the Steadicam™? *Le Technicien Film & Video*, no. 452, pp. 31–3.

Brown, G. (1980) The Steadicam and '*The Shining*'. *American Cinematographer*, August, pp. 26–32.

Brown, G. (1982) Using the Steadicam. From the notes for the seminar *Una citta per il cinema*, Aquila, Italia, October 1992.

Brown, G. (1988) Ancient history: the Brown Stabilizer. *Steadicam Letter*, 1(3), December, pp. 1, 8–9, 13

Brown, G. (1989) The Iron Age. *Steadicam Letter*, 1 (4), March, p. 6.

Brown, G. (1989) The contraption war. *Steadicam Letter*, 2 (1), June, pp. 1–3, 8–10.

Brown, G. (1991) Skyman. *Steadicam Letter*, 3 (2), April, pp. 1–5.

Brown, G. (1993) Forgotten techniques. *Steadicam Letter*, 4 (1), July, pp. 1, 4–6.

Buccheri, V. (1996) Vent'anni dopo. *Segno Cinema*, Nov.–Dec., XVI (82), 2.

Burch, N. (1969) *Praxis du cinema*. Paris: Editions Gallimard.

Casetti, F. (1986) *Dentro lo sguardo*. Milano: Gruppo Ed. Fabbri, Bompiani, Sonsogno.

Casetti, F. and Chio, F. (1990) *Analisi del film*. Milano: Ed. Strumenti Bompiani.

Cerchi Usai, P. (1981) Effetto Shining tecnica ed espressione. *Segno Cinema*, 1–3, (1), 37.

Chatman, S. (1978) *Story and Discourse: Narrative Structure in Fiction and Film*. Ithaca, NY: Cornell University Press.

Chell, D. (1987) *Intervista con Allen Daviau.* Le Mille Luci di Hollywood, Milano: IHT. Gruppo Ed. pp. 12–42.

Chiarini, L. (1965) *Arte e tecnica del film*. Bari: Ed. Laterza.

Chion, M. (1981) A propos de 'Coup de torchon' et 'The Shining': le systeme Steadicam. *Le Journal des Cahiers*, 19, 7–8, in *Cahiers du Cinéma*, 2 (330).

Chion, M. (1982) *La voix au cinema*. Paris: Editions de l'Etoile.

Churchill, T. (1983) Steadicam: an operator's perspective part I. *American Cinematographer*, April, (64) (4), pp. 36–39, 113–20.

Churchill, T. (1983) Steadicam: an operator's perspective part II. *American Cinematographer*, May, (64) (5), pp. 35–47.

Collet, J. et al. (1978) *Attraverso il cinema*. Milano: Longanesi.

Comer, B. (1992) Steadicam hits its stride (part 1). *American Cinematographer*, June, 73 (6), 85–92.

Comer, B. (1992) Steadicam hits its stride (part 2). *American Cinematographer*, July, 73 (7), 77–80.

Comer, B. (1992) Steadicam hits its stride (part 3). *American Cinematographer*, September, 73 (9), 82–84.

Comer, B. (1993) Steadicam hits its stride (part 4). *American Cinematographer*, February, 74 (2), 73–78.

Comolli, J. L. (1982) Tecnica e ideologia. Parma: Pratiche.

Consiglio, S. and Ferzetti, F. (1983) *La bottega della luce – I direttori della fotografia*. Milano: Ubulibri.

Contino, V. (1983) Il nuovo mondo dell'immagine elettronica – Dalla macchina a mano alla Steadicam di Garrett Brown. *Cinema Nuovo*, XXXII (283), 13.

Costa, A. (1985) *Saper vedere il cinema*. Milano: Strumenti Bompiani.
Cosulich, C. (1978) *Hollywood Settanta*. Firenze: Vallecchi Ed.
Crabe, J. (1977) The photography of 'Rocky'. *American Cinematographer*, February, 58 (2), 205.
Cremonini, G. (1988) *L'autore, il narratore, lo spettatore*. Torino: Loescher Ed.
Cuccu, L. and Sainati, A. (1987) *Il discorso del film*. Napoli: Edizioni Scientifiche Italiane.
D'Agnolo Vallan, G. (1998) Morte al Casinò. *Ciak*, no. 11, November, pp. 72–75.
De Bernardis, F. (1997) L'enigma della macchina da presa. *Segno Cinema*, no. 86, p. 2.
De Bernardis, F. (1990) Il carrello temporizzatore. *Segno Cinema*, no. 46, p. 21.
De Bernardis, F. (1996) 'Strange Days'. *Segno Cinema*, XVI, no. 78, p. 54.
Deleuze, G. (1984) *L'immagine in movimento*. Milano: Ubulibri.
Dellario, F. (1997) Interview with Garrett Brown. *Filmcrew*, no. 16, p. 15.
Di Giammatteo, F. (1984) *Dizionario universale del cinema: Vol.1; I film; Vol. II, Tecnica, Generi, Istituzioni, Autori*. Rome: Editori Riuniti.
Di Giammatteo, F. (1996) *Dizionario del cinema americano*. Rome: Editori Riuniti.
DiGiulio, E. (1976) Steadicam-35 – a revolutionary new concept in camera stabilization. *American Cinematographer*, July, 57 (7), 786.
Ejzenstein, S. M. (1981) *La natura non indifferente*. Venezia: Marsilio Ed.
Fisher, B. (1993) Haskell Wexler, ASC: innovation with integrity. *American Cinematographer*, February, 74 (2), pp. 44–52.
Franco, A. (1999) Un intervista stabile e dinamica. *Millecanali*, no. 277, March, pp. 98–102.
Gardies, A. (1993) *L'éspace au cinéma*. Paris: Méridiens Klincksieck.
Gaudreault, A. (1989) *Du litteraire au filmique*. Paris: Méridiens Klincksieck.
Gaudreault, A. and Jost, F. (1990) *Le recit cinematographique*. Paris: Natham Université.
Genette, G. (1972) *Figures 3*. Paris: Editions du Seuil.
Ghezzi, E. (1983) *Stanley Kubrick*. Milano: Il Castoro Cinema, La nuova Italia.
Grisolia, R. (1987) La Steadicam imprigiona corpo e mente del regista. *Cinema Nuovo*, 307 (3), 15.
Guidorizzi, M. (1988) *Cinema Americano 1960–1988*. Verona: Mazziana & Lanterna Ed.
Henderson, S. (1977) The Panavision story. *American Cinematographer*, April, 58 (4), 430–432.
Holway, J. (1998) *The Steadicam Workshop Workbook*. Philadelphia: PA.
Jost, F. (1987) *L'oeil-camera*. Presses Universitaires de Lyon.
Kaminsky, S. M. (1985) *American Film Genres*. Chicago: Nelson-Hill.
Katz, E. (1998) *The Film Encyclopedia*, Third Edition. New York: Harper Collins Publishers.
Konigsberg, I. (1998) *The Complete Film Dictionary*. Second Edition. New York: Penguin Reference.
Kozloff, S. (1988) *Invisible Storyletter*. London: University of California Press.
La Polla, F. (1987) *Sogno e realtà americana nel cinema hollywoodiano*. Bari: Laterza.
Lawson, H. (1964) *Film: the Creative Process*. New York: Hilland Wang.
Liberti, F. (1997) *John Carpenter*. Milano: Il Castoro Cinema.
Ligthman, H.(1980) Photographing 'The Shining': an interview with John Alcott. *American Cinematographer*, 61 (8), pp. 780–5, 840–5.
Linehon, G. (1985) Skycam on stage. *American Cinematographer*, August, 66 (8), 101–105.
Lucchesi, M. (1986) Steadicam do's and don'ts. *American Cinematographer*, May, 67 (5), 87–89.

Maffei, L. and Fiorentini, A. (1995). *Arte e cervello*. Bologna: Zanichelli Ed.
Mamet, D. (1991) *On Directing Film*. New York: Penguin Books.
Marchese, A. (1983) L'*officina del racconto*. Milano: Mondadori Ed.
Marner, T. S. J. (1987) *Grammatica della regia*. Milan: Lupetti & Co.
Mereghetti, P. (1996) *Dizionario dei film 1996*. Milano: Baldini & Castoldi.
Metz, C. (1968) *Essais sur la signification au cinéma*. Editions Klincksieck.
Metz, C. (1972). *Semiologia del cinema*. Milano: Garzanti.
Metz, C. (1977) *Le signifiant imaginaire, psychanalyse et cinema*. Paris: Union Générale d'Edition.
Metz, C. (1980). *Cinema e psicanalisi. Il significante immaginario*. Venezia: Marsilio.
Metz, C. (1991a) *A Semiotics of the Cinema*. The University of Chicago Press (French edition 1974).
Metz, C. (1991b) *L'énonciation impersonelle, ou le site du film*. Paris: Méridiens Klincksieck.
Metz, C. (1991c). *Film Language - A Semiotics of the Cinema*. Chicago : The University of Chicago Press.
Metz, C. (1995). *L'enunciazione impersonale o il luogo del film*. Napoli : Ed. Scientifiche
Micalizzi, P. (1983) A l'Aquila i fotografi: veri autori, grandi star. *Segno Cinema*, no. 6, pp. 62–63.
Mitry, J. (1963) *Esthétique et psychologie du cinéma*. Paris: Encyclopédie Universitaire.
Mitry, J. (1978) *Storia del cinema sperimentale*. Milano: Longanesi.
Molina, Fox V. (1981) Entretien avec Stanley Kubrick. *Cahiers du Cinéma*, January, 319, 5–12.
Muro, J. (1987) Steadicam goes creative and low budget. *American Cinematographer*, June, 68 (6), 84–88.
Nepoti, R. (1988) *Storia del documentario*. Bologna: Pàtron Ed.
Nepoti, R. (1995) *Brian De Palma*. Milano: Il Castoro Cinema Ed.
NUOVOCINEMA/Pesaro no. 38 (1991) *Off Hollywood*. Venezia: Marsilio Ed.
Pasculli, E. (1990) *Il cinema dell'ingegno*. Milano: Nuove Ed. G. Mazzotta.
Piccardi, A. (1992) *John Boorman*. Firenze: Il Castoro Cinema, La Nuova Italia.
Pincus, E. and Ascher, S. (1984) *The Filmmaker's Handbook*. New York: Penguin Books.
Pinel, V. (1981) *Techniques du cinéma*. Paris: Presses Universitaires de France.
Pistoia, M. (1995) Le rovine della ragione: architettura nel cinema di Stanley Kubrick. *La nuova città*, August, no. 8, pp. 93–100.
Pudovkin, V. (1984) *La settima arte*. Roma: Ed. Riuniti.
Rondolino, G. and Tomasi, D. (1995) *Manuale del film*. Torino: UTET Libreria.
Rosenbaum, J. (1982) Tournage 'The Thing': Mefiez-vous des imitation. *Cahiers du Cinéma*, September, 339, 24–26.
Ruffell, B. (1998) *Steadicam: A Resource Manual*. Submitted in completion of the 700 level major project for the Bachelor of Broadcasting Communications at the New Zealand Broadcasting School.
Salt, B. (1992) *Film Style and Technology: History and Analysis*. Second edition. London: Starword.
Salvagnini, R. (1991) *Hal Ashby*. Il Castoro Cinema, La Nuova, Italia.
Samuelson, D.W. (1984) *Motion Picture Cinema Techniques*. London and Boston: Focal Press.
Schatz, T. (1981) *Hollywood Genres: formulas, filmmaking and the studio system*. New York: Random House.
Semprini, A. (1990) *Lo sguardo semiotico*. Milano: Franco Angeli Libri srl.
Silvestri, R. (1996) *Macchine da presa. Il cinema verso il nuovo millennio*. Rome: Minimum Fax.

Smith, G. (1995) Kathryn Bigelow. *Filmcomment*, September–October, 31, 47–60.

Soare, D. (1982) *Il cinema thrilling*. Rome: Fanucci Ed.

Stam, R., Burgoyne, R. and Flitterman-Lewis, S. (1992) *New Vocabularies in Film Semiotics*. London and New York: Routledge.

Swanson, E. (1994) http//www.steadicam-ops.com. Eric Swanson's Steadicam FAQS hosted by Kiwi Film (copyright 1994).

Tavernier, B. (1982) Un lettre, Chion M. Un response. (polémique sur le Steadicam et 'Coup de torchon'), in *Le journal des Cahiers*, no. 21, p. XII. *Cahiers du Cinéma*, February, no. 332.

Tritapepe, R. (1991) *Le parole del cinema*. Rome: Gremese Ed.

Tritapepe, R. (1989) *Linguaggio e tecnica cinematografica*. Torino: Ed. Paoline.

Truffaut, F. (1985) *Il Cinema Secondo Hitchcock*. Parma: Pratiche Ed.

Uccello, P. (1987) *Cinema – Tecnica e Linguaggio*. Milano: Ed. Paoline.

Vedovati, F. (1994) *Dizionario dei termini cinematografici*. Rome: Ente Spettacolo Editore.

Villain, D. (1985) *L'oeil a la camera*. Paris: Cahiers du Cinéma, Editions de l'Etoile.

Zagarrio, V. (1980) *Francis Ford Coppola*. Firenze: Il Castoro Cinema, La Nuova Italia Ed.

Index

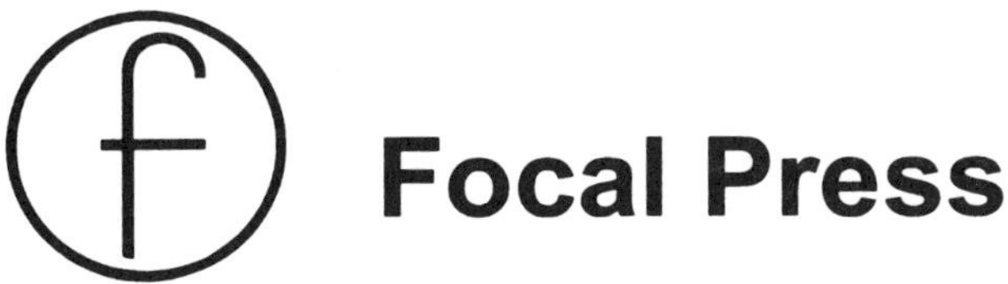

http://www.focalpress.com

Join Focal Press On-line

As a member you will enjoy the following benefits:

- an email bulletin with **information on new books**
- a bi-monthly **Focal Press Newsletter**:
  - featuring a selection of new titles
  - keeps you informed of **special offers, discounts and freebies**
  - alerts you to **Focal Press news and events** such as author signings and seminars
- complete access to **free content** and reference material on the focalpress site, such as the focalXtra articles and commentary from our authors
- a **Sneak Preview** of selected titles (sample chapters) *before* they publish
- a chance to have your say on our **discussion boards** and **review books** for other focal readers

Focal Club Members are invited to give us feedback on our products and services. Email: worldmarketing@focalpress.com – we want to hear your views!

Membership is FREE. To join, visit our website and register. If you require any further information regarding the on-line club please contact:

Emma Hales, Promotions Controller
Email: emma.hales@repp.co.uk
Fax: +44 (0)1865 315472
Address: Focal Press, Linacre House,
Jordan Hill, Oxford,
UK, OX2 8DP

Catalogue

For information on all Focal Press titles, we will be happy to send you a free copy of the Focal Press catalogue:

USA
Email: christine.degon@bhusa.com

Europe and rest of World
Email: carol.burgess@repp.co.uk
Tel: +44 (0)1865 314693

Potential authors

If you have an idea for a book, please get in touch:

USA
Terri Jadick, Associate Editor
Email: terri.jadick@bhusa.com
Tel: +1 781 904 2646
Fax: +1 781 904 2640

Europe and rest of World
Christina Donaldson, Editorial Assistant
Email: christina.donaldson@repp.co.uk
Tel: +44 (0)1865 314027
Fax: +44 (0)1865 315472